Blogging

for Fame and Fortune

Jason R. Rich

Jere L. Calmes, Publisher
Cover Illustration: Tom Burns
Cover Design: Desktop Miracles, Inc.
Book Design and Production: MillerWorks

This publication is designed to provide accurate and authoritative information
in regard to the subject matter covered. It is sold with the understanding that the
publisher is not engaged in rendering legal, accounting or other professional services.
If legal advice or other expert assistance is required, the services of a
competent professional person should be sought.

Library of Congress Cataloging-in-Publication Data

Rich, Jason.
Blogging for fame and fortune / by Jason R. Rich.
    p. cm.
    ISBN 1-59918-342-0 (alk. paper)
    1. Blogs. 2. Computer network resources. I. Title.

HD30.37.R524 2009   006.7′52--dc22
2009001595

Printed in Canada

14 13 12 11 10 09   10 9 8 7 6 5 4 3 2 1

contents

Contents

Contents

acknowledgments

Thanks to Jere Calmes, Courtney Thurman, and Ronald Young at Entrepreneur Press for inviting me to work on this project. This book is also possible because of the editing and design work of Tricia Miller and everyone at MillerWorks.

My never-ending love and gratitude goes out to my life-long friends: Mark, the Bendremer family (Ellen, Sandy, Emily, and Ryan), and Ferras, who are all extremely important people in my life. I'd also like to offer a shout out to my other close friends: Garrick Procter, Christopher Henry, Chris Coates, and Kiel James Patrick.

Thanks also to all of the bloggers and blogging experts who agreed to be interviewed within this book, including Perez Hilton, Chris Crocker, Ben Jelen, Patrick W. Gavin, and Kiel James Patrick.

I also extend a sincere thank you to the folks at Blogger.com (Google), TypePad (Six Apart), Unique Blog Designs, and Dotster, Inc., who also made valuable contributions to this book.

Finally, thank you to my family for all of their support, and also to my Yorkshire terrier, Rusty (MyPalRusty.com). Yes, he has his own website, so please check it out! To visit my website, point your browser to JasonRich.com. You'll find my personal travel blog at JasonRichTravel.com.

preface

Blogging for Fame and Fortune is all about blogging, vlogging, podcasting, webcasting, and how to share your ideas, opinions, creativity, knowledge, rants, and personality with people all over the world, including through participation on the popular online social networking sites such as MySpace, Facebook, Twitter, and LinkedIn.

This book is an information-packed resource for anyone interested in creating, publishing, managing, and promoting any type of blog, whether it's being produced for fun, or to entertain, educate or promote something to its intended audience.

Millions of people just like you have already discovered how fun and rewarding blogging can be. This book can be your personal roadmap for creating a blog that truly stands out, captures the attention of its audience, and has the potential to generate revenue for you, plus serve as a launching pad to make you famous or advance your career.

Blogging for Fame and Fortune offers a tremendous amount of step-by-step and how-to information and advice of interest to anyone looking to start a blog. It also features in-depth and exclusive interviews with some of the world's best-known bloggers (like Perez Hilton and Chris Crocker), plus several people who are considered the world's foremost experts when it comes to blogging.

One of the truly wonderful things about blogging is that virtually anyone can do it! All you really need to get started is access to the internet and the information contained within this book. After reading *Blogging for Fame and Fortune*, you'll definitely have the know-how to publish a blog, plus have a good understanding about what it takes to truly make your blog successful, and even profitable.

To achieve success as a blogger, absolutely no programming knowledge or skill is required. There are also few costs involved. What is necessary is a great idea, a tremendous amount of creativity, the ability to communicate effectively with your audience, and plenty of persistence. A bit of marketing and promotional savvy will also come in handy.

It's true, the steps for creating and publishing a blog are relatively straightforward. But if you want your blog to attract and maintain an audience, you'll need to become an expert in online promotions, plus create truly original blog content that stands out from the millions of other blogs and websites already out there. This book explains exactly how to do this.

People opt to create blogs for many different personal and professional reasons. Regardless of what your blogging goals are, *Blogging for Fame and Fortune* will help you achieve them as quickly and efficiently as possible, based on the resources you have at your disposal.

You're about to discover there are tremendous opportunities available to bloggers, and with the information offered throughout this book, you'll have a distinct advantage when it comes to creating, publishing, managing, and promoting your blog, potentially generating an income from it, and/or using it as a way to transform yourself into a "cyberstar."

introduction

So you're interested in starting a blog? Well, you're not alone! As a blogger, you'll be joining millions of other people, just like yourself, who have adopted the internet as their personal forum for sharing their thoughts, ideas, opinions, talents, knowledge, rants, photos, videos, audio files, or music, for example.

The good news is, just about *anyone* with access to the internet can create, publish, and manage a basic blog extremely easily and rather quickly. Using the free tools and resources available on the web, the process requires absolutely no programming skills whatsoever—none. If you can surf the web and string together a bunch of words to make a sentence, you can blog. Or, if you have the ability to communicate well in front of a video camera (or webcam), you can vlog.

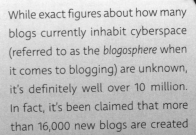

Tip

While exact figures about how many blogs currently inhabit cyberspace (referred to as the *blogosphere* when it comes to blogging) are unknown, it's definitely well over 10 million. In fact, it's been claimed that more than 16,000 new blogs are created every single day.

Blogs, Vlogs, Podcasts, and Webcasts—This Book Covers It All!

Before we go any further, let's clarify some basic terminology. Throughout this book, the term *blog* is used as an all-encompassing word that includes traditional text-based blogs, photo blogs, audio podcasts, vlogs (video-based blogs), and webcasts.

In situations where information being conveyed applies just to one of these categories, such as vlogging, for example, this will be clarified. Each of these terms and how they use different media (such as text, photos, audio, video, or other multimedia content) to communicate with an online-based audience will be explained within Chapter 1.

The Answer to a Very Common Question

If blogging is so easy, why do you need to read an entire book about how to do it? Well, the answer to this question is simple. Creating and publishing a basic blog is simple, but (yes, there's a but) if you want people to access your blog and read it, you'll need to design it properly and promote it effectively. Plus, if you want your blog to truly stand out and get noticed, you'll need to become more than just another run-of-the-mill blogger.

Yes, *Blogging for Fame and Fortune* will teach you everything you need to know to create, publish, manage, and promote your blog. But it will also teach you proven strategies and secrets for driving traffic to your blog, creating a following, generating income from your blog, and even how to become famous as a blogger. Oh, and this book will also teach you how to create new, original, innovative, creative, entertaining, and potentially informative content that will help to set your blog apart from others.

As you're about to discover, blogging is a way for people, just like you, to communicate with a handful of your closest friends or family members, members of a group or organization you belong to, people who share similar interests as you, or a large audience of people who develop an interest in what you have to say or share.

Blogging is all about personal expression, creating and using your own voice, not having to worry about being censored, and having the ability to communicate with the masses. Once you publish a blog (or podcast or vlog), anyone with access to the internet, located virtually anywhere in the world, can access it instantly. The trick (and one of the biggest challenges bloggers face), as you'll soon learn, is properly promoting a blog and driving a constant flow of people to it.

For many people, blogging offers the ability to share what's on their mind and vent. However, blogging can also be used by companies to boost brand awareness and interact better with customers and clients. And blogs can be used as a launching pad for a career or to help advance someone's career as an expert in their field, for example.

When it comes to blogging, no topic is off limits. You can blog about anything at anytime. The trick, however, is finding an audience for what you have to share, and then catering your blog to that audience so it becomes popular.

What This Book Offers

While anyone can blog (and countless millions of people already do), few are able to generate enough success that they can become rich and/or famous from blogging. That's where *Blogging for Fame and Fortune* comes in. From this book, regardless of what your goals for blogging are, you'll acquire the knowledge and skills you need to be successful. Armed with this knowledge, your ability to create a blog that'll reach thousands or millions of web surfers on a regular basis will depend on your own creativity, persistence, and hard work.

One of the most intriguing aspects of this book, however, is not the easy-to-understand, step-by-step directions you'll soon be reading to help you create, launch, manage, and promote your blog. What truly makes this book unique, and an incredible resource, is that it features in-depth and exclusive interviews with some of the world's best-known bloggers, as well as with blogging experts.

From these people, you'll discover true secrets and strategies for creating an amazing blog that's uniquely your own, and one that will attract a huge audience (if that's your objective). You'll learn how people like Perez Hilton and Chris Crocker have become rich and famous as bloggers, and how you, too, might be able to follow in their footsteps.

Don't be misled, however. Not everyone who creates a blog will become rich or famous. Just because you work extremely hard and invest your heart and soul into creating what you believe to be an amazing blog, this does not guarantee your success. Out of the thousands of new blogs published each day, only a small fraction of them will ever attract a decent sized audience.

What sets the most successful bloggers apart from run-of-the-mill bloggers is creativity, talent, persistence, and knowledge. It's true—knowledge is power! And by reading *Blogging for Fame and Fortune,* you will acquire the knowledge needed for success. What you need to bring to the table is originality, creativity, persistence, and uniqueness. All of this, and how it applies to blogging, will be explained a bit later.

What you need to understand, right from the start, is that if you want to become a blogger, you should get started immediately. Don't let anything hold you back. Everyone has something to share, so don't allow fear, insecurity, laziness, or procrastination to stop you. If you believe there's a successful blog inside you that's waiting to be created, use this book as your roadmap to make your ideas and goals a reality!

You can't use the excuse that it costs too much money to start a blog. Even if you don't own a computer or have access to the internet from home or work, as long as you can obtain access to a computer that's connected to the web (at a public library, for example), you can start a blog for free—yes, free. You can even blog from your cell phone or wireless PDA (including your Blackberry or Apple iPhone). In fact, if your blog ever becomes a little bit successful, it could actually start to generate revenue for you.

There are plenty of bloggers out there who earn money from their blog, which can also be used as a launching pad to become an online celebrity. Yes, just by creating a blog, people just like you have become rich and famous.

All of the Information You Need in One Easy-to-Read Book

As it turns out, there's a lot you need to know to create, publish, manage, and promote what will ultimately become a mega-successful blog, and this book will walk you through each step of the process.

Starting in Chapter 1, you'll discover what a blog is, who can blog, what some of the perks and benefits of blogging are, and develop a better understanding of the different aspects of blogging, vlogging, podcasting, and/or webcasting.

In Chapter 2, you'll learn what it takes to get started blogging, plus what equipment, tools and resources you'll want at your disposal. Chapter 3 focuses on some of the most popular blog hosting services, like Blogger.com, TypePad, and WordPress, as well as MySpace, Facebook, and other social networking services.

Chapter 4 talks about how to go about creating and planning your blog from the ground up, while from Chapter 5, you'll learn about blog layout and design techniques. Need ideas about what to blog about? No problem. Chapter 6 offers

101 proven blogging topics and subject matters, plus offers tips for making your content appeal to your target audience.

As a blogger, you will face a tremendous amount of competition on the web. But you can still achieve success by creating content that truly appeals to your audience and that's also unique and creative. From Chapter 7, you'll discover some of what it takes to make an awesome blog.

Because vlogging (video-based blogging) has become so incredibly popular, thanks to services like YouTube, Chapter 8 focuses exclusively on vlogging and webcasting.

If you're hoping to become famous as a blogger, you'll discover the secrets for becoming a cyberstar from Chapter 9, while Chapter 10 covers many different ways you can promote your blog to generate traffic and an audience for it. As you'll discover, properly promoting a blog will mean the difference between success and failure in terms of building a dedicated audience and a constant flow of traffic to it.

Before you begin blogging, it's important to think about your goals. What do you want your blog to be? What do you want to get out of it? If one of your goals is to generate revenue from your blog, there are many ways to do this. From Chapter 11, you'll learn some of the secrets for earning mega-bucks from your blog.

One of the things you'll discover early on as you read this book is that a lot of thought and planning needs to go into creating, publishing, managing, and promoting what will hopefully become your own successful blog. No matter how much planning and hard work you put into it, however, things can go wrong. Chapter 12 explains ten of the most common mistakes bloggers make and will teach you how to avoid them.

All of the information bundled into Chapters 1 through 12 will provide a comprehensive education into the wonderful world of blogging and the blogosphere. What Chapters 13 and 14 offer, however, is something really special—the opportunity to meet, get to know, and learn firsthand from a handful of the world's most famous and successful bloggers.

That's right, people like celebrity gossip god Perez Hilton, online celebrity Chris Crocker (of "Leave Britney Alone" fame), recording artist/environmental activist Ben Jelen, political blogger Patrick W. Gavin, and fashion designer/model Kiel

James Patrick, all share their personal stories, advice, insight, and tips about what it takes to be a successful blogger. This truly is valuable information you won't find anywhere else!

Pay Attention to Tips and Warnings!

Throughout this book, you'll find *Tip* and *Warning* boxes that contain extremely useful tidbits of information that deserve your special attention. Here you'll find useful strategies, links, and practical advice.

What's Next?

For much of my professional life, I have been writing informative how-to books. I'm also a regular contributor to numerous national magazines, major daily newspapers, and popular websites. To learn more about my work, please visit my website at JasonRich.com.

As you've probably guessed, I have my own blog as well. *Jason Rich's Travel Blog* (JasonRichTravel.com) offers travel-related tips for leisure and business travelers, as well as vacation planning ideas and destination reviews. This traditional text and photo-based blog is hosted by Google's Blogger.com service, which is described in Chapter 3. It incorporates some of the widgets, functionality, and revenue-generating techniques described throughout this book, so feel free to refer to it as a very basic example of what's possible.

You're about to discover firsthand how fun, rewarding, and potentially challenging blogging can be! If you're ready to get started, turn the page to learn all about what blogs are, so you can better formulate your own blogging ideas and goals.

Hopefully, this book will help you develop realistic expectations for your blog, plus teach you what it'll take to meet or surpass your blogging goals.

Now, if you're still on the fence about whether or not you have what it takes to be a blogger, this book should quickly convince you that blogging is a wonderfully therapeutic, eye-opening, challenging, exhilarating, and empowering activity. So, in the words of the advertising gurus who work for Nike, "Just do it!"

Chapter 1
Blogging 101

So you have something to say that you believe other people might like to hear or be interested in. Perhaps you have expertise in a specific area, you've had experiences others might want to know about, or you have strong opinions about a certain topic. Maybe you have a sense of humor you'd like to impart with the world, or perhaps events continue to occur in your life that you'd enjoy sharing with others. Do you have secrets you'd like to reveal or information that could somehow benefit others? Is there something that's really angered you that you'd like to complain about in a public forum? If so, becoming a blogger might be just what you're looking for.

Thanks to the internet, you now have a potentially worldwide forum and the ability to easily create and share information with the masses in a variety of formats. In the not-so-distant past, if you wanted to share your thoughts, opinions, or knowledge with a large group of people, you needed to write and publish a book, contribute to established newspapers or magazines, host your own television or radio show, or become famous in the real world.

Today, virtually anyone can use a computer, cell phone, or wireless PDA that's connected to the internet to become a blogger. Becoming a blogger offers quick and easy access to an audience comprised of potentially millions of people.

Thanks to free services like Blogger.com, TypePad.com, WordPress.com, Facebook.com, and MySpace.com (all of which you'll learn more about in Chapter 3), millions of otherwise ordinary people (and plenty of seemingly crazy folks as well) have become bloggers. In fact, as you begin reading this book, you'll discover just how quick and easy it is to establish your very own blog.

Some people get started blogging simply to share thoughts, ideas, opinions, or information. Others opt to create and publish a blog in an effort to become famous,

> **Tip**
>
> The secret to creating a successful blog is to create and publish informative, entertaining, compelling, and original content that your target audience will be interested in. Then, you'll need to market and promote your blog in order to build up a dedicated following. Simply creating and publishing a blog isn't enough, especially if your goal is to become rich and/or famous as a blogger.

while others use this medium as a way to generate revenue and/or to promote themselves or their business. Whatever your reason or rationale is for becoming a blogger, this book will provide the information you need to create and publish a blog on the internet.

Sure, there are plenty of books about blogging that will help you get started, but as the title of this book suggests, *Blogging for Fame and Fortune* is all about how you can actually become famous as a blogger, and at the same time, potentially generate a significant income from your efforts.

This book reveals secrets and proven strategies for promoting your blog and building a potentially worldwide following, with little or no initial out-of-pocket expenses. The trick, as you'll discover, isn't just to create a blog that stands out and that captures the attention of its intended audience. If you want to become rich and/or famous as a blogger, you'll need to properly promote your blog, build a dedicated following for it, and commit to keeping your blog updated with new content on a regular basis.

Individuals just like you have utilized today's blogging technology to become famous—not just on the internet, but in other forms of media as well. Others have used a blog to launch and/or advance their career. Meanwhile, businesses of all sizes and in all industries have discovered ways of using blogs to effectively communicate with their clients and customers.

The great thing about becoming a blogger is that it's an opportunity that's available to almost anyone. There's just a small learning curve to get started, little or no start-up costs (as long as you have access to the internet), and the possibilities are truly limitless in terms of what information you can share, via your blog, with the world.

Perhaps you already have an idea for a blog that you believe can help you become rich and famous, or at least be used as a powerful tool to advance your career (because it will allow you to position and showcase yourself as an expert in your field), promote yourself, and provide you with a forum for sharing your thoughts and opinions. As you'll soon discover, people blog about anything and everything. The only thing limiting you is your creativity, imagination, and ability to create new and original content for your blog. (Chapter 6, for example, will help you flush out potential blogging ideas and topics, plus assist you in keeping your blog's content new and fresh.)

Since they were originally created, blogs have morphed into being much more than digital, text-based diaries created by serious web surfers, nerds, and computer geeks. Today's blogs can incorporate text, graphics, photographs, sound effects, music, video, and other multimedia content in order to entertain, educate, or inform your audience.

Depending on the digital media you utilize, the terminology used to describe your blog will vary. In the past, a blog was typically comprised of just text. If you utilized audio (as opposed to text), it was referred to as a *podcast*. If, however, you use video to share your thoughts, ideas and opinions, it's often referred to as a *vlog*.

For the purposes of this book, we'll use the term *blog* as an all-encompassing term. Thus, you'll learn how to seamlessly incorporate text, graphics, photographs, sound effects, music, video and other multimedia content in order to share your thoughts, ideas, opinions, and information with your audience using a variety of tools and resources that are available to you.

Based on the information you want to convey, your talents, skills, creativity, and your potential audience, you might opt to use only a traditional text-based blog. However, you might find that recording or videotaping your information and distributing it as audio or streaming video content via the web is more appropriate. Some people choose to simply share collections of digital photographs or images, with or without text-based captions, to communicate with their target audience. (This is referred to as a *photo blog*.)

Many of the free and fee-based blogging services available to you right now (including those described within Chapter 3) allow you to quickly and easily create and publish blogs that seamlessly incorporate one or more types of text, graphic, audio, video, and/or multimedia content. Best of all, absolutely no programming skill or knowledge is required to get started.

What's a Blog, Anyway?

In short, a blog is an online-based journal with multiple entries. Originally, blogs were designed to be websites (or pages within a website) created to simulate a traditional, text-based written diary. The term "blog" is derived from two words—*web* and *log*.

Blogs continue to provide a forum for creating a digital journal displayed as individual entrees in reverse chronological order (based on the date each entry is created and published). The person who creates or writes the blog is referred to as a *blogger*, and the process of creating and publishing a blog is known as *blogging*.

As you already know, today's blogs take on many digital formats and styles, plus utilize one or more types of digital content, including text, graphics, photographs, sounds effects, music, video, and other multimedia content. In some cases, blogs have become interactive, feature-packed, and visually complex online communities, while others continue to maintain the more traditional digital diary format.

With the ever growing popularity of services like iTunes (from Apple), podcasting has allowed people to easily record and publish audio content, while YouTube, Stickam, and BlogTV have helped make *vlogging* an extremely popular way for everyday people to share their thoughts, ideas, and opinions using video.

Today, the line between blogs, podcasts, vlogs, and web pages is blurred. Thus, your own blog can realistically become anything you want it to be. There are no rules! There are, however, millions of blogs out there in cyberspace, with many more being added every single day.

Blogs have changed the way people, businesses, and even news organizations disseminate information. Blogs give everyday people a voice and the opportunity to communicate and share information, thoughts, ideas, and opinions in an open and public forum where freedom of speech is practiced each and every day. There are no rules, no editors, and no governing authorities. No topics are taboo or forbidden.

Anyone is free to publish widely accepted or highly controversial content—comprised of fact and/or fiction. Blog content can be true or false; straightforward, or contain information that some would find to be highly misleading propaganda.

Content can also be based on someone's opinion. In a nutshell, anyone can write, say, or publish just about anything at any time, plus take full credit for their work or publish it totally anonymously.

Some believe that with this unlimited freedom comes some level of responsibility that the blogger should (but does not have to) accept. Traditional television, radio, and print news organizations, for example, follow a strict code of conduct when it comes to their reporting practices (or at least they're supposed to) in order to provide accurate, unbiased, and timely information. These rules don't apply to, nor are they enforced among, bloggers.

Many feel it's misleading and a disservice to the general public to promote information in a blog as 100 percent true or fact, for example, when that content is in reality pure fiction, or based on lies that are designed to be propaganda or simply someone's opinion. At this point, however, how much responsibility you take on as a blogger when you create and publish your content is entirely up to you. Hopefully, you will use the potential power, fame, and influence you acquire as a blogger responsibly.

Anyone Can Become a Blogger

It's easy to make the all-encompassing statement that "anyone can become a blogger," because when it comes to creating and publishing a blog, anyone, yes anyone, with access

Warning!

While there are no rules when it comes to publishing content within your blog, copyright and trademark laws do apply. Laws regarding slander and defamation can also apply, depending on the type of content you're publishing as part of your blog. Be sure to obtain permission before utilizing any content that someone else owns the rights to. You could be held legally liable for stealing (plagiarizing) copyrighted information or misusing a company's trademark if you're not careful.

If the content of your blog could be considered highly controversial or go beyond the freedoms granted by the first amendment of the Constitution (freedom of speech), consider consulting with an attorney before publishing your blog.

If you're publishing original content within your blog, take steps to copyright your work. For information about copyrights and trademarks, visit the websites operated by the United States Copyright Office (copyright.gov) and United States Patent and Trademark Office (uspto.gov).

> **Tip**
>
> The equipment, tools, and resources you'll need to get started blogging are described within Chapter 2. You'll discover, however, that as long as you have access to the internet, the equipment that's actually required to get started is minimal. Thus, the cost to start blogging can be totally free (although there are fee-based services and high-end equipment you can purchase to increase the functionality and improve the overall appearance of your blog).

to the internet can become a blogger quickly and easily. However, whether or not their blog will generate a following, capture the attention of people, and appeal to its target audience is another issue altogether.

Anyone who can write, speak, talk in front of a video camera (or web cam), take pictures, or create any type of multimedia content has the ability to become a blogger. Using one of the established and popular blogging services, it's not necessary for a blogger to have any programming or technical knowledge whatsoever. In fact, it's not even necessary for a blogger to be an expert on or have credible knowledge about any topic. Blogging is truly a public forum that's open to anyone and everyone, regardless of their age, sex, income, education level, political affiliation, sexual orientation, geographic area, or occupation.

So, what does it really mean that *anyone* can become a blogger? This book is chock full of examples of how everyday people, students, business professionals, entrepreneurs, politicians, and celebrities, for example, use blogging to share information, as well as their ideas, thoughts, and opinions with their target audience. At the end of this book (in Chapters 13 and 14), you'll read in-depth interviews with a handful of well-known and successful bloggers who share their advice, as well as details about their blogging experiences.

The Benefits of Blogging

People from all walks of life have become bloggers for many different personal, professional, and financial reasons. As you'll soon discover, there are limitless advantages and benefits to becoming a blogger. And yes, many people have gotten rich and/or famous simply from blogging (which is the focus of this book).

What you ultimately get out of the experience will depend a lot on the following:

- Your unique goals
- The blogging approach you take

- The topic or purpose of your blog
- The actual content of your blog
- Your target audience
- Your ability to attract an audience by regularly offering new and fresh content
- How well you promote your blog (as well as yourself)
- The strategies you incorporate to generate revenue from your blog.

Start Setting Your Goals and Expectations

As you begin to focus on why you want to become a blogger and what you want to get out of the experience over the short and long-term, ask yourself the following questions to help you set realistic goals:

- Why do you want to become a blogger?
- What topic(s) do you plan to blog about?
- What information, expertise, opinions, or ideas do you have to share?
- What will make your blog unique and help to set it apart from the millions of other blogs out there?
- Who is the target audience for your blog? Are you looking to disseminate information just to friends and family, communicate with existing customers/clients, generate new business leads, or reach a vast (potentially worldwide) audience made up of people with a special interest?
- What type(s) of content will you create as part of your blog that will be unique, original, entertaining, informative, or of interest to your target audience?
- How will you utilize text, graphics, photographs, sounds effects, music, video, and/or other multimedia content within your blog?
- How much time will you realistically be able to dedicate to creating and updating your blog's content on an ongoing basis?
- How much time and what resources (financial or otherwise) will you be able to dedicate toward marketing and promoting your blog?
- What are some of your short and long-term goals for your blog? For example, are you looking to become famous and develop a large following in cyberspace and in the real world? Are you hoping to better promote your business

and communicate more effectively with your customers? Would you like to generate revenue directly from your blog?

Depending on what you'll be blogging about, your target audience, and how much time and effort you plan to invest into this endeavor, it's important to create realistic expectations for your blog in terms of how quickly and easily you'll be able to generate the desired results.

For example, while you can potentially create and publish a basic blog within a few short hours, it could take days, weeks, months, or even a few years for you to begin generating hundreds, thousands, or even millions of hits (visits) to your blog on a daily or weekly basis, and to build up the dedicated following that's necessary for you to become rich and famous as a blogger.

Just because you publish a blog that you believe offers superior content that millions of people will want to access, don't assume that your intended target audience will magically find out about your blog and then automatically start accessing it on a regular basis. Creating a dedicating following for your blog will take extensive (and ongoing) marketing and promotional efforts on your part. You'll also need to take steps to ensure that the content of your blog stands out in a positive way from the countless other blogs already out there.

The Costs of Getting Started as a Blogger

If you already have a computer with access to the internet, you can create and publish a basic blog for free using one of the popular blogging services, such as Blogger.com, VOX.com, WordPress.com, MySpace.com, or Facebook.com, just to name a few. These services provide their blog creation tools, service, and hosting for free to bloggers.

While bloggers can always add their own ads to generate revenue from their blog (a topic covered in Chapter 11), if you're utilizing a free blogging service, you may be forced to display a pre-determined number of ads on behalf of the hosting service you use. For companies and bloggers looking to promote a more professional image or have total control over their blog's content and appearance, utilizing a free service (that displays ads) might not be appropriate or ideal.

To save money and get your blog up and running quickly, first check out the features and functionality offered by the popular and free blog hosting services that are described in Chapter 3. Based on what you're looking to do with your blog and the type of content you plan to include, choose a service that offers the functionality, capabilities, and online-based tools and templates you'll need.

Keep in mind, some services allow users to create more traditional, text-based blogs and offer limited ability to add photos, audio, video, or other multimedia content, while other services offer more robust tools for creating, formatting, and publishing multimedia blog content.

You'll also discover there are blogging services, like Google's Picasa, that offer more specialized tools for photo-based blogging, while services like YouTube are primarily for publishing free video-based vlogs.

These days, unless you're developing an independent website-based blog or vlog (which requires you to purchase website hosting service from an internet service provider), or you want your blog to be advertising free (so you have total control over any content that is displayed), you should easily be able to find and sign up for a free blogging service that'll meet your needs.

Tip

While all of the free blogging services offer you a unique domain name so people can access your blog, the URL provided for free might be long and complex. Bloggers often find it easier to register their own custom blog domain name with any domain name registrar (such as GoDaddy.com), and then have their easy-to-remember, custom domain name automatically forwarded to the blog they've created. For example, the "Jason Rich Travel" blog was created using Blogger.com and can be accessed by pointing a web browser to jasonrichtravel. blogspot.com. However, to make it easier for visitors, the domain name "JasonRichTravel.com" was acquired separately (at a cost of under $10 per year) and is forwarded to the Blogger.com assigned URL.

Thus, your only costs will be for whatever equipment you need to purchase to produce your blog (see Chapter 2), or for any paid marketing or promotional efforts you undertake to build your blog's audience (see Chapter 10).

In addition to the free blogging services (as you'll discover from Chapter 3), there are also paid services that also allow people to create and publish blogs. These services tend to offer a much more robust set of tools and templates, allowing bloggers to add a greater sense of professionalism to their blog. With the paid services, you don't have to display ads if you don't want to. GoDaddy's Quick Blogcast service,

Tip

In Chapter 3 and 13, you'll also learn more about TypePad, which is an extremely popular fee-based blogging service.

which is priced between $3.49 and $13.99 per month depending on the plan you register for, is just one example of a comprehensive blogging service that offers the online-based tools for creating a blog that utilizes text, graphics, photographs, sounds effects, music, video, and/or other multimedia content.

Regardless of what blogging service you utilize, chances are the basic tools needed to create and publish your blog will be provided. However, you'll need to purchase or have access to the computer hardware, peripherals, and software needed to access the internet and develop the content for your blog.

A blog that utilizes photographs will require additional equipment—such as a digital camera and photo editing software. If you choose to record your blogs and produce podcasts, for example, you'll need some type of digital audio recording equipment and editing software. Likewise, for vlogs, a video camera (or webcam) and video editing software will be necessary. If you want to do live webcasts, a webcam and a computer with a high-speed internet connection are musts. This is all equipment and software you might have to purchase before you can create your blog.

Tip

Apple's iMac and MacBook computers (apple.com) are equipped with all of the software and peripherals needed to become a blogger, including the built-in iSight digital still/video camera and video/photo editing software. There are also several different applications for Apple's iPhone that include all of the tools you'd need to create and publish text-based, photo, or audio blogs while on the go.

As you determine what type of blog you plan to create and what type of content it will incorporate, you'll be able to more accurately access your hardware and software needs. The good news is that even the fee-based blogging services require only a minimal initial financial investment, which can start under $5 per month.

You, Too, Can Become Rich and Famous as a Blogger

While everyone has a unique reason for becoming a blogger, many choose to create and publish a blog in hopes of becoming famous—at least in cyberspace. Some bloggers have also used their blog as a launch pad for their career, or to advance their career in the real world. It can also be a powerful networking tool for meeting and building professional relationships with other people in your field, as well as potential customers, clients, service providers, and/or vendors.

Many bloggers have been "discovered" on the web and have been offered recording contracts, modeling jobs, acting jobs, television production deals, and even hosting jobs on radio and television. Bloggers have also been offered jobs in many other industries as well, after showcasing their knowledge, skills, personality, and expertise through their blog.

Chapter 9 focuses on how you, too, can become famous as a blogger, and follow in the footsteps of people like Chris Crocker (mschriscrocker.com) of "Leave Britney Alone" fame or Perez Hilton (perezhilton.com), who, with more than 38 million visits to his blog per week, has become a driving force in the mainstream entertainment industry.

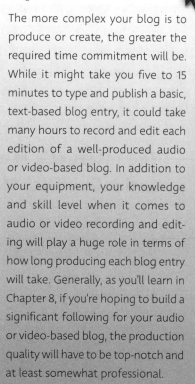

Tip

The more complex your blog is to produce or create, the greater the required time commitment will be. While it might take you five to 15 minutes to type and publish a basic, text-based blog entry, it could take many hours to record and edit each edition of a well-produced audio or video-based blog. In addition to your equipment, your knowledge and skill level when it comes to audio or video recording and editing will play a huge role in terms of how long producing each blog entry will take. Generally, as you'll learn in Chapter 8, if you're hoping to build a significant following for your audio or video-based blog, the production quality will have to be top-notch and at least somewhat professional.

By offering something new, unique, or memorable within your blog, or somehow setting your blog apart from the many other blogs out there, you should be able to build up a large and dedicated following. As your blog receives more and more hits, you can incorporate advertising into your blog in order to generate revenue. In Chapter 11, you'll also learn other proven strategies for generating an income online via your blog.

Ultimately, in addition to creating a blog that people want to read, see, or listen to, you'll need to become an expert at promoting your blog in order to continuously generate traffic to it and build your following. The more creative you are when it comes to how you market your blog, and the more experience you have at marketing in cyberspace, the greater your chances will be of success. However, Chapter 10 will teach you the basic skills you'll need in order to get started when it comes to advertising, marketing, and promoting yourself and your blog both in cyberspace and in the real world.

Every minute of every day, millions of people are online throughout the world and turn to blogs as a way to obtain information, entertain themselves, stay informed, share ideas, and occupy their time. If done correctly, your blog will be

The Internet's Most Famous and Influential Bloggers

Just as *People* magazine publishes its lists of best and worst dressed celebrities and hottest celebrities, Forbes.com publishes an annual list of the most famous bloggers and web-based personalities, which includes the most influential people sharing their thoughts, ideas, expertise, and opinions on the web.

From entertainment reporters/gossip columnists to political commentators and technology gurus, in December 2007, the top names on the Forbes.com list included: Perez Hilton (perezhilton.com), Michael Arrington (techcrunch.com), Mark Frauenfelder (boingboing.net), Seth Godin (sethgodin.com/sg), Matt Drudge (drudgereport.com), Gina Trapani (lifehacker.com), Facebook.com founder Mark Zuckerberg, Harry Knowles (aintitcool.com), and Robert Scoble (scobleizer.com). Other notables on the list include Jeff Jarvis (buzzmachine.com), Glenn Reynolds (pajamasmedia.com), and Fake Steve Jobs a.k.a Dan Lyons (realdanlyons.com).

Simply by frequenting these blogs, you can learn more about what makes a blog successful, entertaining, and informative, plus see what it takes to create content that attracts millions of daily or weekly visitors. What these bloggers all have in common is that they focus their content on a specific and popular topic or overall theme, they offer timely content that gets updated daily, they incorporate quotes and interviews with well-known celebrities or experts, and they take full advantage of text, photos, video, and/or audio footage to make their content compelling and entertaining.

able to capture the attention of these demanding web surfers and allow you to become both rich and famous as a blogger.

What's Next?

Developing the perfect idea for a blog and then creating a unique approach for it is essential. Before you get started, however, you'll need to either purchase or obtain access to the computer hardware, peripherals, software, and tools you'll need to be a successful blogger. You'll also require internet access. Chapter 2 will help you determine all of your needs, based on the type of blog you're planning to publish.

Chapter 2
What You'll Need to Get Started

In addition to the computer hardware, peripherals, and software you'll need to create and publish your blog, podcast, or vlog, what you'll also need is creativity and a flair for capturing your audience's attention and keeping it. This chapter, however, focuses on gathering the hardware and resources you'll need to get started blogging, plus reviews some of your potential costs.

If you already have a computer with access to the internet, you can probably get started blogging for little or no money, since there are a handful of blog hosting services that are available for free (see Chapter 3). To create a more professional looking or sounding blog, podcast, or vlog, however, an investment in extra peripherals, equipment, or software may be required. You might also opt to invest in a fee-based blogging service, so you'll have greater control over your blog's appearance, user interface, and content.

What you'll need to get started blogging can be broken up into five categories:

1. Computer Hardware
2. Software
3. Peripherals and Additional Equipment
4. Internet Connection
5. Blog Hosting Service

Now, let's take a closer look at each of these categories so you can gather all of the resources you'll need to create and publish your blog.

Required Computer Equipment

One of the great things about blogging is that anyone can do it and the initial start-up costs are extremely low (or nothing) if you already have access to a computer that's connected to the internet. If all you'll be doing is writing and publishing a text-based blog that might incorporate some digital photographs, and you plan to use one of the free blog hosting services, almost any PC or Mac-based computer that's capable of connecting to the internet can be used as your primary blogging tool.

For podcasters who plan to record, edit, and publish audio content, a slightly more powerful computer with a good-sized hard drive (for data storage) will be required. However, almost any current model computer should be able to handle the job with no problem whatsoever, once you install the appropriate audio recording and editing software.

A vlogger who plans to record, edit, and publish video using a computer will require a higher-end PC- or Mac-based computer that contains a fast processor, plenty of RAM, and a large hard drive. Editing video files requires significantly more computing power than editing audio files.

Any computer retailer will be able to recommend a computer system configuration once you determine what applications you'll be utilizing to create and publish your blog. One decision that's required of you is whether you want to invest in a desktop or notebook computer. You also need to choose between a PC and Mac-based computer.

You'll definitely get more computing power for the buck if you go with a desktop computer. However, if you plan on blogging while on the go or you tend to travel a lot, investing in a nicely-equipped notebook computer will probably better suit your needs.

Choosing between a PC or Mac-based computer is a personal decision, since the operating system and user interface of these two types of machines is somewhat different, although these days their capabilities are very similar. Bloggers often opt for a Mac-based computer because these systems come with virtually all of the computer hardware and software a blogger needs to create and publish a blog, podcast, or vlog.

For example, all of the Apple iMac (desktop computers) and MacBooks (notebook computers) have a built-in iSight still/video camera, along with good quality microphone and speakers. The Mac OS X Leopard operating system (which comes standard with all Mac-based computers) also has a handful of powerful

applications built in for editing and storing digital photographs, as well as recording images
or still video.

A basic Apple iMac or MacBook computer
starts in price around $1,000, which is a bit
more than a similarly equipped PC-based desktop or notebook computer that runs Windows
applications. However, many Apple users prefer the Mac OS X operating system's interface,
the sleek design of the computers, and the fact

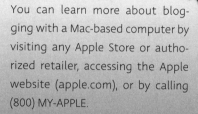

Tip

You can learn more about blogging with a Mac-based computer by
visiting any Apple Store or authorized retailer, accessing the Apple
website (apple.com), or by calling
(800) MY-APPLE.

that Mac users don't have to worry about viruses or spyware when they're surfing
the web. For bloggers, the easy-to-use iSight camera, microphone, and speakers,
plus the many features of the operating system, are also beneficial.

If you opt to go with a PC-based computer to do your blogging, you're certainly
not alone. However, everything you need to get started blogging will probably
not be included in the box when you first purchase your computer. Chances are,
you'll need to invest in a webcam, microphone, speakers, photo or video editing
software, and/or other equipment. Because PCs tend to cost a bit less than Macs,
the extra money you'll invest in PC-based peripherals and software will probably
balance out the costs between the two types of computer systems.

Any computer retailer or consumer electronics superstore can help you choose
the most suitable computer system to meet your blogging needs. In general, invest in
a computer that has the fastest microprocessor, the most RAM, and the largest hard
disk you can afford. The quality and size of the monitor (display) and the computer
graphics card are also important considerations, especially if you'll be editing photos
or video. To save money, consider shopping online for your computer equipment.
Once you know exactly what you want to purchase, you can often find better deals
online. Use a comparison shopping website (such as Nexttag.com) to help you find
the best prices for your computer equipment, peripherals, and software.

Required Software

For a basic text blog that will incorporate a few digital photos, consider using a
word processor with a spelling and grammar checker to do your writing. While

Tip

If you're shopping for an Apple Mac-based computer, prices for these systems are pretty consistent among all Apple Stores and authorized Apple dealers/resellers. Thus, it doesn't matter where you purchase your Apple computer. Where you can save money, however, is by shopping for your peripherals and additional equipment online.

many of the free blog hosting services have built-in text editors, few will correct your spelling and/or grammar. Because one of the best strategies for being taken seriously as a blogger is to offer well-written and error-free content, you're better off doing your writing using Microsoft Word (microsoft.com), for example, and then cutting and pasting or importing your text into whatever blogging software you'll be using.

Once you determine how you'll be creating your blog's text, next consider what type(s) of graphics and/or photos will be utilized. Will you be incorporating pre-existing digital images into your blog entries, or creating original graphics or photos from scratch?

If digital images will need to be edited, cropped, or touched up, consider investing in some type of photo editing software, such as Adobe Photoshop Elements ($79.95–$99.99), Adobe Photoshop CS4 ($699), or another popular photo editing application. If you're using a Mac, iPhoto is bundled with the Mac OS X Leopard operating system. It can handle a wide range of basic photo editing and cropping tasks. A more advanced Mac program, which is more equivalent to PhotoShop CS4 in terms of functionality, is Apple's Aperture 2 software ($199). Paint Shop Pro Photo X2 ($69.99) from Corel is a popular photo editing application for the PC.

Tip

If you don't want to purchase Microsoft Word, you can download an open source word processor, like Writer, which is part of the Open Office suite of applications (openoffice.org), and get virtually the same functionality as Microsoft Word (for Windows or Mac OS X), but the software is totally free. For Mac users, a less expensive word processing alternative to Microsoft Office is Pages '09 (which is part of the iWork '09 suite of applications from Apple, $79).

Many of the blog hosting services and the free online photo archiving services also offer basic online-based photo editing and cropping tools.

To learn more about photo editing software and online-based services, visit these websites:

- Adobe PhotoShop Elements or CS4 (adobe.com)
- Apple iPhoto or Aperture 2 (apple.com)
- Corel Paint Shop Pro Photo C2 (corel.com)
- Google's Picasa Online Photo Editing/ Archiving (picasa.google.com)
- SnapFish Online Photo Editing/ Archiving (snapfish.com/editphotos)

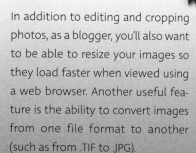

Tip

In addition to editing and cropping photos, as a blogger, you'll also want to be able to resize your images so they load faster when viewed using a web browser. Another useful feature is the ability to convert images from one file format to another (such as from .TIF to .JPG).

For podcasters, you have two major considerations when it comes to creating audio content. First, you need to record your digital audio. This can be done using your computer with specialized audio recording software, or you can use a digital recorder (sold separately), such as the Edirol R-09HR by Roland recorder (which is priced at less than $300 at rolandus.com/products); it allows bloggers to record extremely high-quality audio in almost any setting using a battery-powered, handheld device.

Once your audio is recorded, you'll need editing and mixing software to properly edit your audio into a professional-sounding podcast. This might mean utilizing digital multi-track recording options to add sound effects, music, or multiple vocal tracks to your podcasts.

Depending on whether you're using a PC or Mac-based computer, there are a wide range of audio recording and editing software packages available. The following list is just a small sampling:

- Adobe SoundBooth CS4; PC or Mac, $199 (adobe.com/products/soundbooth)
- Audacity; PC or Mac, free download (audacity.sourceforge.net)
- EPodCast Creator, PC, $89.95 (industrialaudiosoftware.com/products/ epodcastcreator.html)
- GarageBand '09, Mac, $79 (apple.com/ilife)
- GoldWave Digital Audio Editor, PC, $45 (goldwave.com)
- Logic Pro 8, Mac, $499 (apple.com/logicstudio/logicpro)
- Propaganda, PC, $49.95 (makepropaganda.com/products.html)

- ProTools, PC or Mac, price varies based on version (digidesign.com)

- Record For All, Windows, $39.95 (recordforall.com/recordforall.htm)

- TwistedWave, Mac, $79.90 (twistedwave.com)

Vloggers also have two major considerations in terms of creating their video blogs. First, the video needs to be recorded. This can be done in several different ways. You can use a traditional video camcorder, or you can attach a webcam directly to your computer and use video recording software to create your vlogs. Once the raw footage is shot, however, you'll then need to convert the video footage into a popular video format and edit the footage before it can be published as a vlog.

Apple offers several easy ways to record and edit video using an iMac or MacBook, for example, using the computer's built-in iSight camera and microphone, along with the iMovie '09 software (which is part of the iLife '09 application suite from Apple which is priced at $79). For more professional-quality video editing, you'll need a high-end Mac computer plus the Final Cut Express 4 ($199) or Final Cut Studio 2 ($1,299) software from Apple (apple.com).

Video editing software for the PC or Mac is also available from many different third-party software developers. For example, there's Adobe Vlog It! ($29, adobe.com/products/vlogit) or Microsoft Windows Movie Maker (free with many versions of Windows Vista, microsoft.com).

From Adobe, there's also Premier Elements 7 ($99.99, adobe.com/products/premiereel), which is a powerful, popular, and relatively easy-to-use video editing software application for the PC that is suitable for many vloggers. Adobe also offers Premier Express

Tip

Many freeware and shareware applications for podcast recording and editing can be found online. PC users should visit Download.com, while Mac users should visit apple.com/downloads, for example. Also, using any search engine (such as Google), search for the phrase "podcast recording software" or "podcast editing software." Many of the applications listed in this section have free 30-day trial or free demo versions available for download from their respective software publishing company's website.

(adobe.com/products/premiereexpress), which is also video editing software ideal for vloggers and amateur videographers.

Pinnacle Studio Version 12 ($49.99, pinnaclesys.com) is a Windows application that allows you to edit video footage, add Hollywood style special effects, plus incorporate other multimedia elements into your vlogs, and then automatically publish your creations on services like YouTube.

From Roxio, Creator 2009 ($99.99, roxio.com) also offers easy-to-use yet powerful video editing functionality that works with most well-equipped PCs. As with all of these video-editing applications, you'll need a computer with a fast microprocessor, plenty of RAM, plus a large hard drive to truly be able to edit high-quality (or High Definition) video footage.

Peripherals and Additional Equipment

Once you have your computer and software (for blogging, podcasting or vlogging), depending on the types of content you'll be creating, you may need additional peripherals, equipment, and/or accessories, such as a:

- **Digital audio recorder.** Forget about cassette or microcassette recorders. The newest handheld digital audio recorders offer top quality, stereo recording capabilities at a very low cost.

- **Digital camera.** If you'll only be using the camera to publish photos on the web as part of your blog, a camera with eight-megapixel or better resolution will be ideal. As you'll discover, digital cameras come in all shapes and sizes, and they range in price from under $100 to over $3,000.

- **External hard drive.** If you'll be recording, editing, and archiving a lot of photos, audio, or video, you'll probably want or need additional hard disk storage for your computer.

- **Microphone.** Used for recording audio directly to your computer, without using a separate digital audio recorder. Several companies offer studio-quality USB microphones that can be connected directly to a PC or Mac. The Samson C01U USB Studio Condenser Microphone ($129) or the Samson C03U USB Microphone ($169), for example, connect directly to a computer via the USB port and allow for top-quality, professional recording of voice and/or music.

Tip

For a blogger who wants to be able to take good-quality photos almost anywhere, the Olympus Stylus 850 SW camera is a handheld, point-and-shoot camera featuring eight megapixel resolution, a 3x optical zoom lens, and a 2.5-inch LCD display. What makes this camera idea for bloggers is that it's also waterproof (up to ten feet), drop-proof (up to five feet), weather proof (down to −14 degrees Fahrenheit), and virtually crush proof. It's also easy to use and automatically takes excellent pictures in almost any lighting situation. For more information about this camera, which is priced under $250, visit olympusamerica.com/cpg_section/product.asp?product=1365. It can be purchased from camera stores or consumer electronics retailers nationwide.

For more professional-quality digital photographs, consider investing in a full-size, digital SLR camera, such as the Canon Digital Rebel XTi or Digital Rebel SX ($599–$699, usa.canon.com). The popular digital SLR cameras have interchangeable lenses and can shoot at 8, 10, or 12 megapixel resolutions, depending on the model. In addition to Canon, Nikon, Minolta and Sony also make excellent digital cameras that can create professional quality images.

- **Scanner.** Scan images, photos, or graphics and transform them into a digital format that can be incorporated into your blog.
- **Speakers/Headphones.** Be able to listen to audio being played back on your computer.
- **Video camera.** Record video footage virtually anywhere using a stand-alone handheld video recorder. Opt to use the best quality video recorder possible in order to create the sharpest looking video and achieve professional quality production values.
- **Webcam.** A video camera that gets connected directly to your computer via a USB or Firewire cable. Logitech (logitech.com) is just one of several well-known webcam manufacturers. When shopping for a webcam, look for a unit with the highest resolution possible (at least two megapixels) to ensure the best quality video images can be recorded. Plan on spending between $50 and $200 for a good quality webcam.

Internet Connection

As a blogger, your computer must have access to the internet in order to publish and distribute your blog. While a slow, dial-up connection is suitable if you'll be publishing a text-based blog, podcasters or vloggers will definitely require a high-speed broadband or DSL internet connection. Plan on spending between $19.95 and $39.95 per month for a high-speed internet connection.

A high-speed internet connection (which is available from your local phone company and/or cable television company) is what allows your computer to access the internet. You will still need to utilize some type of online blog hosting service to publish and distribute your blog (see Chapter 3).

Blog Hosting Service

Just as someone who publishes a website requires a website hosting service or Internet Service Provider (ISP) to host their site, a blogger must utilize some type of blog hosting service to publish and distribute their blog, podcast, or vlog. Some blog hosting services are available to bloggers for free. For example, there's Blogger. com, VOX.com, and WordPress.com, along with MySpace.com, Facebook.com and YouTube.com (for vloggers).

If you require ultimate control over your blog content and don't want your audience to be exposed to ads from other companies, you might opt to utilize a fee-based blog hosting service. These services typically give you greater control over the user interface, appearance, and functionality of your blog, plus put you in control of what advertising, if any, your audience sees or hears. More information about free and fee-based blog hosting services can be found in Chapter 3.

The Mobile Blogging Option

Not everyone wants to be stuck at home or in their office in order to create and publish new entries for the blog. Thanks to the latest wireless personal digital assistants (PDAs) and Smartphones (such as the Apple iPhone), as well as notebook computers that can be wirelessly connected to the web, blogs that include digital photos, podcasts, and even vlogs can be created while on the go and uploaded/published directly to the web using a wireless internet connection. Chapter 5 offers more information on mobile blogging.

Cost Calculating Worksheet

The following worksheet will help you calculate the start-up and monthly costs of creating and maintaining a blog. Over time, your costs will vary based on what types of content you create. Also, the price of computer hardware and related technology will change and the technology will become more advanced as new breakthroughs occur.

Blog Expense Worksheet

Product or Service	One-Time Purchase Cost ($)	Monthly Fee ($)
Computer System		
Word Processor		
Photo Editing Software		
Audio Editing Software		
Video Editing Software		
Microphone		
Computer Speakers/Headphones		
Webcam		
Video Camera		
Digital (Still) Camera and Memory Card(s)		
Digital Audio Recorder and Memory Card(s)		
Video/Photo Lighting Equipment and Backdrop		
Scanner		
External Hard Drive (for data storage)		
Internet Connection (through ISP)		
Blog Hosting Service		
Mobile Blogging (Wireless Internet) Service and Equipment		
Other		
Other		
Total Costs		

What's Next?

The next chapter focuses on various free and fee-based blog hosting services and will help you select a service based on your needs, budget, and goals. While these services are designed to make your blog, podcast, or vlog extremely easy to publish and distribute, you might also opt to create and host your blog on your own, or make it part of your existing website.

Chapter 3
Choosing a Blogging Service

Just like a stand-alone website, a blog requires an online host to call home. Your blog must be stored on a server that's permanently connected to the internet so web surfers can access it 24-hours-per day.

While some bloggers add their blog to an already existing website and use the same hosting service as their website, a more common option is to take advantage of a popular blog hosting service. Even if you already have a website, using a blog hosting service to host your blog is more convenient since the blog design and publishing tools are provided by the blog hosting service. You can always add a link from your website to your blog, so visitors can access your blog seamlessly, without knowing they're being switched to a separate hosting service or server.

There are seven main reasons to take advantage of a blog hosting services:

1. The services provide your blog with its own, unique website address (URL)

2. All of the tools you'll need to create, manage, and publish your blog are made available to you by the service and are online-based, so you typically require no special software and absolutely no programming knowledge. (Basic HTML programming knowledge is helpful in order to fully customize your blog's design, but it's not required.)

3. The blogging services offer dozens, sometimes hundreds of professionally designed templates, so you can create a

Tip

Before choosing a blog hosting service, plan out your blog on paper. Determine what types of content, functionality, and features you'll want to incorporate and make sure your technical needs will be met by the service you ultimately select. If you plan to include a lot of audio or video content, your needs will be vastly different from bloggers who incorporate mostly text and photos into their blog entries.

blog that looks professional, that's easy to navigate, and that follows a traditional blog format, with no graphic design knowledge or skill required. (Again, graphic design and photography skills are useful if you want to create original graphics for your blog without hiring freelance experts to do this on your behalf.)

4. Because the blogging services are online-based (as are all of the blogging tools needed), you can access your blog to update it or add new entries from any computer or mobile device that has access to the internet

5. There are literally thousands of *widgets* (downloadable applications) that can be added to a blog, for free, in order to add functionality and interactivity. These widgets are fully compatible with the popular blog hosting services and, in some cases, can be auto-installed to any one of them.

6. If you want or need assistance designing your blog, there are plenty of highly skilled graphic artists and web designers who specialize in doing custom design work for blogs. Many of these freelance professionals, who charge a fee for their work, are highly proficient using the various popular blogging services. More information about hiring a freelance blog designer can be found later in this chapter and in the interview with John Mullineaux from Unique Blog Designs, LLC (uniqueblogdesigns.com), which is featured in Chapter 13.

7. Perhaps the most alluring feature of the popular blog hosting services is that they're available to bloggers for free (at least most of them are free). There no start-up or ongoing hosting fees to create, publish, and manage a blog using many of the popular blog hosting services. It's possible to create and launch a blog, for free, within a few hours.

This chapter offers an introduction to several of the most popular blog hosting services and offers summaries of the features and functionality each offers. Because each of these services offers slightly different features, interfaces, and functionality, the one you choose should be based on the goals and plans you have for your specific blog. After learning about what each of these services offer, you may discover that one of these services is more suitable for your needs than the others.

Meet Your Hosts

Here are the details about a handful of popular blog hosting services.

Blogger.com

Company: Google

Price: Free

Tip

In addition to the free blog hosting services described within this chapter, there are many fee-based blog-hosting services that typically charge a one-time set-up fee, plus a monthly hosting fee to bloggers. Some of these services offer additional functionality that aren't available from the free services, while others are more suited to business-oriented blog applications.

Way back in 1999 (ancient times as far as internet technologies go), a small San Francisco-based company called Pyra Labs launched what is now Blogger.com. The company was created and initially operated by three friends. Although it experienced some hard times due to lack of funding, by 2002, Blogger.com had amassed several hundred thousand users—dedicated bloggers who used Blogger.com as their blog's hosting service. It was around this time that the popularity of blogging, and the Blogger.com service, caught the attention of Google, which ultimately purchased the company and has been operating it ever since.

Today, Blogger.com is one of the largest and most popular free blog hosting services in the world. The company has a powerful suite of online-based tools that allows virtually anyone with access to the internet to create and publish a blog in a few easy steps and in a matter of minutes. Blogs created and published with Blogger.com can incorporate text, photos, graphics, audio, and video, as well as third-party widgets.

Blogger.com features hundreds of templates to choose from, and allows you, the blogger, to customize fonts, text colors, text alignment, and other formatting elements as you compose new blog entries. There's also a built-in spell checker.

While a working knowledge of HTML programming is not required to create, publish, or manage a blog, the service offers a full-featured HTML editor that allows you to customize your blog if you so desire.

Blogger.com's blog creation and publishing tools are all offered free of charge. In addition to free tools and blog hosting, each blog is given a free domain name; however,

Tip

Because Blogger.com is part of Google, the service is compatible with many of Google's other online-based services, including Gmail (e-mail), Picasa (online photo storage and editing), and Google Video (YouTube). To learn about some of the third-party applications (widgets and gadgets) that are compatible with Blogger.com, point your browser to help.blogger.com/bin/answer.py?answer=42347.

you can register your own custom domain name if you wish (for a low annual fee).

Once your blog is published, you can incorporate widgets and gadgets easily to add functionality and interactivity, plus easily begin to generate revenue from your blog by agreeing to display AdSense text-based (context sensitive) ads within your blog. Google offers a handful of its own gadgets and widgets for adding polls, quizzes, and slideshows to your blog, for example, but Blogger.com is also compatible with a wide range of other widget services including widgets offered by WidgetBox.com.

For your blog's visitors, Blogger.com has a powerful commenting feature built in that allows people to post feedback and comments about individual blog entries. As the blogger, you can moderate the comments that are left, before they get published. Blogger will even keep people who frequent your blog up-to-date via e-mail every time your blog is updated.

Blogger.com currently supports 41 languages and offers a variety of tools for mobile bloggers and team bloggers. (Team blogging is when multiple people can contribute to a single blog and have equal access to blog administration tools and functionality.) New features and functionality are always being added to make the service easier to use and more powerful. A special blog, called Blogger Buzz (buzz.blogger.com), helps keep bloggers up to date on the latest developments with Blogger.com. If you're thinking about signing up with Blogger.com and having this service host your blog, be sure to read Blogger Buzz to obtain extremely useful how-to advice. Because Blogger Buzz is, of course, created and hosted using Blogger.com, this blog also serves as a great example of what's possible in terms of functionality.

While Blogger.com is extremely powerful and highly customizable, it's also easy to use and allows new bloggers to get started very quickly. The following are the nine steps required to create and publish a blog with Blogger.com.

1. Create a Google account. To do this, you'll need to provide your e-mail address and a unique password for the account. You'll also be asked to create a "display name" and accept the Blogger.com terms of service in order to continue.

2. The next Blogger.com registration screen requires you to "Name your blog." This is the blog's title that will appear when the blog is published.

3. Every new blog created using Blogger.com receives a unique blogspot.com URL ([YourNameHere].blogspot.com). You must select your blog's URL, but can also register your own domain name (that does not incorporate 'blogspot.com') using a service such as GoDaddy.com. There is an annual fee to register a separate custom domain name, but this is highly recommended.

4. Blogger.com will automatically host the blog you create and publish. However, you can also opt to use Blogger.com to create and publish your blog, but host it on another server (such as the service that hosts your existing website). If you opt to do this, complete the "Advanced Blog Setup" questionnaire available from the Name Your Blog registration screen. Be prepared to supply your FTP server information, FTP path, FTP username, and FTP password; this information will be provided by your current Internet Service Provider/ website hosting service; it will be used to identify exactly where the Blogger. com blog creation tools should actually publish the content you create.

5. The next step in creating your blog with Blogger.com is to choose a template. At any time you can switch templates. You'll be given over a dozen options to choose from, each of which can be fully customized. Once you choose your template, you can always hire a professional designer to create your own template or modify an existing one.

6. At this point, you're ready to begin creating posts for your blog. The Blogger. com Posting screen looks like an on-screen text editor. Using the on-screen icons, you can format your text, plus add and format photos. As you create each new blog entry, at anytime you can *Publish* the post (meaning it goes live and people will be able to read it), or you can *Save Now* (which saves your post, but does not make it available to the general public). You can also *Save As Draft* and return to the editing and formatting process later.

7. Below the text editor, on the Posting screen, is a field that allows you to enter labels for your post. Use this field to enter keywords related directly to the content of that specific blog entry. For example, if you're blogging about your trip to Orlando, some of the labels you might enter include: vacation, Orlando, Florida, Disney World, and travel. Blogger.com will create a searchable directory of your entire blog using these keywords to help visitors find the content they're looking for. These keywords will also help with categorizing your blog and blog entries with search engines, including Google.

8. Once a blog entry is completed (even after it's published) it's possible to edit it anytime.

9. From Blogger.com's Setting screen, you can customize the overall settings for your blog. In addition to being able to edit your blog's main title, you must enter a text-based description of your blog (up to 500 characters in length), and choose whether or not to add your blog to Google's blog directory and the various search engines. You can also make it possible for people to e-mail posts from your blog to their friends and determine whether or not your blog contains adult-oriented material.

Tip

The Blogger.com Setting and Layout screens allow you to fully customize the look and formatting of your blog, plus control much of its functionality. These two screens offer access to a wide range of features and commands that are at the blogger's disposal. How proficient you become using these features will determine how unique your own blog will ultimately look and what functionality it includes.

Using the Blogger.com Layout screen, you can further customize your template and determine the overall look and layout of your blog. The Page Elements section allows you to decide where various content and elements of your blog (including the header, blog posts, blog archives, gadgets, the About Me section, and other content) will be placed. All of these options are drag-and-drop, so no programming is required. At any time, you can choose the "View Blog" command to see exactly what your visitors will see when they access your blog. Once your blog is operational, you'll use the Blogger.com Dashboard to access the various screens and available commands as a blogger.

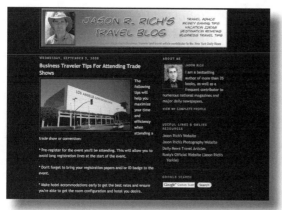

The Jason Rich Travel Blog was created using the Blogger.com service. While the content took time to create, the blog itself was designed and published in less than one hour.

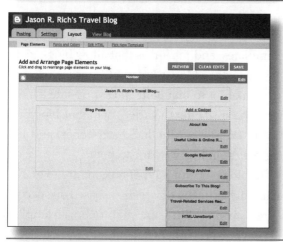

Using Blogger.com's Layout screen, you can create the layout of your blog and position various content elements, including the Main Title Banner, About Us, Archives, Links, and ads.

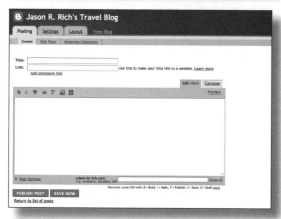

From the Posting screen of Blogger.com, you can create and publish new text-based blog posts, plus incorporate photos and other multimedia content into your blog entries. Basic text editing functionality is available to you.

To learn more about blogging using Blogger.com, be sure to read the interview with Taj Campbell, one of the product managers of Blogger.com at Google. The interview appears in Chapter 13.

TypePad.com

Company: Six Apart, Ltd.

Price: $4.95 to $29.95 per month (after free 14-day trial). Discounts are offered for annual subscriptions, and there is separate pricing for business-oriented blogs.

Created in 2003 by a talented team of dedicated bloggers, TypePad has become one of the most popular, fee-based blog hosting services in the world. Like Blogger.com, TypePad.com is a full-featured, online-based blogging service that offers a wide range of tools, customizable templates, and resources that allow bloggers to quickly and easily create, publish, and manage a blog. While a blogger can use any computer that's connected to the web in order to maintain and/or update a blog, TypePad.com is one of several services that also offers a variety of mobile blogging tools for wireless PDAs, Palm OS and Windows Mobile Smartphones, and the Apple iPhone. The service also integrates seamlessly with Facebook.

Included in the toolset available to bloggers from TypePad.com are over 100 fully customizable and professional templates, many of which are based on specific themes (including sports and leisure, travel, politics, and nature, for example). Bloggers can adjust the color scheme, layout, and other elements of each template, plus add widgets to increase the functionality and interactivity of their blog.

TypePad has its own widget gallery (sixapart.com/typepad/widgets) that offers dozens of first- and third-party widgets that can be immediately added to a blog. However, widgets from other sources (such as WidgetBox.com) will work as well.

Like Blogger.com, all of the online-based tools for creating, publishing, and managing a blog

Tip

To learn more about TypePad as a blogging service, plus learn free tips and tricks for properly using this service, be sure to read the official *Everything TypePad* blog (everything.typepad.com).

are designed with ease-of-use in mind, even for people who don't consider themselves to be at all technologically savvy. If you opt to learn basic HTML programming, for example, you can utilize more complex tools to further customize your blog and make it more functional. But if you have the ability to surf the web and do basic word processing, you already have the skills and knowledge necessary to launch a blog.

One of the nice features of TypePad blogs is that they're automatically made to be search engine optimized. This means that your blog and your blog entries will be listed with the popular search engines, including Google. Because this is a paid service, the decision about whether or not advertising appears within your blog is entirely up to you, plus you get to keep the revenue if you opt to display ads.

Tip

To learn about many popular blogs and be able to preview them as you develop plans for your own blog and kick around ideas for your blog's design, be sure to check out Blogs.com (blogs.com). It's an online guide to the world of blogging and offers links to popular and highly recommended blogs that cover a wide range of topics—from entertainment to news and politics to technology.

Unlike many of the free blog hosting services, because you're paying for TypePad, technical support is available to you 365 days per year, plus there's an extensive and interactive online-based support center designed to address the most common questions and problems encountered by bloggers.

In addition to providing the tools needed to create and publish your blog, TypePad offers powerful tools and resources for managing your blog, including real-time access to traffic stats and traffic analysis tools. Bloggers also have the ability to create and publish podcasts, plus add web pages to their blog.

If your goal is to generate revenue from your blog, TypePad offers multiple ways to do this, by displaying text-based ads or display ads. Partnerships have also been developed with Amazon.com, eBay.com, and PayPal, so eCommerce elements and content can be added to a blog, allowing people to make credit card or PayPal purchases directly from your blog.

Depending on the goals you have for your blog, TypePad offers more flexibility and customizability than some of the free blog hosting services, but whether or not you need this added functionality (and whether it's worth it for you to pay a

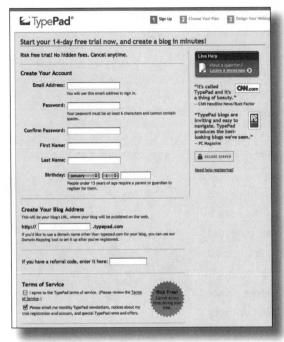

When you sign up for TypePad account, which takes just minutes, you can receive a free, 14-day trial of the TypePad blogging service.

monthly or annual fee) is entirely up to you. As you'd expect, TypePad is an ever-changing blogging platform that's continuously adding new features and functionality. In fact, in Summer 2008, TypePad underwent a massive update in order to provide cutting-edge features to its bloggers.

Also available from Six Apart, Ltd. is VOX.com, a totally free blog hosting service that offers scaled-down functionality compared to TypePad.

WordPress.com

Company: WordPress

Price: Free for the basic WordPress blogging service, however, a fee applies for using "premium features," such as extra storage, the ability for an unlimited number of simultaneous visitors to access your blog, and custom CSS functionality.

WordPress.com is a hybrid between a totally free blog hosting service and a fee-based one. While the majority of casual and non-business-related bloggers will find the free services offered by WordPress.com more than adequate, for more advanced functionality, premium services can be paid for on an a la carte basis.

In terms of the free service, it works pretty much like Blogger.com in that all of the tools needed to create, publish, and manage a blog are online based and available to anyone, from anywhere, with a computer that's connected to the internet. A basic (free) blog allows the blogger to utilize up to three gigabytes (3GB) of online storage space, which is more than enough to publish thousands of text-based pages or up to 2,500 photographs, for example. Additional online storage space is available for an annual fee.

Once you set up your personal account as a blogger with WordPress.com, you'll be given access to the online-based tools needed to create, publish, and manage your blog. This includes access to more than 60 fully customizable templates. If you have basic programming knowledge or wish to hire a freelance programmer, your blog design can be custom-created from scratch.

When it comes to creating individual blog entries, WordPress.com offers access to a highly functional word processing system that's online based. This word processor also has built-in page design features that allow you to incorporate photos or other types of content into your blog with a few clicks of the mouse. When it comes to managing your digital images and multimedia content, WordPress.com is compatible with services like Flickr, Photobucket, YouTube, and Google.

As you're creating your blog entries, you can create a list of tags (keywords) that are relevant to that entry. WordPress.com will use your keyword list to properly categorize your blog and automatically promote it using popular search engines, including Google. This is a powerful tool for helping you quickly generate traffic to your blog.

Like many of the other blogging services, WordPress.com has powerful anti-spam tools that prevent people from posting spam comments within your blog. In addition to providing interactive online support, WordPress.com's technical support team can help you solve programs via e-mail.

In addition to offering real-time traffic stats for your blog, WordPress.com allows you to monitor comments posted by your visitors. The service also allows you connect

Tip

If you've already created and published a blog using another blog hosting service, WordPress.com offers free tools to quickly and easily copy your existing blog content and transfer it to the WordPress.com service.

independent web pages to your blog, so you can easily add an "About Me" section, for example.

As you're developing and designing your blog, you'll have access to hundreds of free widgets and gadgets that can be used to add features and functionality to your blog, with no programming knowledge required.

WordPress.com is operated using an open source business model, which means that not only is almost everything offered for free, the service is constantly evolving and being improved upon. The developers boast that new features are added based on requests from its bloggers. One of the more recent additions to the service has been mobile blogging capabilities. For example, special Apple iPhone blogging software for WordPress.com can be downloaded from the Apple iTunes App Store.

While WordPress.com offers online tools, there is also downloadable software that can be used for creating and managing blogs. This software can be downloaded, for free, from WordPress.org.

WordPress.com, which is based in San Francisco, was created in 2003 by Matthew Mullenweg. Since launching WordPress, Mullenweg has been named one of the "50 most important people on the web" by *PC World* magazine. He publishes his own blog, called MA.TT (ma.tt/). As of late August 2008, WordPress.com hosted more than 3,899,958 active blogs.

From the WordPress home page (WordPress.com), you can create your own blog or access any of the other blogs currently hosted by this popular service.

Blogster.com

Company: Blogster.com

Price: Free

Although not as popular as Blogger.com (and not to be confused with it), Blogster. com is a free blog hosting service that provides all of the online-based tools needed to create, publish, and manage a blog. The service also offers online photo storage, making it easy to showcase digital images within your blog entries plus keep a remote backup of your photos. In a nutshell, Blogster.com refers to itself as a "vibrant virtual community built and inhabited by people who love to blog."

When you first visit the Blogster.com website, you can't do too much until becoming a member and initially setting up your blog. This is a quick and straightforward three-step process, which involves providing basic information about yourself and the blog you intend to create.

Step one requires you to give your blog a main title (which can be changed at anytime). You'll also need to select a free blog address (also referred to as your *member name*). This is a URL that ends with ".blogster.com". Once your blog is established, you can register your own custom domain name using a domain registrar service, such as GoDaddy.com, for a low annual fee.

Step two in the Blogster.com registration process requires new users to provide their name, gender, birthday, and zip code, while step three asks fo your e-mail address and a password for the account. Once you agree to the Blogster.com Terms of Service (done by placing a checkmark where appropriate using your mouse), you're in business and ready to begin blogging. The whole registration process takes about two minutes.

Upon completing the registration process, the main Blogster.com Dashboard screen will be displayed. It's from here you can create new blog entries and manage your blog. Start by clicking on the "Customize Blog" menu option to upload a photo of yourself (to be displayed within the heading of your blog) and create an "About Me" section.

If you opt to incorporate photos into your blog, you must first upload your images by clicking on the "My Photos" menu option and create an image database.

Warning!

Blogster.com offers far fewer features than its competitors, especially in terms of layout and design options, for example. As of September 2008, the service offered no blog templates or customization options, but a message stated that this functionality was "coming soon."

Then, when you select "Write Post" to create a new blog entry, the images in your database can be selected and incorporated into your blog.

The Write Post feature is a basic text editor that's online-based and allows you to write and format your blog entries. For each blog entry, you can choose one of several hundred pre-created categories, plus manually create a list of tags for each entry. Tags are keywords used to make it easier for visitors to find specific information within your blog, plus they're used by Blogster.com to categorize your blog in its own directory and when your entry is being listed with the search engines. Between two and five relevant tags are recommended for each blog entry.

Each blog entry requires is own title. This is different from the main header or main title of your blog itself. In terms of the body text for each blog entry, Blogster.com allows for basic formatting and the use of **bold**, *italic*, <u>underlined</u> and ~~strike thru~~ text. You can mix and match these typestyles as you see fit (using ***bold and italic text***, for example).

It's also possible to created bulleted or numbered lists, indent paragraphs, as well as right/left align or justify your text. Blogster.com offers about 25 different fonts to choose from, and allows you to select a font size between 8- and 36-point type. All of these options are controlled using on-screen command icons and pull-down menus that are displayed as part of the Write Post screen.

Additional blog formatting and creation options that available from the "Write Post" screen allow you to:

- include hyperlinks within your text
- add photos
- add emoticons (e.g., smiley faces)
- perform a spell check on your text (highly recommended before publishing a blog entry)
- select the color of your text and/or highlight your text with a color of your choice

- embed multimedia content (audio, video, animations, etc.) within your blog entry. Blogster.com is compatible with Flash, QuickTime, Shockwave, Windows Media, and Real Media content

- incorporate HTML code into your blog entry using the HTML editor; this allows you to add compatible widgets and gadgets, or custom design the appearance of your blog, plus add functionality if you're familiar with the HTML programming language. When adding a gadget or widget, however, you'll be provided with the appropriate code to cut and paste into this area.

After creating each blog entry, you have the option to either save the blog entry (and not publish it right away), or publish the entry and make it available immediately for the world to access. Once a blog entry is published, your visitors can post comments.

If you're looking to get a basic blog up and running quickly and don't want to spend any money or waste too much time creating a fancy design for your blog, Blogster.com offers a viable but not as robust solution as its competitors. The biggest drawback to Blogster.com is that all of the blogs look very similar due to limited design customization capabilities.

Tip

Aside from these general interest-free blogging services that welcome bloggers to create blogs about virtually anything, there are some topic-specific blog hosting services that are also offered free of charge. For example, there's SmugMug.com for creating photo blogs, and a wide range of services, like TripAdvisor.com, TravelBlog.com, and Travellerspoint.com, that welcome vacation or travel-specific blogs within their online communities. For people who have experienced divorce, the Divorce360.com site invites bloggers to create and manage blogs that share their personal relationship experiences. The MobileMe service from Apple allows Mac-users to create their own blogs as part of its fee-based service.

Additional Blog Hosting Options

Blogger.com, TypePad.com, VOX.com, and WordPress.com are four extremely popular online-based blogging services that combined host the majority of the millions of blogs currently in existence. However, there are also many other blog hosting services worth mentioning, including several of the popular social networking sites that offer blogging capabilities.

FaceBook.com

Company: Facebook

Price: Free

Facebook.com has become one of the most popular and populated social networking sites on the web. According to its developers, "Facebook gives people the power to share and makes the world more open and connected. Millions of people use Facebook everyday to keep up with friends, upload an unlimited number of photos, share links and videos, and learn more about the people they meet."

This is a free, advertiser-supported service that allows members to create detailed profiles about themselves, send messages to their friends, meet new people, upload and display photos and videos, plus create their own blog.

While Facebook offers full blogging capabilities, this is not primarily a blogging service. Facebook is designed to allow people to meet and communicate with each other through messaging, e-mailing, and real-time chatting.

In addition to being available via any computer that's connected to the internet, Facebook can also be accessed using many wireless PDAs, Smartphones, and cellular phones. There's even a special Facebook for iPhone software package available for free from the Apple iTunes App Store, so people can communicate with their Facebook friends from virtually anywhere.

Tip

In addition to displaying photos and text-based blogs, many vloggers use Facebook and MySpace to post and distribute their vlogs (video blogs). These services, in addition to YouTube, for example, provide an excellent tool for building up an audience for your blog.

One feature that Facebook (and MySpace) offers is a one-line status line, which begins "[Your Name] is..." It encourages users to continuously add one line of text about what they're currently doing. In essence, users are creating single line blogs that are automatically shared with their friends. This is a very quick and easy way for people to get started blogging. A similar one-line blogging concept used by Twitter, and Plurk ask the question, "Where are you and what are you doing?"

MySpace.com

Company: MySpace.com

Price: Free

Although the MySpace.com user interface is vastly different from Facebook.com, the functionality between these two services is similar. MySpace.com is primarily an interactive social networking site that allows people to meet and communicate in cyberspace. However, Myspace.com also offers powerful blogging tools and offers a forum for distributing and promoting blogs.

In fact, regardless of what blog hosting service you use, it's an excellent strategy to establish and maintain an active MySpace and Facebook page in order to promote your blog (or vlog) and develop a large group of online friends. One nice feature of MySpace is that members can post bulletins, which are public messages that automatically can be read by all of their friends. So, if you add hundreds or thousands of MySpace friends, you can quickly notify them when you've posted a new blog or vlog entry using a bulletin.

Within your profile on MySpace (or Facebook), you can include as much personal information as you desire, allowing people to get to know you. You can also post links to your blog or website(s), and display your personal contact information (although as you'll learn from Chapter 10, you should think twice about doing this).

Using the people search tools available on MySpace and Facebook, you can find and meet people with similar interests and add them as friends in order to stay in contact with them through the service. Because your MySpace and Facebook profile page is extremely customizable, you can determine what it looks like, plus add widgets to improve its interactivity and functionality.

Using a bit of creativity, bloggers and vloggers have discovered many ways to promote themselves and their blog using MySpace and Facebook, plus use these services as powerful (and free) marketing tools for their blog and to help

Warning!

Facebook and MySpace allow businesses, recording artists, artists, and other professionals to set up accounts and use them as a promotional tool for themselves and their work. However, there are strict rules in place that prevent business operators from spamming or using their Facebook page for many types of commercial purposes. Failure to adhere to the Facebook terms of service will result in an account being deleted.

them become famous in cyberspace. It's not uncommon for popular MySpace or Facebook users to have tens of thousands of friends, although building up this type of following will typically require a significant time investment and a dedication to becoming an active social networker (in addition to a blogger).

Twitter.com

Company: Twitter, Inc.

Price: Free

Twitter.com was originally created in March 2006 (and launched publicly in May 2007). It quickly became something of a worldwide phenomenon. It basically bridged cell phone text messaging with online social networking and blogging, but made the whole process extremely simply, fast, and effortless. Twitter is an online-based social networking site with just one purpose—to inform your online friends about what you're doing and/or where you are.

Instead of creating elaborate blogs and profiles, producing vlogs, or having to maintain contact with friends through long and detailed e-mails or text messages, Twitter allows you to answer just one simple question (in one or two sentences) and keep your online friends informed.

Each time you log into Twitter (via computer, wireless PDA, or cell phone), you'll be asked one simple question which you must answer in 140 characters or less. The question is, "What are you doing?" Your response is then displayed for all of your friends and followers to see. As a Twitter member, you're encouraged to update your entry throughout the day as you create an ongoing series of one line blogs that chronicle your life, your emotions, your thoughts, and your activities.

On the surface, Twitter may sound like an overly simplistic waste of time; however, millions of bloggers, web surfers, and social networkers have literally become addicted to this service and stay connected to Twitter throughout the day from their computer, wireless PDA, or cell phone.

The Twitter service was created by Jack Dorsey, who wanted to create an easy way to keep tabs on what his friends were doing.

Tip

Plurk.com is a micro-blogging service that's very similar in functionality to Twitter.

According to the company, "The result of using Twitter to stay connected with friends, relatives, and coworkers is that you have a sense of what folks are up to, but you are not expected to respond to any updates unless you want to. This means you can step in or out of the flow of information as it suits you and it never queues up with increasing demand for your attention. Additionally, users are very much in control of whose updates they receive, when they receive them, and on what device."

> **Tip**
>
> To see a comical explanation of what Twitter is all about, check out the video created by independent vlogger Lisa Nova, called "Twitter Whore." (This video is not actually produced or endorsed by Twitter, but it's funny and explains the addictiveness of the service.) It's available on YouTube. com. You can follow Lisa's daily life on Twitter (twitter.com/Lisa_Nova).

If you're new to blogging and not sure you want to invest the time and energy to create and maintain a traditional blog, Twitter is an ideal way to get your feet wet and start experimenting. After all, you can probably come up with just one sentence to write a few times throughout any given day.

As you read other peoples' Twitter posts, you'll discover some users take this service very seriously, while others use it to post extremely funny, creative, or thought-provoking content (again in 140 characters or less). Twitter is also a powerful tool for meeting new people and for promoting your existing blog, and it's a fun and addicting way to interact with people around the world.

LinkedIn.com

Company: LinkedIn Corporation

Price: Free, however, there is a fee-based premium service available.

LinkedIn.com is an online social networking service designed exclusively for business professionals. It's a free tool (although fee-based services are also offered) for creating and managing professional relationships, networking, and exchanging information among professional colleagues. As of mid-2008, LinkedIn boasted more than 25 million members representing more than 150 industries.

LinkedIn.com is successfully used by business people to find potential clients, service providers, subject experts, and partners who come recommended. It can also be used for finding new business opportunities, finding new job opportunities, and for meeting like-minded people who work in your industry.

For bloggers catering to business people and entrepreneurs, LinkedIn represents a powerful tool for building a following and promoting a blog. The service allows you to create a detailed online profile about yourself that can summarize your professional accomplishments. It also allows you to create, build, and manage a network of online-based contacts.

YouTube.com

Company: YouTube is an independent subsidiary of Google

Price: Free

If you're a vlogger (or contemplating becoming one), it's essential that you become familiar with and an active participant on YouTube. This has become the premier vlog distribution and promotion vehicle for video-based vlogs.

Since it was founded in February 2005, YouTube has become the undisputed leader in online video and the world's most popular online destination for watching and sharing original videos (and vlogs). Upon registering for a free membership, anyone can upload and share their own videos (vlogs) and make them available to the world.

Tip

As a vlogger, you'll probably want to post links to your vlogs on your own website or blog, but you'll definitely want to make them available on YouTube, as well as other web-based video services, such as Yahoo! Video (video.search.yahoo.com/video) and AOL Video (video.aol.com). For additional information about vlogging, be sure to read Chapter 8.

Videos that are hosted on YouTube can be accessed from the YouTube website, but they can also be embedded within independent websites and blogs (including MySpace and Facebook pages), sent to others via e-mail, or accessed from wireless PDAs, cell phones, and Smartphones (including the Apple iPhone).

All videos posted to YouTube are categorized and searchable by keyword, so content is typically easy to find once it's been posted. Thus, YouTube provides an ideal forum for promoting and distributing vlogs. As a vlogger, YouTube allows you to create your own channel that people can subscribe to, so they automatically get notified when you post a new vlog, plus they can view all of your posted vlogs in one place.

YouTube also makes it easy to track online stats and traffic for your vlogs, plus the service encourages people to post feedback and comments, and rate videos that are posted to the service.

According to Google, YouTube has more than 200 million unique members (as of March 2008) that include an equal number of males and females, typically between the ages of 18 and 55. More than half of YouTube's active members access the service at least once per week.

Tip

All of the main steps involved with creating, designing, and publishing a traditional blog can be found within Chapters 1 through 6. These chapters will walk you through the process of brainstorming ideas, designing your blog, creating blog entries, publishing and then managing your blog. If you're more interested in vlogging or podcasting, you'll also find the information within Chapter 8 to be extremely useful.

What's Next?

The next chapter focuses on the different types of blogs you can create, plus discusses some of the other important things you'll need to consider as you initially create your blog. For example, you'll learn how important it is to develop a memorable main title for your blog. You'll also learn how and why maintaining a positive online reputation as a blogger is essential to your success as a blogger, plus how what you blog about can impact your personal and professional life outside of cyberspace.

Before kicking off your blogging efforts, it's important to develop a well-thought-out and organized approach, not just in regard to the content of your blog, but about all aspects of your blog—from its appearance to your intended audience, and how you'll promote it to the public. As you get started, you'll also want to establish clearly defined goals for your blog.

Chapter 4 explores how you can utilize text, graphics, audio and video to help achieve your blogs goals, how you can better get to know your target audience, how to register a custom domain name (URL) for your blog, plus how to establish a unique, consistent voice and tone for your blog.

Chapter 4
Creating Your Blog

Depending on your goals, blogging can be a fun and rewarding experience. A blog can also be a powerful business tool, or simply used as a forum for quickly, easily, and inexpensively sharing information, thoughts, ideas, and opinions with friends and family, coworkers, customers, clients, members of a group/association/club, or the general public.

A well-written or professionally produced blog, podcast, or vlog is an excellent tool for marketing and promoting yourself, as well as your business and its products or services. A blog can also help you gain notoriety, popularity, and fame in cyberspace, as well as in the real world, and it can be used as a revenue-generating tool.

This chapter begins by exploring the different types of content you can create, and then delves into some of the steps required to actually get started blogging. For example, you'll discover how important it is to give your blog a catchy title, and then how to register an easy-to-remember (and spell) domain name for your blog.

Choosing a topic or theme for your blog is also an important consideration. Deciding what you can actually blog about is touched on within this chapter, but is focused on more in Chapter 6.

Before you can create and launch a successful blog, no matter what your goals for the blog actually are, it's essential that you carefully define who your target audience is, and then ensure that you cater specifically to that audience in order to develop a large and ever-growing following.

Just as if you are marketing or selling a product or service to a target audience, knowing exactly who your intended audience for the blog is will help you cater to that audience's wants, needs, interests, and expectations. It will also help

Tip

As you begin developing your blog, you'll probably want to incorporate different types of content, including text, graphics, photos, audio, video, and other multimedia elements. Choosing the right elements to use throughout your blog will help you more effectively communicate with your audience and more easily get your point(s) across. Your target audience will help dictate the types of content that are appropriate for your blog. Once you know what type of content you'll need to produce, you can acquire the appropriate tools and resources to make developing that content easier. Keep in mind: Your audience will have expectations for your blog, in terms of production quality and appearance, as well as content. To achieve success, it's essential that you meet or exceed those expectations.

you more easily select topics and approaches for each blog entry that are appropriate to your audience, and allow you to develop a blog that people within your target audience will want to access on a regular basis.

Finally, this chapter explores the need to keep your blog's content new and fresh with regular updates, and focuses on why it's important to establish a consistent voice or tone for your blog.

Types of Blogs and Content

The whole blogging phenomenon began as people, just like you, from all walks of life, started posting text-based entries online using a digital journal format. Instead of keeping a traditional, handwritten, and secret personal diary in a hard copy format, people began opting to share their innermost thoughts and feelings by making their blog entries available to the public. In the early days of blogging, only text was used to create blogs.

Today, depending on what blogging, podcasting, or vlogging services and tools you utilize, it's easy to incorporate text, photos, audio, video, animations, and other multimedia elements into your blog. Or, you can focus on producing an audio-based blog (podcast) that people can download and enjoy on their Apple iPod (or .MP3 player), for example, or listen to using their computer (assuming it has speakers attached to it).

Most recently, as internet connections have become faster and computer technology has become more advanced, recording, editing, and publishing vlogs (video-based blogs) has become commonplace. For any of these blogging, podcasting, or vlogging methods, absolutely no programming is required, so it's relatively easy for anyone with a bit of creativity to write, edit, produce, and publish almost any type of blog content using tools available on their computer or through the online-based blogging service being used.

Before you decide what type(s) of content to create for your blog, make sure you have the know-how, necessary equipment and software, budget, and time available to create the most professional-quality content possible in order to meet or exceed the expectations of your target audience.

Many of the most popular blogs, podcasts, and vlogs feature text that's equally or better written than what you'd find in major daily newspapers or popular magazines, for example. As for podcasts and blogs, people often expect a production quality that's equivalent to professional radio or television broadcasts. In other words, how you present your content is often as important as the information you'll be attempting to convey.

What to Consider Before Creating Text-Based Content

Creating a text-based blog is the easiest in terms of the resources and time commitment involved. You can use any text editor or word processor to create your content, and then use a blogging service to publish that content. You can even create blogs while on the go using a wireless PDA or cell phone (such as the iPhone).

If you opt to create a text-based blog, what will be required of you are basic writing skills. If your blog will utilize text, that text must:

- be well-written
- be easy-to-understand
- be concise
- contain no spelling or grammatical errors.

If you're not comfortable with your ability to write in a compelling, entertaining, and/or

Tip

For Apple's iPhone, there are several third-party software packages available, either for free or for a small fee, which allow you to create and publish text-based blogs from anywhere and upload them to popular blogging services. To see what iPhone applications are available for text or photo-based blogging, visit the iTunes App Store and click on the "Social Networking" software category. TypePad is a free application for creating text and photo-based blogs via an iPhone. There are also iPhone versions of MySpace and Facebook, both of which allow for the creation of blog entries.

Warning!

Professional writers, well-known journalists, and bestselling authors all rely on highly skilled editors to edit their work. Be sure to have someone proofread your text-based blogs before publishing them if you're trying to communicate in a professional manner via your blog. Some people focus on keeping their blog extremely informal; for these types of blogs, the audience's expectations are lower, and what you have to say becomes far more important than how you say it. If, however, your blog is being used for business purposes or you're trying to develop a professional reputation, creating well-written and error-free text is essential.

informative style that caters to the demands of your target audience, consider producing a podcast or vlog that better utilizes your verbal communication skills. With practice, most people can fine-tune their writing skills, but becoming a good writer requires creativity and is an art form onto itself.

What to Consider Before Creating Audio Content (Podcasts)

Producing a podcast (audio-based blog) requires more steps and more of a time commitment than creating a text-based blog. Instead of writing, however, you'll be communicating with your fans and followers using your voice and sound. In addition to creating compelling and informative content, you'll need to concern yourself with production quality issues and how your podcast sounds.

Therefore, the additional skills that are required might include:

- **Public speaking.** The ability to speak clearly and effectively in order to convey your information. Are you able to speak well and utilize a sufficient vocabulary to get your points across? Is the tone of your voice pleasant? Are you able to successfully convey emotion using just your voice? Are you able to speak extemporaneously or can you read from a script and make yourself sound natural?

- **Audio recording.** You must have the ability to record your podcasts in a quiet environment using quality recording equipment. Depending on the computer equipment you'll be using, this might include investing in a quality microphone, headphones (or speakers), and a high-end digital voice recorder. While Apple iMacs and MacBook computers have a webcam (iSight camera), microphone, speakers, and software for recording audio and/or video built in, PC-based computers require you to purchase these peripherals and software-based tools separately.

- **Audio editing.** Very few people can record content from start to finish without making a mistake. Audio editing skills (and tools) allow you to edit your recordings before publishing them. Part of the editing process might include incorporating music, sound effects, or other audio clips into your podcasts. There is a wide range of software packages available to help you record, edit, and publish podcasts. More information about the necessary equipment

Need Help with Your Public Speaking Skills?

There are a wide range of how-to books, audio and video-based courses, plus in-person classes and workshops you can participate in to fine-tune and improve your public speaking skills and your vocabulary.

To learn about public speaking classes being taught in your area, contact your local community college or adult education program. Toastmasters International (949-858-8255/toastmasters.org) is a worldwide organization with local chapters in many cities across America that is open to anyone interested in improving their public speaking skills. Toastmasters offers regularly held meetings and workshops, plus offers a wide range of instructional materials. Membership to the Toastmasters organization is extremely affordable.

Instructional audio book producers, including Nightingale Conant (800-560-6081/nightingale.com) offer audio CD and .MP3-based courses designed to help people improve their vocabulary and public speaking skills. According to the company, *Stand and Deliver: The Dale Carnegie Method for Public Speaking Mastery* ($79.95 to $89.95), for example, "gives you everything you need to know to become an incredibly poised, polished, and masterful communicator. Someone who can hold an audience of one, 10 or 1000 in the palm of your hand, from the first word you speak to them until the last." *WordSmart Deluxe Edition* ($288) is an audio-based course designed to help you improve your vocabulary by quickly teaching you more than 5,000 new words.

Additional audio-based instructional programs can be purchased and downloaded from Audible.com and listened to using an iPod or any .MP3 player.

Tip

When acquiring music or sound effects to incorporate into your blog, podcast, or vlog, look for music that is "royalty-free." This means you only pay a one-time charge to use the music, but don't have to pay a recurring fee for each use.

and software required can be found within Chapter 2. Be sure to invest the time necessary to become proficient using this equipment to ensure the production quality of your podcasts is as professional as possible.

Depending on the topic of your podcast (audio blog) and how much effort you want to invest, you might want to incorporate sound effects, background music, and other audio content. To make this easier, you can purchase or license royalty-free music and sound effects from various companies that can easily be incorporated into your podcasts. You can also hire a production company to create radio-quality intros, "bumpers," and "sweepers" to help make your podcasts sound more like professionally produced radio programs.

The following is a sampling of music and sound effects you can acquire to incorporate into your podcast. For additional resources, use any internet search engine and enter the search phrase, "royalty free background music," "sound effects," or "radio sweepers." In most cases, music and sound effects can be downloaded in .MP3 or .WAV format. The one-time fee associated with acquiring the rights to use the music will vary by company. In some cases, the audio content is offered free of charge; in others, there is a low, one-time fee for each track you wish to use.

Music and Sound Effects Companies

The following is a sampling of music production companies that offer extensive libraries of royalty-free music that can be acquired and downloaded for use in podcasts or vlogs. You'll find that these companies divide their offerings into categories or genres (such as classical, jazz, rock, holiday, new age, or pop), and then offer individual music tracks in various lengths, including 30, 60, and 90 seconds.

- Audio Jungle: royalty-free music (audiojungle.net/category/music)
- Audio Sparx: royalty-free music and sound effects (audiosparx.com)
- Free Play Music: royalty-free production music (freeplaymusic.com)
- Opuzz: royalty-free production music (opuzz.com)

- Partners In Rhyme: sound effects library (partnersinrhyme.com)
- Royalty-Free Music: royalty-free music (royaltyfreemusic.com)
- Sound Rangers: sound effects library (soundrangers.com)
- SoundSnap: sound effects library (soundsnap.com)
- Stock Music: royalty-free music and sound effects (stockmusic.net)
- Stock Music Store: royalty-free music (stockmusicstore.com)

One way to boost the production quality of your podcast or vlog is to incorporate professionally produced intros, sweepers, stingers, or bumpers. These are short audio clips created by professional announcers/broadcasters that can be used to introduce your podcast or vlog, and quickly capture someone's attention. These audio elements are typically used on radio stations for station IDs and other purposes. They can be between five and 15 seconds in length.

Radio Voice Imaging (radiovoiceimaging.com) is just one example of a production company that produces extremely professional sounding and attention getting intros, bumpers, stingers, and sweepers for radio stations, but that also offers its services to podcasters and vloggers for as little as $13 per sweeper (up to 15 seconds in length) or $21.99 per stinger (a highly produced intro that's less than five seconds in length that can be used to promote a blog name or slogan).

The Radio Voice Imaging website offers an online demo of this company's work, or you can visit jasonrich.com or mypalrusty.com to hear actual samples of sweepers produced by this company. Once you place your order and submit a script, production takes less than one week and the final product(s) are e-mailed in .MP3 or .WAV format for easy incorporate into your podcast or vlog.

To find additional companies that offer this type of production services, use any search engine and enter the search phrase "radio

Warning

Utilizing music or sound effects without permission violates copyright laws. Therefore, you should not simply download (pirate) music or sound effects and incorporate them into your blog. Purchasing or licensing royalty-free music and sound effects is the easiest and most economical way to legally use music in your blogs, unless you write and record your own music or create and record your own sound effects from scratch.

imaging." A small sampling of production companies that offer inexpensive intros, sweepers, bumpers, and stingers to radio stations and bloggers (for a fee) include:

- DJ Drop Ins (djdropins.com/index.html)
- Jack Murphy Productions (jackmurphy.com)
- Jeff Radio (jeffradio.com)
- Long Train Audio Production Company (longtrainproductions.com/radio-imaging.html)
- ProVoice USA (provoiceusa.com/radio-sweepers.htm)
- Radio Sweepers (radiosweepers.com)
- Radio Tool Kit (radiotoolkit.com)

What to Consider Before Creating Vlogs (Video-Based Blogs)

If you opt to produce a vlog (as opposed to a text-based blog or an audio podcast), you now have three major elements in terms of production to worry about:

1. **Your blog's content.** This includes what you have to say, how you'll say it, and what content you'll use within each vlog entry.

2. **How your vlog sounds (audio quality).** This includes all audio elements that will be incorporated into your vlog, such as your voice, sound effects, and music. It also involves editing out or eliminating unwanted background noise.

3. **The video production quality of your vlog.** Your own appearance, lighting, and your "set" or "background" are among the visual elements you'll need to take into account when creating a vlog.

Vlogging means you'll be using video (in addition to other multimedia elements, like sound, music, graphics, and animations, for example) to showcase and distribute your content. Thanks to services like YouTube.com, vlogging has becoming more popular than ever and has been a launching pad for numerous people to become online celebrities.

Producing a vlog allows people to both see and hear you. However, producing and editing quality video can be a time consuming process and takes specialized software, computer hardware, and skill. Some vloggers, however, like Chris Crocker, go with a grassroots approach to their production and have achieved tremendous success. The level of production quality your vlog will require will depend on your target audience and your content, as well as your own personal preference. Obviously, a vlog that offers top-notch production will have much more credibility than something that looks thrown together using a low-end camcorder or webcam.

Depending on your equipment, you can shoot your vlog using any type of video camcorder and then edit the footage on your computer before publishing it. You could also use your computer's webcam (or built-in video camera) to record your vlog entries, and then use video editing software to edit and publish your vlog. To obtain the highest production quality possible without filming your vlog in a television or motion picture studio, you'll need to invest in some high-end, high definition video equipment and become proficient in video editing software.

Choosing What to Blog About

When it comes to choosing a topic to blog about, your options are truly limitless. As you'll discover in Chapter 6, you can choose to convey facts or information within a blog; voice your personal opinions or thoughts; distribute propaganda; discuss topics that are of interest to you; or share information about yourself, your life, your products, or your services.

Choosing the right topic for you will take a bit of creativity and should be based on what you're interested in and are truly passionate about. The overall topic you opt to blog about should be one that can be expanded or built upon, so you can create ongoing entries that are innovative, new, informative, entertaining, and/or provocative for your audience.

There are no rules about what you can or can't blog about, but before you get started, spend some time fleshing out your idea and developing a way to convey your content that will inform and/or entertain your intended audience. Focus on what type of image or reputation you're looking to create for yourself over the long-term, plus how you'll be able to use your blog (and its content) to achieve your overall goals.

Defining Your Target Audience

Just like any TV show, radio program, newspaper, magazine, website, traditional business, online-based business or service, your blog should have a primary target audience (and perhaps a defined secondary audience as well).

For your blog to ultimately achieve success, you'll want to carefully and thoroughly define your target audience and then cater to that audience's wants, needs, desires, interests and personality. This section will help you do all that.

Remember, it's to your benefit to know and understand as much about your target audience as possible. This will typically require that you conduct research and really get to know these people as a group. Ultimately, as you begin to develop your blog's content as well as all of your marketing materials, you'll want to put yourself in your target audience's shoes and think the way they think. The better you relate to your audience, the more favorably they'll respond to your blog and its content.

Establish Your Own Niche

Most bloggers find it infinitely easier to select topics to blog about that cater to a small niche audience. By doing this, it becomes easier to understand your potential audience and address their wants, needs, desires, interests, and concerns, as well as specifically cater all of your blog's content to this defined audience.

A niche audience can be any group of people that you define to be your target audience. It can be based on a single defining factor, such as a special interest. For example, if you're blogging about golf, the single criteria you might use to define your target audience is people who play golf, enjoy watching golf on TV, or who belong to a golf club.

You can more narrowly define this audience by focusing on just male or female golfers, golfers who earn a specific income, golfers who live or play golf in a specific geographic region, people who are members of a private golf club, golfers who are retired, or golfers who are left-handed, for example.

The more narrowly you define your audience, the easier it is to ascertain their wants and needs, and then cater your blog's content to those people. Of course, your blog's content might appeal to several unique target audiences, in which case, you'd want to define and address each of these audiences separately in order to maximize your audience and build the largest following possible.

Before you can define your niche audience, however, spend as much time as is necessary to get to know absolutely everything there is to know about the topic(s) you'll be blogging about. Discover why the topic will appeal to your intended audience. Also, invest the time needed to learn about competing blogs so you can develop a more innovative way to communicate your information, or at least differentiate your blog from the many others out there.

Defining Your Audience

You already know how important it is to understand and know your target audience. Use the worksheet on pages 66-67 to help you fine-tune exactly who comprises this audience. Think about what your blog will be about, who it will primarily appeal to, who will be reading, hearing, or viewing it, what needs it addresses, how it will potentially solve a problem, and who will benefit from it and why.

Doing Your Market Research

Approach your research from several angles. First, focus on the blog idea or subject matter itself and to whom it will appeal. Next, research your competition; what approach are other bloggers taking? Who is their target audience? Based on your knowledge of the topic and your target audience, how can you improve or build on what your competition is doing in order to build your own audience?

Next, do as much research about your target audience as possible. Based on the profile you create for the people you believe will be your primary audience, learn as much as possible about their likes and dislikes, their wants, their needs, their interests, and what problems they're facing in their daily lives. Focus on how you can use this knowledge to generate as much interest in your blog as possible.

Finally, focus on the best way to distribute your blog and convey your information in a succinct, easy-to-understand, and cost-effective way that will capture your target audience's attention. This will mean figuring out if a text-based blog, podcast, or vlog is most appropriate.

A wide range of online-based elements can be used within a blog, but they must be used effectively to truly make an impact on your audience. Having a bunch

Target Audience Worksheet

For each category, check all that apply specifically to your primary target audience. Once you've carefully narrowed down your target audience, complete this worksheet a second time to define the secondary potential audience for your blog.

Gender: ❑ Male ❑ Female ❑ Not Applicable

Marital Status: ❑ Single ❑ Married ❑ Divorced ❑ Widowed ❑ Not Applicable

Age: ❑ Child ❑ Teenager ❑ Age 18-24 ❑ Age 25-49 ❑ Age 50-65 ❑ Age 66+ ❑ Not Applicable

Race: ❑ White ❑ African American ❑ Hispanic ❑ Asian ❑ Other:_____ ❑ Not Applicable

Sexual Orientation: ❑ Straight ❑ Gay ❑ Bisexual ❑ Not Applicable

Income Level (per year): ❑ Under $15,000 ❑ $15,001 to $25,000 ❑ $25,001 to $45,000 ❑ $45,001 to $55,000 ❑ $55,001 to $99,999 ❑ $100,000 to $500,000 ❑ $500,000 to $999,999 ❑ $1,000,000+ ❑ Not Applicable

Education Level: ❑ Some High School ❑ High School Graduate ❑ College Graduate ❑ Advanced Degree ❑ Not Applicable

Occupation: _____ ❑ Not Applicable

Religion: _____ ❑ Not Applicable

Political Affiliation: ❑ Republican ❑ Democrat ❑ Other:_____ ❑ Not Applicable

Geographic Region: ❑ Specific City/State: _____ ❑ Not Applicable ❑ United States ❑ Canada ❑ Europe ❑ Asia ❑ South America ❑ North America ❑ Africa ❑ Australia ❑ Antarctica

Physical Attributes: ❑ Tall ❑ Short ❑ Average Height ❑ Thin ❑ Overweight ❑ Average Weight ❑ Not Applicable

Housing: ❑ Owns Home ❑ Rents Home ❑ Rents Apartment ❑ Owns Condo ❑ Rents Condo ❑ Lives with Parents ❑ Lives with Spouse ❑ Lives with Spouse and Children ❑ Lives with Roommate(s) ❑ Other: _____ ❑ Not Applicable

Primary Computer and Internet Usage:

❏ At Home   ❏ At Work   ❏ Internet Café/Wi-Fi Location

❏ Wireless PDA or Smartphone   ❏ Apple iPod/iTouch (.MP3 Player)

❏ Desktop Computer: ❏ PC ❏ Mac   ❏ Notebook Computer: ❏ PC ❏ Mac

❏ Not Online*

Primary Internet Connection:

❏ Dial-Up   ❏ Broadband ❏ DSL   ❏ Wireless PDA/Cell Phone

Type of Blog Content Your Audience Would Prefer or Best Relate To:

❏ Text Only   ❏ Text and Graphics (Photos)   ❏ Photos Only

❏ Audio (Podcast)   ❏ Video (Vlog)   ❏ Other

Hobbies/Special Interests: _____ ❏ Not Applicable

Club/Association Membership: _____ ❏ Not Applicable

Spending/Shopping Habits:

❏ Typically Shops at Retail Stores   ❏ Shops Often Via Mail Order

❏ Comfortable Shopping Online   ❏ Readily Uses Credit Cards

❏ Readily Uses a Debit Card   ❏ Writes Checks for Purchases

❏ Possess a PayPal Account   ❏ Has Below Average or No Credit

Driving Habits:

❏ Drives a Compact Vehicle   ❏ Drives an SUV or Van

❏ Drives a Pick-Up Truck   ❏ Drives a Sports Car

❏ Drives a Luxury Sedan   ❏ Drives a Hybrid Vehicle

❏ Owns Their Vehicle   ❏ Leases Their Vehicle

❏ Drives Less Than 15,000 Miles/Year   ❏ Drives More Than 15,000 Miles / Year

❏ Commutes Daily To Work   ❏ Carpools

❏ Other: _____   ❏ Not Applicable

Media Habits:

❏ Primarily Watches TV   ❏ Primarily Reads Newspapers

❏ Primarily Reads Magazines   ❏ Primarily Surfs The Web

❏ Not Applicable

Other Relevant Attribute: _____ ❏ Not Applicable

Other Relevant Attribute: _____ ❏ Not Applicable

Other Relevant Attribute: _____ ❏ Not Applicable

*If you check this box, stop reading this book because the audience for your online-based blog idea does not exist!

Tip

Once you define your target audience, put yourself in their shoes and start to think as they think. One way to do this is to read the other blogs, newspapers, magazines, books, and special interest publications they'd typically read. For example, if your blog will appeal to mothers of infants and preschool children, make a point to start reading many different parenting blogs and magazines, and visiting all of the parenting websites you can find. This is ongoing research that will help keep you in the know about current trends, issues, concerns, new developments, and information that's of interest to your target audience.

Another way to get to know your target audience is to spend time with them in person. The more time you spend with people in your target audience, the more obvious their wants, interests, and needs will become, and the easier it will be for you to address them as you begin blogging.

of flashy bells and whistles in a blog that look amazing but that make your blog confusing to navigate, or that say little or nothing about what you're actually blogging about, is virtually useless.

Giving Your Blog a Catchy Name or Title

Just as products, companies, stores, movies, TV shows, and songs, for example, have catchy titles or names to capture the attention of their intended audiences, your blog should also have a catchy title or name that somehow describes what it's all about. The main title of your blog should also be memorable and easy to spell. After all, you want to attract people to read, listen to, or watch your blog, plus talk about it with their friends, coworkers, and relatives.

Some people opt to incorporate their own name, company name, or product name into their blog; for example, my blog is JasonRichTravel.com. An alternative is to coin a unique word as the title of your blog, like Gizmodo (gizmodo.com).

In addition to naming your blog, include a headline or main title to each individual blog entry. These titles should somehow incorporate descriptive keywords based on the content of each entry in order to make it easier for internet search engines to categorize and list your blog and make it easier for new people to find online. You also want to make it quick and easy for people who visit your blog to be able to access exactly what they're looking for.

Writing a Succinct Blog Description

When you register your domain name with a registrar, as well as when you register it with the popular internet search engines (Google, Yahoo!, etc.) and/or with the various blog, podcast, or vlog directories, you will be required to provide a short description of your blog.

In two sentences or less, create an attention-grabbing description of your blog that will make people want to visit or access it. The description you create should include what the blog is about (the overall topic or theme), as well as information about you, the blogger.

The description you create should appeal to your target audience, plus, just as importantly, incorporate as many keywords or phrases as possible. It should also answer the questions, "Why should I read/access this blog?," "What does the blog offer?", and "What's so special about this blog?"

Tip

Some people opt to also create a logo for their blog, just as a company would create a logo for itself. This can help you establish your blog as a brand and make it more unique and identifiable to your intended audience. Any freelance graphic artist can be hired to create a professional-looking logo on your behalf. Online-based companies such as LogoWorks (logoworks. com) will create a customized logo starting at $99. You can find and hire a freelance graphic designer using a service like guru.com or eLance.com, or using any internet search engine, use the search phrase "logo design."

Since it will probably be your short description that people read in order to learn about your blog before they read or access it in its entirety, this description should use powerful language with no grammatical or spelling mistakes.

Choosing and Registering Your Blog's Domain Name

After selecting the name of your blog, you'll need to register your blog's specific URL (internet address). This process takes just a few minutes and will cost under $10 per year, per URL, if you use an internet registrar such as GoDaddy.com (godaddy.com).

The first step in this process is to brainstorm the perfect custom domain name for your blog. Ideally, the domain name you select should be easy to remember, easy to spell, and obvious to potential web surfers. For example, if the name of your blog is "Joe Hates Politics" you might want your website address to be "JoeHatesPolitics.com."

Obviously, with so many website and blog URLs already in existence, many domain names are already taken. However, with more than 31.7 trillion domain names ending with the ".com" extension possible, there are still plenty of appealing domain names available.

From a technical standpoint, every website/blog is assigned a unique IP address, which is comprised of a series of numbers, between zero and 255. An IP address might look like this: "135.52.0.255." To the layperson, this numeric combination means nothing. But to a computer, this is how an internet browser finds your website/blog in the vastness of cyberspace.

Instead of making web surfers memorize a bunch of confusing number combinations for the websites or blogs they're looking for, a system of URLs has been created.

A typical URL has three main components. The first part typically begins with "www." or "http://" The second part of a URL is what you actually must select.

The third part of a URL is its extension, which is typically ".com". However, a variety of other extensions are available, such as .edu, .org, .net., gov, .info, .TV, .biz, .name and .us. Some of these extensions have specific uses. For example, a website or blog that ends with the extension ".gov" is typically government operated.

Most web surfers are accustomed to URLs ending with the popular ".com" extension, so ideally, you want your URL to use it. Otherwise, potential blog readers might get confused trying to find your blog if it utilizes a less popular extension.

Of course, the same blog can have many different URLs that lead to the same place. So, you could potentially register "JoeHatesPolitics.

Tip

In addition to using a search engine to find the websites/blogs they're looking for, most web surfers also rely on their common sense. For example, if someone is looking for a specific company or individual's blog, they'll enter "[companyname].com" or "[name].com" into their web browser. Knowing this, you'll want to choose a URL that your potential customers will be able to figure out for themselves and then remember.

com," "JoeHatesPolitics.biz" and "JoeHatesPolitics.info," to ensure web surfers will be able to find you.

As you brainstorm the perfect URL for your blog, the part of the address that you create can only use letters, numbers and the hyphen symbol "-". No other special characters or punctuation marks (such as '!', "#", "$", or ",") can be used. Also, no spaces can be used within a URL. You can use an underscore ("_") to represent a space, but this can be confusing to web surfers, so it's not advisable.

The customizable part of a domain name and the extension (".com", for example) can be up to 63 characters long. As a general rule, the shorter the domain name, the easier it is to remember and type into a web browser accurately. Virtually all of the one, two, three, and four character-long domain names have long since been taken, however.

Most importantly, the customizable part of the domain name you select must be totally unique and not have already been registered by another person or company. It also may not violate someone else's copyrighted name, company name, or product name.

Domain names are not case sensitive, so you can mix and match upper and lowercase letters to make a domain name easier to read and promote. For example, you could promote your domain name as "JoeHatesPolitics.com" or "joehatespolitics.com" or "JoeHATESPolitics.com."

While you're in the process of brainstorming the perfect domain name for your blog, come up with at least five to ten options you like. When you're ready to register your domain name, you'll first need to determine if the domain name you've selected has already been registered by someone else. This process takes under one minute. Simply go to the website of any domain name registrar, such as GoDaddy.com, Register.com, NetworkSolutions.com, or MyDomain.com, and enter your desired domain name in the field marked "Start a domain search" or "Find a domain name." If the domain name you've entered is available, for an annual fee, you will have the opportunity to register it on the spot. If, however, it is already taken, you have three options:

1. You can choose to register an alternative domain name (after finding one that nobody else has.

2. You can contact the person or company that owns the domain name that's taken and offer to purchase or lease it. This will typically cost much more than registering a domain name that isn't already taken. Acquiring a domain name from someone else or another company can cost anywhere from under $100 to $1,000,000, depending on the domain name.

3. You can be put on a waiting list and be notified when and if the domain name you want ever becomes available. The chances of this happening within a reasonable timeframe, however, are relatively slim.

After you've determined that the domain name you want is available, you'll need to register it with an internet domain name registrar. There is an annual fee to register a domain name. Depending on the registrar, registering a single domain name will cost between $5.95 and $39.95. Obviously, choose a company with the lowest rates. GoDaddy.com (godaddy.com) tends to offer very competitive rates for domain name registrations, plus this company makes the process extremely fast and easy.

Registering your domain name will require you to provide details about yourself and your company, including your name, address, phone number, and credit card information (for paying the annual fee). The process will vary based on which domain registrar you use, but it should take no more than five to ten minutes to complete. After you've set up an account, registering additional domain names can be done much faster.

Part of the domain name registration process will most likely involve the need to provide the registrar with your Internet service provider's IP address. You may also need to provide what are called DNS numbers to the registrar. This is information that will be provided by your internet service provider (or your blogging service provider), if applicable. The internet service provider or blogging service provider is the company that will be hosting your blog (see Chapter 3).

Ideally, you want your blog to have a single domain name that you can promote and that will be easy to remember. However, since some people have trouble spelling or get easily confused, you might want to register multiple domain names with slightly different spellings. This way, if someone accidentally types the wrong domain name into their web browser, they'll still wind up at your blog. Think about some of the common typos or ways someone might misspell your domain name, and register those domain names as well.

Also, to ensure you generate the most traffic possible to your website, consider registering domain names that relate to the topics you'll be blogging about. Think about the search phrases, keywords, or terms someone might use who is looking for your blog online, and incorporate those terms into your blog's domain name. Be creative as you register your domain names, keeping in mind that it's perfectly okay to have 10 or more domain names ending up at the same blog.

If you're using an established blogging service to host your blog, that service will assign your blog its own URL. However, that URL will most likely be long, difficult to remember, and incorporate the name of the blogging service within it. In this situation, you can still create and register your own domain name and have that domain automatically forwarded to the provided URL. This is a service most domain name registrars offer for free (or for a low annual fee).

Yet another option for allowing people to access your blog, if you already have a website, is to create an easily identifiable link from your website's home page or main menu to your blog. It's become extremely common for companies to incorporate blogs, podcasts, and/or vlogs into the overall content of their websites. This foregoes the need for a unique URL for your blog, plus allows you to promote your blog to your website's existing traffic.

Finding Your Blogging Voice and Attitude

What you say within your blog and the content you create is, of course, extremely important. However, equally important is the writing style, voice, or overall attitude you convey throughout your entire blog.

Your blog's unique voice or attitude should remain consistent and somehow showcase your own unique personality. This will help you establish your online reputation and gain notoriety.

Your blog's voice should also give your audience a firm indication of what they can expect from your blog in terms of its content. For example, the overall tone could be pompous, egotistical, humorous, extremely serious, light-hearted, whimsical, angry, controversial, opinionated, gossip-oriented, or always take a straightforward approach to conveying facts and information.

Think carefully about how you want your audience to perceive you and what type of online reputation you wish to create for yourself. Also consider how this reputation will impact other aspects of your personal and professional life. Once you publish a blog and make it available online, assume that anyone will have access to it. Thus, if you blog about how much of a jerk your boss is, or why your coworkers are totally incompetent, you can bet that the people you write about will eventually see your blog and hold what you wrote or said against you.

No matter what topic you opt to blog about, chances are there are dozens, perhaps hundreds or thousands of other blogs covering that same subject matter. What will help to set your blog and its content apart is your personality and the attitude and style you incorporate into your overall blog, as well as each blog entry. The layout and design of your blog (a topic that's discussed in Chapter 5) will also play a large role in setting your blog apart from others.

Keeping Your Blog New and Fresh

As a general rule, your blog is only as interesting, entertaining, informative, and engaging as your last entry. If you fail to meet the expectations of your audience and don't continue to provide the same level or better content that your previous blog entries, you'll quickly discover that your repeat audience will dwindle quickly.

One of the biggest challenges you'll probably face as a blogger is keeping your content new, timely, unique, and fresh, so there's something relevant and interesting in each and every new entry. Maintaining this level of originality will take considerable creativity on your part, but it's absolutely necessary if you want to keep your audience coming back for more.

If you commit to updating your blog on a daily, weekly, or monthly basis, make it clear to your audience how often and exactly when they can expect to be able to access new content, and then stick closely to that schedule. If people expect a new blog entry every Monday afternoon at noon, you'll disappoint them and lose their interest if you fail to deliver.

Knowing there's a need for you to develop and publish new blog content on a regular basis, pace yourself and plan ahead. It's wise to outline topics for your blog up several entries in advance and to maintain a list of relevant topics you'd like to blog about in the future. This way, if you're working under a tight deadline or experience writer's block, for example, you have pre-planned ideas you can fall back on.

A common mistake made by bloggers is to create and post last-minute blog entries that have little or no thought put into them. If your audience perceives you're wasting their time, they'll stop accessing your blog. Be sure that you maintain a level of respect for your audience and cater to their wants and needs. Refer to Chapter 6 for ideas on what you could potentially blog about and what approaches you can take for each topic idea.

Incorporating Keywords in Your Content

Many blogs feature advertising as a way to generate revenue for the blogger. The more people who access your blog and see the ads that are displayed, the higher your revenue potential becomes. One way to increase traffic to your blog is to incorporate as many relevant keywords or phrases into the site's text-based content as possible. Not only will this impact the relevancy of the ads being displayed if you're using a service like Google AdSense (see Chapter 11), but it will also impact how your blog and each blog entry is listed with the various search engines. These search engines pick up on keywords and match them up with the words or phrases being used by web surfers in search of specialized content.

As a general rule, if you're trying to broaden the reach of your blog, you'll want to incorporate relevant keywords in your blog's main title, it's description, within each blog entry's headline(s), as well as within the text-based content. For podcasts or vlogs, keywords are particularly important in the title and in the descriptions you create.

After you have developed and fleshed out the overall idea for your blog, its approach, and its title, develop a detailed list of descriptive keywords or phrases that best describe its content, approach, theme, and audience. With a

Tip

If your blog is about cars, sample keywords might be: cars, autos, automobiles, transportation, Ford, General Motors, GM, or BMW. Examples of relevant phrases: antique cars, sports cars, hybrid cars, used cars, or new cars.

bit of brainstorming, you should be able to develop a comprehensive keyword list, containing at between 10 and 20 relevant keywords.

Create Your Blog's Unique Keyword List Now

Develop a list of keywords that you believe people might enter into a search engine in order to find your blog or content that's directly relevant to what you're blogging about. Keywords can include names, titles, locations, things, and other descriptive words or phrases.

Start creating your blog's keyword list right now. Over time, as you add new blog entries, you'll probably want to update and fine-tune your keyword list. Once you have this list created, make an effort to incorporate these words and phrases (two or three words used together) into your blog's title, description(s), headings, text-based content, photo captions, etc. Avoid using keywords that are irrelevant to your blog's content.

1. _____
2. _____
3. _____
4. _____
5. _____
6. _____
7. _____
8. _____
9. _____
10. _____
11. _____
12. _____
13. _____
14. _____
15. _____
16. _____
17. _____
18. _____
19. _____
20. _____

If you need help selecting appropriate and relevant keywords, there are several free, online-based tools designed to help you with this process. For example, there's Google Trends Labs (google.com/trends), the Google AdWords Keyword Tool (adwords.google.com/select/KeywordToolExternal), and Niche Bot (nichebot.com).

Additional information about how to utilize keywords within a blog can be found at the Blogsessive website (blogsessive.com/blogging-tips/blog-seo-tips-keyword-optimization/).

What's Next?

Now that you've selected a blogging service to host, publish, or distribute your blog and you've begun to formulate ideas and goals for your blog, the next chapter focuses on specifically how to format and design your blog. It discusses how to develop a unique appearance, format, and/or design elements for your blog. Chapter 5 also focuses on mobile blogging; how to maintain your blog from anywhere using a laptop computer, cell phone, or wireless PDA that has access to the internet.

Warning

Many search engines calculate how often individual keywords are used throughout your blog when indexing and listing your blog. The frequency of these keywords is based on their positioning among other words in blocks of text. For example, if you're blogging about birds, you can keep using the word "bird" in sentences through your blog's text-based content in order to establish a higher level of relevancy. You should not, however, simply repeat the keyword repetitively in within your blog in order to trick the search engines. For example, adding the word "bird" a few dozen or several hundred times repeatedly (i.e., "bird, bird, bird, bird, bird...") will actually hurt your positioning and how your blog is categorized with the popular search engines.

Chapter 5
The Anatomy of a Blog

I f you're hoping to generate a large following for your blog, generate revenue from it, or use it as a launching pad for your personal fame, one of the things you'll need to concern yourself with when it comes to creating and publishing your blog is its appearance.

You already know that the title of your blog, what you have to say, and how you say it are all equally important when it comes to blogging. This chapter, however, focuses exclusively on your blog's appearance. As you'll discover, the visual aesthetics of your blog (what people see on their screen when they access it), will dramatically impact how people perceive it and whether or not they'll return often.

The Appearance of Your Blog is Important

As you focus on your blog's visual appeal—this pertains to blogs, as well as what people see when they attempt to acquire or download your vlog or podcast—

you'll definitely want to consider every aspect of your layout and design so that your blog is visually appealing, welcoming, easy to navigate and uncluttered. Visitors should be able to find exactly what they're looking for in seconds and be able to access that information or content with the fewest mouse clicks possible.

As you focus on the appearance of your blog, some of the things to consider include:

- **The overall page layout.** This takes into account where information and content is placed on your page. For example, your

Tip

The majority of information covered within this chapter caters to traditional blogs, as well as vloggers and podcasters who will be distributing their content via a website or traditional blog. For tips on producing a vlog or podcast, and to learn how to distribute it through services like YouTube or iTunes, see Chapter 8.

main title banner should always be at the top of your main page, followed by a brief text-based description of your blog and the main menu options. How you utilize on-screen columns and your use of "white space" will impact how cluttered your on-screen content looks. There's a fine line between providing the right amount of information and content within a blog and creating pages that are cluttered with too much content, too many options, and visual complexities that will confuse your visitors. Again, this is why understanding your target audience and being able to cater to it is essential.

- **The color scheme.** This includes the color of the text, graphics, backgrounds, etc., and how the colors are used in conjunction with each other. If you choose the wrong color scheme for the background and text, for example, your text or graphics could become too difficult to read or be strenuous to the eyes. Certain color combinations could prove too distracting for the reader.

- **The fonts and typestyles.** Choosing a font that is visually pleasing, easy to read, and that looks good is essential. You'll also need to consider the best ways to use typestyles, like **bold**, *italics*, underlined text, and various combinations of typestyles—*italicized bold type that's underlined,* for example, to most effectively convey your information. The size of the fonts you use is also important to insure readability. Type that is too large (aside from headlines) can be distracting, while type that's too small will be difficult to read.

- **The use and placement of graphics,** including photos, illustrations, clip art, and animations. As that age-old saying goes, a picture can be worth a thousand words. However, the photos, graphics, and visual content you use should all contribute to the message you're trying to convey. Cluttering your blog with random eye-candy can be distracting and make your blog confusing. Focus on the best way to utilize visuals and how they can make the most impact.

- **How and where applications (including widgets) will be used** within your blog to enhance interactivity (a concept described later within this chapter).

- **The placement of on-screen menus and the available menu options.** Visitors will expect certain menu options at the top or bottom of the screen to help them navigate your blog. These menu icons should all be easily identifiable, easy to find, and intuitive.

- **The availability of a search feature** to help people find the exact content or blog entries they're looking for, based on keywords or search phrases.
- **How and where advertisements are utilized and displayed throughout your blog.** This includes display ads, as well as text-based ads (i.e. Google AdSense ads).

While having some graphic design skill will be beneficial when designing your blog's appearance, you can benefit from the skill of graphic art professionals by utilizing blog templates offered by the various blogging services. You can also hire a freelance graphic artist to help you with the visual design and page layout aspects of your blog. Utilizing your own common sense will also go a long way when it comes to design choices. If you truly understand your blog's target audience, you should be able to look at the draft of your blog (before publishing it) and easily determine whether or not it will appeal to your audience.

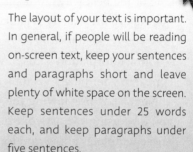

Tip

The layout of your text is important. In general, if people will be reading on-screen text, keep your sentences and paragraphs short and leave plenty of white space on the screen. Keep sentences under 25 words each, and keep paragraphs under five sentences.

Large blocks of text, especially if they're displayed on-screen using a small typestyle and a busy font, can be extremely intimidating for a reader. It's always better to break up large blocks of text into multiple paragraphs, and to potentially break up groups of paragraphs into several screens worth of information.

Now that you have a general understanding of the visual components of your blog that you'll need to properly deal with, let's take a closer look at each of these elements so that you'll be able to make intelligent layout and design decisions that are appropriate to your blog.

The overall appearance of your blog will help you instantly set a tone and convey an attitude. The decisions you make should relate to your topic(s) and overall theme of your blog, plus appeal directly to your target audience. Young girls, for example, will relate to a blog that incorporates lots of bright colors, along with artistic and flashy fonts, while an adult business person will relate more to more neutral color schemes that are easier on the eye.

Layout and Design Fundamentals

One of the best ways to begin planning the layout and design of your blog is to first determine exactly what content you wish to incorporate into your blog and how you'd like it to appear visually on the screen. Next, visit a handful of blogs to see how information is displayed and choose design elements you believe would appeal to your blog's visitors.

Next, start previewing the various blog templates offered by the blog service you'll be using to host your blog (several of them are featured within Chapter 3). These templates allow you to customize professionally-designed blog formats to which you can add your own text, graphics, and other elements in order to create a blog that's truly yours, but that requires absolutely no programming or graphic design knowledge or experience on your part.

If you'll be using a template, choose one that offers the visual design and layout you believe will most appeal to your target audience and that conveys the attitude you're hoping to convey through your blog.

While you can always hire a freelance graphic designer or webpage designer to create a totally original look and design for your blog, this is typically not necessary, since the majority of available templates are highly customizable. These templates become even more flexible if you know basic HTML programming.

Your Blog's Main Title Graphic

To enhance the look of your blog, consider having a custom main title banner graphic created. At the top of your blog, this graphic will display your blog's main title (and can incorporate your photo and/or logo). It will act as the masthead or main title for your blog and be the first thing visitors see when they access your blog.

Many blog templates allow you to create a main heading, using text, for your blog. However, creating and incorporating a main title banner graphic will add to the visual appeal and professional look of your overall blog. A good main title banner will also instantly inform visitors what your blog is all about (using a well-written subtitle or brief, text-based description or tag line). The main title banner can include the title of your blog, a sub-heading, a logo, your photo, or any other

The Main Title Banner for the Jason Rich Travel blog (JasonRichTravcel.com) was created in about 15 minutes using Photoshop CS4 on a Mac. (On the web, this graphic is displayed in full color.) The image size is 800 by 160 pixels.

The Main Title Banner for the KJP Life blog (kjplife.blogspot.com) is another example of how you can easily combine different fonts, photos, and graphic elements to create an eye-catching title for your own blog. (On the web, this graphic is displayed in full color.) The image size is 628 by 90 pixels.

graphic that you want people to immediately associate with your blog. This main title banner is different from the individual blog entry headlines you'll create and publish with each new blog entry added to your blog.

A main title banner can be created using any graphics program, such as Adobe's PhotoShop CS4, Adobe's PhotoShop Elements, PaintShop Pro, or CorelDraw. You can also hire a freelance graphic artist to create this graphic for you. Once the graphic is created, it should be saved in a popular digital format, such as .jpg or .tif, so that it can be easily uploaded and incorporated into your blog.

The size of your banner (how large it appears on the screen) is something you can decide for yourself as a blogger, based on the overall design of your blog. Use this main title banner to help set the tone for your blog, immediately identify your blog to visitors, and create a visual identifier for your blog. In terms of sizing, while there no rules you must adhere to, popular banner sizes for websites and blogs are

Warning

Keep in mind, because the main title banner is a graphic, your blog's title that appears within this image (which will be text), will not be searchable or readable by search engines or blog hosting services that automatically categorize and list blogs based on keywords. The main text of your blog should also incorporate the title of your blog, as well as additional and appropriate keywords. Chapter 10 focuses more on these search engine optimization (SEO) techniques that will help you generate traffic for your blog.

Warning

While there are exceptions to every rule, avoid using an animated background for your blog. If the background is animated or overly colorful, it will be distracting as visitors attempt to read your blog's actual content. A good rule is to keep your background simple; solid colors often work best.

728 x 80 pixels, 468 x 60 pixels, 336 x 280 pixels, or 160 x 600 pixels.

Backgrounds

Behind your text, graphics, menus, and other blog content, you'll need to select a background color or design. Your blog's background can be a single, solid color or a radiant background that transitions from one color to another. You can also use a graphic image or photo as your background (but this might make your text more difficult to read).

As a general rule, it's wise to keep your background as simple as possible. This makes it easier to read any text that's displayed over the background and keeps the background from conflicting visually with any photos or graphics you incorporate into your blog.

The background color you choose should be easy on the eyes and not distract visitors from your main content. Your background should also remain consistent throughout all of the blog in order to create a unified appearance. Continuity is important, especially if your blog will be part of a website.

Fonts

In typography, a font is defined as a complete character set of a single size of a particular typeface. It's the overall design for a set of characters. Your word processor or online-based blog creation tools (provided by your blog hosting service) will offer a selection of headline and body fonts to choose from. A headline font is generally large, bold type and can be visually complex; headers and subheads should be composed in as few words as possible. The main text within your blog should be displayed using a commonly accepted body text font. Body text usually utilizes serif fonts (type that includes the little horizontal lines at the tops and bottoms of characters that make text easier to read), but sometimes sans serif fonts are used as well. Popular body text fonts include Times New Roman, Courier, Georgia, and Cambria; sans serif examples are Arial, Avant Garde, Helvetica, and Verdana.

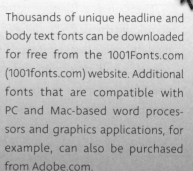

Tip

Thousands of unique headline and body text fonts can be downloaded for free from the 1001Fonts.com (1001fonts.com) website. Additional fonts that are compatible with PC and Mac-based word processors and graphics applications, for example, can also be purchased from Adobe.com.

When choosing a font, it's important to select one that all web browsers will understand and be able to display without special add-ons or additional downloads. Only certain fonts can be incorporated into a blog and appear consistently no matter which web browser is being used. If you really want to use a particular font (and there are literally tens of thousands of available), you can convert your type into a graphic. When type is converted into a graphic form, or *rasterized*, it becomes an object rather than a live font, and it will look the same on all screens.

The font(s) you choose should be based on the overall visual image you're looking to convey, but should focus on readability on-screen and when printed. As a general rule, you should avoid mixing too many different fonts within a document. It's more appropriate to use one font for headlines and subheads, and a separate font for body text.

Typestyles

Once you select a font, you can add visual impact to your text by utilizing various typestyles and font sizes. Most fonts have a normal, **bold**, *italics* and underlined variation. You can also mix and match typestyles, by incorporating text that is **<u>bold and underlined</u>** or ***bold and italicized***. Typestyle variation can be used within a paragraph or sentence to make a word or phrase stand out visually. It's unwise, however, to overuse typestyles or to mix and match them too much within a single blog entry. Visually, this can make text more difficult to read.

The size you display your text is also an important consideration. Headlines should be displayed in a large type to make them stand out. Subheads should use a slightly smaller size text. Meanwhile, your body text font size should be easily readable both on-screen and in print. Font sizes are measured in points. Commonly used font sizes for main body text is between 11 and 13 points. Never use a font size below eight (8) points on-screen, because this will appear too small and be unreadable to many visitors.

Sample Typestyles Using Times New Roman

The following is a sampling of what various font sizes look like using a traditional Times New Roman font:

This is Times New Roman displayed in 8-point normal type.

This is Times New Roman displayed in 8-point bold type.

This is Times New Roman displayed in 8-point italic type.

This is Times New Roman displayed in 10-point normal type.

This is Times New Roman displayed in 10-point bold type.

This is Times New Roman displayed in 10-point italic type.

This is Times New Roman displayed in 11-point normal type.

This is Times New Roman displayed in 11-point bold type.

This is Times New Roman displayed in 11-point italic type.

This is Times New Roman displayed in 12-point normal type.

This is Times New Roman displayed in 12-point bold type.

This is Times New Roman displayed in 12-point italic type.

This is Times New Roman displayed in 13-point normal type.

This is Times New Roman displayed in 13-point bold type.

This is Times New Roman displayed in 13-point italic type.

Line Spacing and Text Alignment (Page Formatting)

The following paragraphs of text show how line spacing and text alignment can impact how your text appears both on-screen and when it's printed:

When it comes to formatting text, you can also control the line spacing and alignment. Again, how you format your text will impact how easy it is to read on-screen and when printed. How you combine your on-screen text formatting with various fonts, typestyles, font sizes, font colors, line spacing, and alignment will determine its appearance. **This is an example of text that's single-spaced and aligned left.**

When it comes to formatting text, you can also control the line spacing and alignment. Again, how you format your text will impact how easy it is to read on-screen and when printed. How you combine your on-screen text formatting with various fonts, typestyles, font sizes, font colors, line spacing, and alignment will determine its appearance. **This is an example of text that's single-spaced and aligned right.**

When it comes to formatting text, you can also control the line spacing and alignment. Again, how you format your text will impact how easy it is to read on-screen and when printed. How you combine your on-screen text formatting with various fonts, typestyles, font sizes, font colors, line spacing, and alignment will determine its appearance. **This is an example of text that's single-spaced and centered.**

When it comes to formatting text, you can also control the line spacing and alignment. Again, how you format your text will impact how easy it is to read on-screen and when printed. How you combine your on-screen text formatting with various fonts, typestyles, font sizes, font colors, line spacing, and alignment will determine its appearance. **This is an example of text that's single-spaced and justified (aligned evenly on the right and left edges).**

When it comes to formatting text, you can also control the line spacing and alignment. Again, how you format your text will impact how easy it is to read on-screen and when printed. How you combine your on-screen text formatting with various fonts, typestyles, font sizes, font colors, line spacing, and alignment will determine its appearance. **This is an example of text that's double-spaced, and justified (aligned evenly on the right and left edges).**

Color Schemes

The colors that appear within your blog, in terms of the background color, headline color and body text color, for example, will impact visual appeal and readability. Using a nicely coordinated color scheme will help set the tone of your blog, promote an added sense of professionalism, and make your blog easier to read. Since current computer monitors are capable of displaying literally millions of colors, website designers and bloggers are no longer limited to a palette of just 216 or 256 browser-safe colors. When it comes to choosing colors and color schemes, the possibilities are truly limitless.

These websites offer free, online-based color scheme generators that can help you pick and choose colors to incorporate into your blog's layout and design:

- wellstyled.com/tools
- colorcombos.com
- colorschemer.com/online.html
- colorsontheweb.com/colorwizard.asp
- design.geckotribe.com/colorwheel

Tip

In addition to using full paragraphs of text within your blog entries, sometimes it's easier to communicate key points using bulleted or numbered lists. When it comes to blogging, using a succinct writing style that communications information as quickly and efficiently as possible typically works best when trying to appeal to people with limited attention spans—i.e., almost all blog readers and web surfers, regardless of their age, sex, reading level, or demographic.

When creating a bulleted or numbered list, it is not always necessary to use full sentences for each point you're trying to make. Focus on how you can communicate your main points as quickly and as clearly as possible.

Incorporating Photos

Adding digital photos, graphics, illustrations, animations, and other visual elements into your blog entries is definitely beneficial, providing that the graphics and photos you use are relevant and clear.

To add to the visual appeal of your photos, you can use specialized software, such as PhotoShop or PhotoShop Elements, for example, to add frames, borders, and other graphic elements to your photos before publishing them as part of a blog entry.

For each photo or image you opt to include within your blog, first make sure you crop it appropriately and save the image in a file format (such as .jpg) and file size that's fast-loading.

Using a digital camera, webcam, or even a traditional film camera, you can take your own photographs that can be incorporated into your blog. These images, however, should be edited (cropped and/or fixed using specialized photo editing software) to ensure they're displayed properly.

Incorporating original photography that you take yourself or own the copyright to will help ensure the content of your site is unique. However, another option is to pay a stock photo agency that can provide you with literally hundreds of thousands of digital images you can incorporate into your blog as they're needed.

The benefit to purchasing or acquiring photos from a stock photo agency is that the images will be the work of professional photographers. The potential drawback is that unless you purchase the photo outright, that same photo could appear in other blogs, websites, newspapers, or magazines.

The following is a partial listing of inexpensive stock photo agencies that offer vast databases of available images that can be downloaded and incorporated into your blog. These stock photo agencies typically operate using one of two pricing models. Fee or membership-based stock photo agencies include:

- Fotosearch.com
- GettyImages.com
- iStockPhoto.com
- Shutterstock.com
- SnapVillage.com

Some stock photo agencies charge a flat monthly or annual fee that would allow you to download and use an unlimited number of images on a royalty-free basis within your blog. For a blogger on a budget, this is typically the best deal financially. Once you subscribe to a stock photo agency, you can search the agency's image database based on specific keywords to quickly find and download the images you want or need.

Tip

It is possible to find royalty-free, public domain images on the web that can be used free of charge. Using any search engine, perform a search using the keywords "free photos" or "free images." The following websites offer databases of free images available to bloggers: free-foto.com and freedigitalphotos.net. Wikipedia offers a list of free online-based image sources at en.wikipedia.org/wiki/Wikipedia:Public_domain_image_resources.

Another pricing model used by stock photo agencies involves paying a licensing fee for each specific image you opt to use. The per-image licensing fee will vary greatly, based on the photographer or agency.

Depending on your needs, it may be beneficial for you to hire a freelance photographer to take professional quality photographs that you can incorporate into your blog and to which you will you own the copyright. You can find freelance photographers in the Yellow Pages or using an online service, such as eLance.com. Professional photographers will typically have a flat fee for a photo shoot, an hourly rate and/or a per-image fee. Be sure to obtain the images in a digital format that can easily be uploaded and incorporated into your blog. For a typical blog, photos with a small file size and a moderate resolution should be suitable.

Menus and Menu Options

Just like a website, a blog must be easy to navigate and extremely intuitive for your visitors. That being said, the easiest way for people to navigate around your blog is to provide them with an easy to find and easy to read on-screen menu. This menu should be placed near the very top of your blog (under the main title or main title banner graphic), or on the left side of the screen. Some people also position menu buttons at the very bottom of the screen.

> ### Warning
>
> Utilizing photographs that you don't own or have not properly licensed is a violation of copyright laws. The copyright of a photograph is typically owned by the photographer (unless it's been transferred to another party or individual) and cannot be used without permission from the copyright owner. Never use photographs within your blog that you have not taken yourself or that you have not purchased or licensed, unless the photo has clearly been placed in the public domain as is being made available as a free (royalty-free) image by the copyright holder.

One trick to making your blog easy to navigate is to provide enough menu options so visitors can find exactly what they're looking for quickly, without offering too many menu options that the choices become confusing. Also, avoid trying to be too creative when choosing the actual wording displayed on each menu button or option. Typically, straightforward and widely used menu terms work best.

While it's assumed that your blog entries will be displayed in reverse chronological order on the main page of your blog, the menu options you opt to add to your blog will vary, based on your personal preferences, your blog topic/theme, and your audience. Common menu options, listed here in alphabetical order, include:

- **About.** Offers a text-based description of who you are and what your blog is about. This can include a personal biography or company background. It's best to keep this information down to one screen's worth of information (under 500 words). It's also acceptable, however, to include one or two photos of yourself as the blogger.

- **Archives.** This section of a blog allows people to access past blog entries based on a list of previous dates or blog entry headlines. This, too, is a tool designed to make navigating around your blog faster and easier.

- **Comments.** Allows visitors to post comments about your blog in general or specific blog entries that can either be private (to be read only by you—the blogger) or posted for all of your blog's visitors to read. It's important to allow visitors to your blog to offer feedback. It creates a more interactive environment and allows others to publicly (or privately) provide you with feedback and/or agree or disagree with what you have to say. Also, the feedback you receive could provide valuable ideas for future blog entries or additional content you can provide.

- **Contact.** Provides information about how your blog's followers can contact you directly by e-mail, telephone, or traditional mail. How much personal information you post in terms of your contact information is something you should consider carefully. Chapter 10 focuses on personal security considerations as a blogger.

- **Home.** Returns visitors to the main home page of your blog (or the home page of your website).

- **Links.** Create and make available a listing of links that are of interest to your audience or somehow related to your blog. These links can be hyperlinks, so visitors to your blog can click on any of them to access them instantly. One drawback to this, however, is that if someone follows a link on your blog, to do so, they'll be exiting from you blog and might not return.

- **Search.** Allows visitors to find specific blog entries or content based on keywords or search phrases. This is a very important tool for bloggers to incorporate into their blogs in order to make them easier to navigate. Many of the online-based blog hosting services (described in Chapter 3) automatically incorporate this feature into blogs.

Displaying Ads

There are definite pros and cons to displaying ads within a blog. The obvious benefit is that by displaying ads, you can derive an income from publishing your blog based on how many hits your blog receives and how many of those visitors respond to the ads by clicking on them.

While Chapter 11 deals specifically with how to generate an income from your blog, when it comes to advertising, you can opt to incorporate text-based (context sensitive) ads, and/or you can showcase graphically based display ads. Many bloggers with a large following are able to generate a respectable income as a result of displaying ads as part of their blog.

The choice to display ads should be based on what your goals are for the blog, as well as how you want to your blog to be perceived. Many web surfers are turned off when they see an abundance of advertising within a webpage or blog, and are more apt to surf elsewhere, so keep in mind there's a fine line between displaying some advertising and having too much advertising showcased within your blog.

Another potential drawback is that if an ad on your blog catches the attention of a visitor, they're apt to click on that ad and leave your blog prematurely, potentially without reading it.

If your business is using a blog to better communicate with customers and clients, for example, displaying ads from other companies within your blog can be counterproductive for your business, not to mention confusing and distracting to your blog's visitors. However, displaying ads for your own products and service within your blog (again, without bombarding the visitor with too many advertising messages) could be beneficial, providing the ads are relevant and unobtrusive.

For personal bloggers, by displaying small, context-sensitive, text-based ads within your blog (in between blog entries or along the right or left margin or sidebars of your blog), it is possible to generate revenue, especially once your blog begins to receive significant traffic. Chapter 11 explains how to incorporate text-based ads using Google AdSense, for example. These ads can be small, contain only text (no graphics), and be context sensitive. Thus, if you blog about your vacation in Orlando, Florida, for example, the ads that will automatically be displayed will relate to airlines, resorts, and other travel opportunities in the Orlando area.

As the blogger, you typically have 100 percent control over whether or not ads are displayed within your blog, as well as how large the ads are and where exactly they're placed on the screen. If you're looking to generate an income from your blog, it's a common mistake to saturate your blog with too many ads. While you might think that doing this would help boost your revenues, in most cases, it will result in more of your traffic simply leaving your blog prematurely out of frustration.

The size and frequency of your ads, as well as their placement, will determine how intrusive they are. If your ads are displayed in the left and right margins, for example, but your main blog content is easily read and uninterrupted as it scrolls down the center of the screen, this will be helpful to your visitors.

A good example of a lot of advertising within a blog that's organized in a reasonably unobtrusive way can be found within entertainment gossip blogger Perez Hilton's blog (perezhilton.com). Relatively small display (graphic-based) ads are displayed in the left and right margins, as well as in between blog entries. My Jason Rich Travel blog (jasonrichtravel.com) is an example of how two content-related, text-based ads (using Google AdSense) can be subtly incorporated into a blog in between each blog entry.

When designing the layout and design for your blog, determine whether or not you plan to display any type of advertising and then allocate space in your design for the ads so that they appear well integrated into your blog.

Multimedia Elements

Because the attention span of web surfers has become so short, and most surfers have become accustomed to flashy graphics, animations, and sound effects incorporated into the websites they visit, viewing a generic, text-based blog may seem boring unless the text really grabs and holds their attention. Many bloggers add animated graphics or short videos into their blog, for example, to make their blog flashier and more interactive.

The decision about what multimedia elements to incorporate into your blog is entirely up to you, based on your content and audience, as well as how much time you're willing to invest in gathering, producing, and then publishing this additional content.

Finally, make sure that whatever multimedia content you incorporate into your blog is

Tip

Adobe's Flash CS4 software (adobe.com) is an ideal tool for creating original animations that can be published as part of a blog. However, there is a significant learning curve associated with this software. Be sure to read Chapter 8 for more information about producing and publishing video-based content.

relevant and works toward achieving your blog's overall goals or objectives. Otherwise, an abundance of eye candy along with flashy bells and whistles could easily become distracting or annoying to your visitors.

Make Your Blog More Interactive with Widgets

Available to bloggers, usually for free, but sometimes for a small fee, are a wide range of "widgets" and "gadgets" that can be incorporated into a blog, typically with no programming knowledge involved.

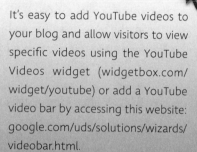

Tip

It's easy to add YouTube videos to your blog and allow visitors to view specific videos using the YouTube Videos widget (widgetbox.com/widget/youtube) or add a YouTube video bar by accessing this website: google.com/uds/solutions/wizards/videobar.html.

Thousands of widgets are available that can be incorporated into a blog that is part of a MySpace or Facebook account, for example, however, there are also plenty of widgets available that can be added to a blog hosted by virtually any service.

The main reason to add one or more widgets to a blog is to give it added functionality and interactivity, making it more interesting for your visitors when they access your blog. Using widgets, you can add questionnaires, quizzes, a live chat feature, maps, a guestbook, photo slide shows (with animations), games, news feeds, sports scores, weather forecasts, news headlines, and a wide range of other content.

The developers of each widget provide all of the tools and programming necessary to add the widget to your blog, with no actual programming required by you. At most, you'll simply need to cut and paste pre-written HTML programming code into the appropriate location of your blog. Complete directions are typically provided by the widget developer, and the process takes just minutes to complete.

For example, if you want to add an animated slide show, featuring an unlimited number of

Tip

The Mashable website (mashable.com/2007/09/06/widgets-2/) also offers links for more than 50 widgets suitable for blogs, while the WidgetBox website (widgetbox.com) maintains a database of hundreds of free widgets for bloggers. To access even more free widgets and gadgets, visit the GoogleGadgets website (google.com/ig/directory).

your digital images (photos) into your blog, you can use a free widget offered at Slide.com (slide.com) to upload your photos and create your slide show. Your slide show can be completely customized with various special effects and captions.

From the Bloggers Blog website (bloggersblog.com/widgetlinks), you can access a listing of widgets available to bloggers. Examples of available widgets include:

- 3Bubbles, Mobber, and Gabbly: live chat tools for blogs

- Babel Fish: a language translation tool for blogs

- Blog Hot or Not: Allows people to vote on whether a blog is hot or not

- Blogthings.com: Incorporate a quiz and publish quiz results into your blog

- ClockLink.com: Display a clock on your blog

- Feedjit: Display web traffic and visitor maps on your blog

- iMood.com: Displays the blogger's mood graphically within a blog

- PollHost.com: Create and display customized polls and results on your blog

- Quizilla: Create customized quizzes as part of your blog

Tip

Using the ScrollFX widget available from WidgetBox (widgetbox.com/widget/scrollfx-1-0-std), it's easy to add a scrolling LCD ticker display within your blog that can be used to communicate news headlines and other important pieces of information to your audience. Like all of the widgets available from WidgetBox, ScrollFx is self-installing and takes just minutes to add to a blog hosted by any of the popular blog hosting services.

As with any type of blog content, focus on adding widgets or gadgets that are relevant and of interest to your audience and tha t will add value to the content of your blog. Using widgets, it's easy to clutter a blog with superfluous content that may look impressive, but that will confuse or frustrate your visitors as opposed to making your blog more informative, entertaining, interesting, or interactive.

Hiring a Professional Blog Designer

If you don't have the skills or creativity to create a truly unique or visually impressive design for your blog, but you have no trouble developing your own content, consider hiring a freelance blog designer to initially help you create a visually pleasing and impressive blog design. The design of your blog relates to where information is positioned on the screen and how it looks in terms of color schemes and how graphics, artwork, and text are utilized. A professional blog designer can have either a graphic design or website design background, for example, and will have already developed an expertise in designing highly functional blog designs for use by individuals, professionals, entrepreneurs, and businesses alike.

While a blog designer will not create your blog's content for you, a skilled blog designer will help you develop a user friendly layout and interface for your blog, create a custom main title banner, plus help you choose appropriate fonts, color schemes, and formatting for your intended audience. Most importantly, a blog designer will know HTML programming, so they can create a totally unique look for your blog, or add features and functionality, plus more customization to a template provided by your blog hosting service.

Most bloggers find that their need for a blog designer is a one-time thing, and that once the design and format for their blog is created, they're able to easily add their own content and blog entries. Thus, once you develop a concept for your blog, if you don't want to invest the time necessary to develop your own design, you can hire a freelance blog designer on an hourly or per-project basis.

In addition to hiring an individual freelancer (whom you can find using a service like Guru.com or eLance.com), you can hire an established blog design firm that has the expertise to help you promote your blog and get it listed prominently with the search engines. These companies are highly proficient using the design tools offered by services like Blogger.com, TypePad.com, and WordPress.com, and can vastly improve the look, visual appeal, ease of navigation, and functionality of any type of blog.

Unique Blog Designs, LLC (uniqueblogdesigns.com) is just one example of an independent blog design firm that has successfully worked with more than 150 clients (as of September 2008), including several of the Top 100 bloggers. Be sure to read the interview with Josh Mullineaux, director of marketing for Unique Blog Designs, which can be found in Chapter 13.

Update Your Blog Anywhere, Anytime with Mobile Blogging

Once your blog is established, updating it while on-the-go from virtually anywhere there's cellular phone service is easier than ever, especially if you have a laptop with a wireless internet card, a wireless PDA/Smartphone, or the Apple iPhone.

Of course, you can also update your blog using any computer that's connected to the internet. If you're traveling, you can take advantage of internet cafes and public libraries, for example, to gain access to the web and post new entries to your blog.

Blogging with a Notebook Computer Equipped with a Wireless Internet Card

Apple iPhone, Palm Treo, and Blackberry users enjoy easy access to the internet from virtually anywhere using their handheld wireless device. This is extremely appealing to bloggers who know the importance of staying connected and require the ability to access their e-mail and blog whenever and wherever they happen to be.

The obvious drawback to accessing the web using a cell phone or wireless personal digital assistant (PDA) is the small screen, limited keyboard, and dramatically scaled down web surfing capabilities these tiny devices offer. As a result, bloggers also tend to travel with a laptop computer, allowing them to access the internet from wireless (Wi-Fi) hotspots or from hotel rooms.

This solution also has its drawbacks. While most airports and hotels offer high-speed internet access, it comes at a cost. Airports, internet cafes, bookstores, and coffee shops throughout the country often charge a daily fee of between $6.95 and $9.95 to connect to the web via a wireless hotspot. Hotels typically charge between $9.95 and $19.95 per night to access the internet from a guestroom. For bloggers who are constantly on the go, these charges can add up quickly.

Tip

The ability to blog while on the go allows your blog's audience to stay up-to-date and literally follow you (in cyberspace) as you travel. Bloggers often enjoy updating their blog from remote locations and don't necessarily want to be tied down to their desk at home or at their office in order to maintain their blog. Acquiring mobile blogging capabilities gives you, the blogger, added freedom and allows you to update your blog with new entries the moment something new or exciting happens or whenever an idea for a blog entry flashes through your mind.

For budget conscious bloggers, it is possible to seek out free, public Wi-Fi hotspots and utilize them during your travels. The jiwire.com website, for example, offers a listing of more than 150,000 free Wi-Fi hotspots worldwide. The wifi411.com website also lists public Wi-Fi hotspots that offer free and paid access in cities across America.

The CyberCafes website (cybercafes.com) provides an online directory listing thousands of internet cafes worldwide that allow users to access the web using supplied desktop computers for a low hourly fee, usually between $5 to $10 per hour.

There is another alternative. For between $39.95 and $79.95 per month, laptop computer users can subscribe to a wireless broadband service offered by Sprint, T-Mobile, AT&T, or Verizon. By connecting an inexpensive wireless modem to a laptop computer, true wireless, high-speed access is available from almost anywhere, especially within major cities. No phone lines or extra cables are required, plus you're not limited to Wi-Fi coverage areas.

When choosing which wireless Broadband internet service provider, don't just compare the price of the monthly service. It's also necessary to evaluate the service coverage map and connection speeds offered by each provider. Also, look at the duration of the required service agreement, the cost of the wireless modem, and whether or not unlimited internet access is granted through the service plan.

For someone who stays in a hotel three to four nights per month, or who needs internet access while on the go, wireless broadband internet is an extremely convenient tool for enhancing productivity and staying connected.

The following is a sampling of the wireless data plans available from the most popular service providers. Terms of service vary by provider. Ask about special promotions and rebates being offered before committing to a plan.

Provider	Phone Number	Website	Monthly Cost	Addition Information
AT&T	(888) 333-6651	wireless.att.com	$60	Unlimited data plan. Two-year agreement required.
Sprint	(866) 866-7509	sprint.com	$59.95	Unlimited data plan. Two-year service agreement required.
T-Mobile	(877) 387-4324	t-mobile.com	$49.99	Unlimited data plan. One-year agreement required.
Verizon	(800) 922-0204	verizonwireless.com	$39.99 to $59.99	50MB or 5GB plan. (Additional MB $.25)

Tip

Google has developed a mobile blogging application that's compatible with many cellular telephones and Smartphones that have wireless internet capabilities. This software allows you to update a blog that's hosted by Blogger.com. To download the free mobile blogging software, visit google.com/mobile/default/blogger.

Apple iPhone 3G

The Apple iPhone 3G is not only an excellent device for surfing the web (using a scaled-down version of Apple's popular Safari browser), it's also now possible to add third-party software applications to the iPhone. Several companies have released blogging tools for the iPhone that make creating and publishing text or photo blogs easy—from virtually anywhere. (Similar software applications are also now available for Blackberry devices and many Windows Mobile Smartphones.)

Some of the blogging tools available for the iPhone (which can be downloaded from the iTunes App Store by selecting the 'Social Networking' category) include:

- **Facebook** (facebook.com): Update and maintain your Facebook page, including your blog(s) (free).
- **LifeCast** (lifecast.sleepydog.net): LifeCast is a blogging and journaling application you can carry in your pocket. Record your daily events and activities using photos and text, plus time-stamp and geo-locate your entries. Using this software, it's easy to set up a connection to your blog and post your entries online (free).
- **MySpace Mobile** (myspace.com): Update and maintain your MySpace page, including your blog(s). (free)
- **TwitterFon** (twitterfon.net): Access and update information on your Twitter social networking account (free)
- **TypePad for iPhone** (typepad.com/features/blog-iphone.html): Update and maintain your blog that was created using the TypePad blogging service (described within Chapter 3) (free)
- **WordPress for iPhone** (iphone.wordpress.org): Update and maintain your blog that was created using the WordPress blogging service (described within Chapter 3) (free)

For more information about the iPhone, visit the Apple website (apple.com), any Apple Store or any AT&T Wireless retailer.

What's Next?

For some bloggers, just coming up with ideas for what to blog about and then developing and fleshing out those ideas is one of the biggest challenges they'll face. The next chapter offers advice about choosing what topic(s) to blog about, plus offers more than 101 proven topics that can be developed into interesting, informative, controversial, and/or entertaining blog entries.

Chapter 6
101 Proven Topics to Blog About

Even if you're the most skilled communicator, choosing what topic(s) to blog about and then being able to develop entertaining, informative, engaging, and unique content on an ongoing basis is a challenge for even the most talented and creative of bloggers. This chapter will help you choose topics to write about and then flesh out those topics into blog entries that will capture the attention of your audience.

There is no simple formula for selecting a topic to blog about. What topic(s) work well for you will be vastly different from someone else, since everyone can incorporate their own unique attitude, personality, philosophy, style, knowledge, experience, and approach to each and every one of their blog entries in order to make it unique, engaging, and appealing.

Depending on the approach you take, the reputation you're looking to create as a blogger, your level of knowledge or expertise on a topic, the types of blog content you'll be creating, and your target audience, what topics are most suitable for you will vary.

As you consider topics to blog about, consider:

- What approach you'll take—will your blog be controversial, informative, thought-provoking, humorous, or satirical?

- Will you be able to flesh out the topic to make what you have to say engaging and comprehensible to your audience?

- How will you make the topic(s) relevant and appealing to your audience?

- The level of knowledge and/or experience you have that relates to the topic(s).

- Whether or not you'll be able to develop new and original content on an ongoing basis that's related to your chosen topic(s). A successful blog must be updated regularly (hourly, daily, or weekly, for example), and maintain the consistent quality of content that your audience expects.

- Using the topics you select, what type of reputation will you develop for yourself as a blogger? What type of attitude or style will you convey to your audience?

- How will the content of your blog be unique, based on the topic(s) you select? Why will your blog appeal to its target audience?

You'll definitely need to invest thought and effort into developing your content and choosing the most appealing, relevant, and engaging topics for your audience.

Just as communicating effectively through text, pictures (or graphics), verbally (via audio), or on video are skills unto themselves that you must possess as a blogger, a successful blogger must also be able to select suitable topics to blog about, and then mold, expand, or transform those topics to create content that's appropriate for their blog. If what you have to say, write, or present resonates in any way (positively or negatively) with your audience, they'll keep coming back for more—which is your goal.

Tip

Once you settle on a topic to blog about, make a list for yourself of five to 10 related topics that you can either incorporate into a single blog entry or blog about in the future. Consider ways you can expand or build on the topic(s) you've selected. Also, make sure the topic(s) you choose are and will continue to be of interest to your target audience, at least for a while. Otherwise, you could quickly become perceived as a blogger who is out of touch with current events, issues, or trends.

101 Topics to Consider Blogging About

Some bloggers focus on transforming themselves into an online personality who can focus on any topic that's on their mind. These people tend to create a following for themselves, just as a celebrity from the entertainment industry might do. These blogs are driven by the blogger's unique personality, attitude, style, appearance, knowledge, sense of humor, or ability to create controversy. These bloggers aren't afraid to put themselves out there and share with their internet audience a piece of themselves. Other bloggers focus on a specific topic they're knowledgeable about and use their blog to convey information about that specific theme, issue, or subject matter. In this case, what you're saying and how you say it will play a much greater role than how you showcase yourself within your blog. The subject matter is the main focus on the blog—not you.

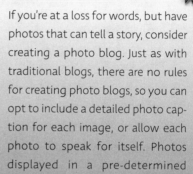

Tip

If you're at a loss for words, but have photos that can tell a story, consider creating a photo blog. Just as with traditional blogs, there are no rules for creating photo blogs, so you can opt to include a detailed photo caption for each image, or allow each photo to speak for itself. Photos displayed in a pre-determined sequence, for example, can be used to tell a powerful story.

Keep in mind, sometimes, the most successful or popular blogs are highly controversial and really anger people. However, a blog can also be humorous, entertaining, or strictly informative.

The following are 101 topics, subjects, issues, or themes worthy of blogging about. This list is presented for brainstorming purposes and is not meant to be a complete list; feel free to tap your own creativity in order to come up with your own blogging topics. You can also modify any of these topics so that they better fit into the overall theme or approach you'll be adopting for your blog.

Remember, once you pick a topic for your overall blog or for an individual blog entry, you'll want to flesh it out, make it your own, and present information or content that is somewhat unique and that will resonate (in a positive or negative way) with your audience.

Blog Topic Idea List

The following list, presented in alphabetical order, is comprised of 101 proven topics you could blog about. However, this list only scratches the surface when it comes to possible topics, themes, issues, or subject matters.

For every potential blogging topic, you can offer your opinions, experiences, commentary, news, how-to information, or any variety of different approaches, and then delve into sub-topics or related themes.

1. Abortion (Your Opinion/Commentary)
2. Abuse (Drugs, Alcohol, Mental, Physical, etc.)
3. Airline Security
4. Art (Favorite/Least Favorite/Your Review)
5. Books (Favorite/Least Favorite/Your Review)
6. Brothers/Sisters
7. Business & Financial News
8. Cars
9. Cell Phones
10. Challenge Your Audience To Do Something Specific
11. Charity
12. Collectibles
13. Commentary on Someone Else's Blog
14. Computers
15. Consumer Electronics
16. Cooking
17. Corruption
18. Create a Parody of Something
19. Credit Cards and Loans
20. Crime
21. Dealing with a Difficult Boss
22. Dealing with Loss
23. Divorce
24. Dream or Nightmare
25. Economic Trends
26. Engage in a Debate about Something with Your Audience
27. Family Vacation (Best or Worst)
28. Fashion
29. Fitness
30. Food/Nutrition
31. Friends
32. Gambling
33. Gas Prices
34. Gay Rights or Gay Marriage
35. Global Warming
36. Government/Government Policies (Local, State, or Federal)
37. Hairstyling
38. Health Insurance (and other types of insurance)
39. Hobbies (Golf, Fishing, Hiking, Camping, Crafts, Knitting, Painting, etc.)
40. Hollywood or Show Business Gossip
41. Home Decorating
42. How-To Instruction (share your expertise on a topic)
43. Interview Someone (Expert, Commentator, Celebrity, Politician, etc.)
44. Investing
45. Iran/Iraq/The Middle East
46. Jewelry
47. Knitting/Sewing
48. Magazine Article (your commentary)
49. Major Trial
50. Medical Issues
51. Mortgages/Refinancing
52. Most Embarrassing Moment

53. Movies or DVDs (Favorite/Least Favorite/Your Review)
54. Music (Favorite/Least Favorite/Your Review)
55. News Event/News Story
56. Office Politics
57. On-the-Job Experiences
58. Operating a Business/Being Self-Employed
59. Opinions about a Politician
60. Parents/In-Laws
61. Paying Off Debt
62. Performance of a Sports Team or Athlete
63. Personal Experience(s)
64. Personal Finances
65. Personal Heroes or Role Models
66. Pets
67. Political Commentary
68. Political Election
69. Pop Culture
70. Problem or Dilemma (Personal or Work Related)
71. Product Review(s)
72. Raising Children or Teenagers
73. Random Rants about Anything—or Nothing
74. Reality TV Commentary
75. Recent Family Event
76. Recycling
77. Religion/Your Religious Views

78. Reveal a Secret
79. Review of Book, TV Show, Movie, etc.
80. School
81. Share Research on a Topic
82. Shoes
83. Shopping
84. Single or Married Life
85. Social Networking
86. Something You Hate or that Makes You Angry
87. Sports
88. Teacher or Professor (Favorite/Least Favorite)
89. Technology Trends
90. Tell Jokes/Present Comedy
91. Terrorism
92. The United States (or any other country)
93. Theatre (Favorite/Least Favorite/Your Review)
94. Travel
95. TV Shows (Favorite/Least Favorite/Your Review)
96. U.S. Foreign Policy
97. Value of the U.S. Dollar (Currency Exchange Rates)
98. War
99. Websites (Favorite/Least Favorite/Your Review)
100. Weight Loss
101. Yourself—Share Something Personal

Developing Your Topic(s) to Make Them Engaging

Once you settle on one or more topics to blog about, you'll want to flesh each out and make it your own. Choose an approach to take by deciding what your overall goal is for the blog or blog entry. Ask yourself:

- What information can you share about the selected topic?
- What are three positive things you can discuss or blog about that are related to your specific topic(s)?
- What are three negative things that you can discuss, complain about, gossip about, or offer personal opinions about that relate to your topic(s)?
- What is your overall goal with the blog or blog entry? What thoughts, emotions or actions are you looking to solicit from your audience?
- Will the topic appeal to your audience and be relevant to it?
- Can you cite three to five well-known and respected sources who will agree or disagree with your position or opinion? How can these sources be used to enhance your credibility and help support your position on a topic or issue?
- How passionate are you about the topic? Will you be able to share your strong conviction, thoughts, or opinions within the blog entry?
- What approach will you take to present the material? Will you adopt a serious or humorous approach, for example?
- Will the topic promote controversy, anger, or disagreement among your audience? If this is something you want to happen, what will you say to spark the controversy or strong reaction from your followers?
- What graphic, visual, audio, or video assets can you incorporate into your blog to properly cover your selected topics?
- Is the topic something your audience will relate to in a positive way? If so, how will you build on those positive feelings?
- What can you share, as the blogger, with your audience to make the content unique?
- Based on the topic, will your blog contain facts and statistics, thoughts and opinions, quantifiable research data, or hypothetical ideas?
- How can you expand on or build up the topic so that it will remain fresh for an extended or ongoing period?

- Is the topic very timely, or will it have long online shelf life? In other words, will people be able to revisit the blog entry in 3, 6, 12 or 24 months, for example, and still find it relevant? Long-term relevance becomes more important if you'll be updating your blog on an infrequent basis, say once per week or month, as opposed to on an hourly or daily basis. If you update very frequently, timeliness of your content is important.

- Does the topic have follow-up potential, so it can be expanded upon in future blog entries?

Consider Your Reputation

The topic(s) you choose to blog about and the approach you take will have a direct impact on your reputation as a blogger and your ability to build an audience. It will also impact what people think about you as a person. It's easy for the general public to misconstrue blog content and make false assumptions about you as a person if you're not careful. For example, if you start blogging about UFOs, ghosts, and conspiracy theories, people might perceive you to be a bit extreme or mentally unstable.

If you choose to cover highly controversial topics, such as politics, war, gay marriage, or abortion, for example, and you present yourself as someone who is strongly for or against the issue, there will be a portion of the population that by default strongly disagrees with you, which could cause extreme resentment.

Many talk radio personalities and talk show hosts that deal with newsworthy topics (hosts of shows on Fox News or MSNBC, for example), try to be highly opinionated and controversial to attract an audience. Opting to share your opinions publicly about highly contentious

Warning

Building a positive reputation as a blogger or as an internet celebrity, for example, could take months or years. However, one simple mistake or misunderstanding could destroy your reputation overnight. Before posting a blog, consider how the public (your audience) might react and what the potential ramifications of those reactions might be. If you become a high-profile blogger, consider what could happen if you receive regional or national publicity in the mainstream media as a result of your controversial blog. How could bad publicity impact your personal and professional life outside of your blog's following?

Tip

Be sure to refer to Chapter 10 in regard to protecting yourself and precautions you might want to take as a blogger.

topics could help you establish yourself as a well-known blogger, or it could backfire and result in a highly unpopular blog, depending on the approach you take and your personal willingness and ability to deal with certain topics.

As you focus on topics, consider that what you focus on within your blog will impact what people think about you, how you're perceived, and how much respect people develop for you. It could also impact your friendships, work-related relationships, and potentially your romantic relationships as well.

There are many approaches you can take when it comes to blogging about almost any topic. The approach you take is as important as the topic itself. It's relatively easy to take a lighthearted topic and transform it into something highly controversial. Likewise, it's also possible to take a hotly debated and controversial topic and create a blog that does not offend or anger your audience.

As you develop the topic(s) you plan to cover, consider several different approaches to them and decide which approach will help you achieve your overall goals or objectives as a blogger.

Consider carefully the ramifications of your words and actions, as well as your thoughts and opinions on various topics before going public with them. Understand that the public's perception of you (which might be based on false assumptions) can be damaging to your blogging career, your professional career and your personal life in the real world, if you're not careful or if you allow a situation to get blown out of proportion.

What's Next?

You're quickly acquiring the knowledge you need to create, publish and manage an awesome blog. The next chapter, however, sums up some of this extremely important information, plus offers additional tips and strategies for making your blog informative, entertaining, and memorable. From Chapter 7, you'll also learn more about how to build up your credibility as a blogger and learn more about cutting-edge blogging trends and technologies.

Chapter 7
Creating an Awesome Blog

As you've hopefully discovered by now, anyone can create and publish a blog quickly (within a few hours) and for little or no money. The problem is, out of the millions of new blogs being created every year, only a few truly stand out and develop a dedicated following.

When it comes to creating a successful and popular blog, many factors are involved. They range from the topic you blog about, to the appearance of your blog, to how well you transform yourself into a likable online personality.

This chapter focuses on ten proven strategies you should utilize to create an awesome blog.

Ten Strategies for Creating an Informative, Entertaining, and Memorable Blog

The following ten strategies summarize many of the concepts explored throughout this book and will help you develop, publish, and promote a blog that will truly appeal to your target audience, and help your blog stand out from the millions of other blogs and websites that currently have a home in cyberspace.

Not all of these strategies will be applicable to your blog, but most of them should be, regardless of your blog's topic, approach, or target audience.

1. Fine-tune and Flesh Out Your Blog Topic or Theme

Simply coming up with a general topic or theme to blog about is an important first step toward creating a new blog, but an equally important ongoing step as you plan, create, and publish plenty of new topic-related content on a regular basis. Once you've thought about what you want to blog about, make a list of at least 10 to 15 potential blog entries you plan to create, and then flesh out those entry topics into full-length posts—always making sure the topics are relevant and of interest to your target audience.

2. Brainstorm New and Original Content

Aside from simply being or becoming an expert on whatever topic(s) you ultimately choose to blog about, one activity that any good blogger should engage in is getting into the habit of regularly reading other blogs, websites, newspapers, newsletters, magazines, and trade journals, for example, that cover the same topic. In addition to helping you stay up-to-date about your topic, this allows you to keep tabs on other sources your audience might already be turning to for information.

From these other sources, you can figure out what approaches work in terms of communicating with your audience, plus you can more easily brainstorm innovative and original ways to better provide your audience with relevant content. Figure out what your competition is doing and discover ways to do it better, more efficiently, and/or in a more entertaining manner. Use your research of other blogs and websites to discover what's missing and what additional content your audience could benefit from.

Furthermore, staying up-to-date on the approach taken by other bloggers that cover the same topic(s) as you offers you the opportunity to exchange links with other online-based information sources in order to further build your audience and boost your own credibility. Many popular search engines take into account how many websites and blogs, for example, link to your blog when positioning

Tip

Remember, there are no rules for achieving success when it comes to blogging. What's required is a tremendous amount of creativity, uniqueness, persistence, and an understanding of your audience. In your mind, you should also have a firm grasp on what you want your blog to be about, and how you as the blogger want it to be perceived. Whether you're using your blog to somehow promote yourself, your company, or a product/service, your blog should be an extension of your personality (or the persona you establish as a blogger). Once your online personality or persona is established, keep it consistent.

or ranking your blog. So, the more links you have established with other websites and blogs, the better. Plus, offering links to online resources offering relevant or related information is a value-added service you can easily provide to your blog's audience.

3. Keep Your Blog Current

Unlike many other media outlets, the internet offers the opportunity to publish information and timely content immediately. As a result, information (such as facts, figures, statistics, and other types of data) quickly becomes outdated. People turn to the internet for up-to-the-minute, cutting-edge news or information. Therefore, it's important that your blog, if applicable, incorporate the most recent data and information available in order to keep your blog timely.

When applicable, base your reporting, opinions, and other blog content on the very latest information available, and keep up as new information or data becomes available. Not only will this help your reputation for being a well-informed blogger, it'll also help you better cater to your audience.

For example, when you're sharing specific facts, figures, or statistics, be sure to list your sources and explain how and when the information was compiled. Presenting old or outdated information and promoting it as current information is irresponsible and provides a disservice to your audience. Plus, it can quickly damage your credibility as a blogger.

If your audience expects you to update your blog on a daily, weekly, biweekly, or monthly basis, be sure to diligently stay on that publishing schedule, so your audience knows what they can expect and when.

4. Get Your Audience Emotionally Invested in Your Blog

Just as you, the blogger, need to be truly passionate about whatever topic(s) you're blogging about, assume your target audience is equally passionate about that topic. Then, use the enthusiasm or emotional connection you know your audience has with the topic to build up their allegiance to you and your blog.

Develop and publish content that your readers can strongly agree or disagree with, learn from, or somehow become emotionally invested in. Encourage your audience to then share their own thoughts and opinions by posting comments

Tip

Incorporating widgets or gadgets into your blog is a fast and very easy way to add functionality and interactivity to a blog, whether it's a survey, quiz, questionnaire, the ability to post comments, the ability to share photos, or the ability to add a live chat feature to your blog.

to your blog entries, take part in online questionnaires or surveys, and become part of an small online social networking environment that you create around your blog.

As you communicate with your audience about a topic, encourage them to take specific actions and provide incentives for them to follow through and become an active participant in your blog—as opposed to a passive reader, listener, or viewer.

Consider adding a specific call to action within your various blog entries. The call to action might be providing an open invitation to agree or disagree with a blog entry, attend a real-world event, make a donation to a charitable cause, purchase a specific product or service, or simply to tell friends about your blog in order to help you generate more traffic.

By creating an online forum or environment where your audience can quickly and easily obtain information that they're passionate about or have an emotional connection with, you're automatically providing a powerful incentive for them to return to your blog in the future.

5. Find Your Voice and Use It Properly

People appreciate what's familiar. If they come to know you as a blogger with a particular point of view, opinion, or approach to a topic, or they begin to follow your blog because they like your personality (or the personality/persona you've created online), they'll expect you to maintain some level of consistency.

If you have an opinion on a topic, state it and then support it with facts, research, and strong arguments, while encouraging opposing points of view. Whatever you do, however, be consistent. Avoid flip-flopping on opinions or publishing false information that you'll later need to correct or retract.

For example, if you follow politics and blog about your political beliefs as they relate to current events, government policy, or the approach of specific politicians, and your followers come to know you as having strong republican or democratic beliefs, don't one day adopt an opposite point-of-view simply to get attention or create controversy or disagreement. This will take away from your credibility and could damage your reputation.

Instead, one approach is to invite others with strongly opposing beliefs to write or create guest blog entries, or post comments with different points of view that you can address within your future blog entries in order to create controversy and make your content more enticing.

As you initially brainstorm ideas for your blog, consider carefully your voice as a writer and develop that voice so it's uniquely you. Your voice should allow you to showcase your personality and create a reputation for yourself that sets you apart from other bloggers and public figures such as TV or radio show personalities.

Warning

No matter how good of a writer or communicator you are, if you personally don't believe in or feel passionate about whatever you're blogging about, this will quickly become obvious to your audience and can damage your credibility.

Are you more apt to believe a religious leader who passionately believes they're spreading the word of God to their followers in order to help people, or a used car salesman who only shows up to work in order to make money by saying or doing whatever is necessary to sell cars? Your true belief in whatever it is you're blogging about will automatically and subconsciously be communicated by you, if that passion is genuine. Even if you're using your blog to promote or sell a product or service, if you believe what you're selling lives up to the hype you create for it, others will take to heart what you have to say.

On the flip side, if it's obvious that within your blog you're being less than truthful or controversial for the sake of creating controversy, this, too, will be apparent by your audience and could damage your credibility and ability to generate an audience. Many talk radio hosts are guilty of spewing out opinions they don't necessarily believe in order to generate calls to their show, create controversy, and boost their ratings. This tactic might work in the short term for a blogger, but when all is said and done, if you don't believe what you're saying within your blog, others won't believe it either and achieving your goals as a blogger will be that much more challenging, if not impossible.

Make sure you are comfortable writing or blogging using the voice and tone you create, so you can more easily maintain consistency and continuity throughout all of your blog entries, even if you take on new topics to blog about that will appeal to your target audience.

6. Create New Ways to Say Old Things, Compared to Other Blogs and Websites

Chances are, no matter what topic(s) you opt to blog about, there will be dozens, maybe hundreds or even thousands of other blogs and websites—not to mention newspapers, magazines, TV programs, radio shows, newsletters, trade magazines, and other media outlets—somehow covering that same topic and communicating somewhat similar information to their respective audiences.

While you might not be able to come up with something that's 100 percent new to say or blog about in terms of an overall topic, you can put your own spin on your topic, share your own personal opinions, and package your content in a way that's different from everyone else. It's how you package the material and make it engaging, interesting, informative, memorable, valuable, and/or entertaining for your audience that will allow you to stand out as a blogger and flourish.

The more often you incorporate a unique point of view, a new fact, or an interesting tidbit of information that's exclusive to your blog, the better. Focus on creating original content by interviewing other experts, doing your own research, and sharing your findings, and by allowing your unique voice and opinions or ideas to be heard. These are just some of the

Tip

Make sure the voice you adopt for your blog is appropriate for your target audience. Consider the vocabulary, slang, colloquialism, and language you use within your blog, in addition to the content itself. Ensure what you say and how you say it is suitable for and understandable by the people you perceive to be your audience.

There's a huge difference between writing in an up-beat, irreverent, and light-hearted or entertaining tone that would be suitable for a blog covering the entertainment industry or celebrity gossip, and the tone you'd adopt to create a blog for conservative followers of a specific religion, or for die-hard believers of a specific topic, such as abortion, same sex marriage, or gun control.

strategies bloggers use to create engaging and unique content.

Yes, there's a lot of competition out there. If you want to stand out from the crowd, tap your creativity and uniqueness as a person to make whatever it is you're blogging about different from what other bloggers, reporters, writers, authors, and journalists are doing.

Whenever possible, bring your own life experiences, emotions, opinions, dreams, knowledge, background, and education into the mix. For example, if you're blogging about your family's trip to Disney World in Orlando, there are countless travel guides and other blogs out there that have "reviewed" the rides or that have helped people understand what a Disney vacation is all about. However, nobody else on the planet has ever experienced the same trip experiences as you did personally. This is unique information you can share. How did you feel when experiencing your favorite Disney rides, shows, and attractions? What was going through your mind at the time? Who were you with? What did they experience, and why? What sights, sounds, smells, tastes, and feelings did you experience? What memories stand out most based on your experience? What would you do differently next time, based on your opinions and experiences? This is all blog content that you can create that would be unique to you.

> ## Tip
>
>
> Sometimes a single photo can convey more information than several paragraphs worth of text. A photo can also stir up emotion and add to the visual appeal of your blog. Whenever possible, try to incorporate relevant photos that add to the overall content of each blog entry. How you utilize photos and artwork is one thing that can help differentiate your blog from the competition.

7. Focus on Building Up Your Credibility and Reputation as a Blogger

People have to believe that you believe what you're blogging about if you want people to take you seriously. Having a passion for what you're blogging about is essential, but equally important is the way you develop and present your content. In order to establish and ultimately maintain your credibility and believability as a blogger, consider incorporating these strategies:

- Make sure the text within your blog contains absolutely no spelling or grammatical mistakes.

- Only publish the truth (unless you're a gossip-oriented blog) or you make it clear that what you're blogging about is based on fiction, opinion, or someone else's perception. Don't intentionally mislead your audience by disguising incorrect or fictional information as truth.

- Consider how what you blog about will impact how you're perceived as a person. If you write about topics that people will react to badly, such as an endorsement of racism, people who read your blog will perceive you as a racist. If you blog about topics like aliens, ghosts, possessions, and communicating with the dead, non-believers might perceive you to be a bit odd. Keep in mind, even if your blog caters to a specific audience, such as UFO abductees, it can be accessed and read by anyone—including your relatives, friends, employer, professors, religious leaders, neighbors, etc. Therefore, what you blog about in cyberspace can easily impact not just what your blog's audience thinks about you, but how you're perceived in the real world by people you interact with on a daily basis. As a result, there can be consequences if someone unexpected gains access to your blog, such as your boss, an important client, or a co-worker, for example.

- Demonstrate you care about your audience and develop a bond with them. It'll be easier for your audience to relate to you and what you have to say if they somehow relate to you as a person and have something in common with you. Use the "About Me" section of your blog, for example, to share some personal information about yourself that might help people relate to you more easily. Try to create a virtual bond with your audience by making it clear you understand them and have something in common with them. For example, if you're seeking out information about how to raise your teenagers as a newly divorced parent, are you more apt to trust a blogger who is a fellow single parent and who has already experienced what you're going through, or someone who has never been married and doesn't even have kids, but who claims to be an expert on the topic?

8. Transform Yourself Into an Online "Personality"

Simply by visiting other blogs and vlogs, you can easily distinguish between people who simply create a blog and those who establish themselves as a personality that distinguishes them from other bloggers—based on their appearance, attitude, voice, opinions, knowledge, and experience.

There are thousands of entertainment gossip blogs that populate the internet, but there's only one Perez Hilton (perezhilton.com). Within seconds of visiting his blog, it's easy to see that every aspect of Perez and what he has to say is unique and different. He's become a personality onto himself. Plus, he offers an expertise and obvious knowledge about the entertainment industry that gives him instant credibility. Perez has become "famous" as a blogger because of what he blogs about, plus because of who he is, what he represents, and the unique way he presents his material.

Obviously, Perez Hilton is an extreme example of what can be done to transform yourself from a run-of-the-mill blogger into a personality. However, valuable lessons can be learned from his success and applied to people blogging about any topic whatsoever. While in some cases, it's important for the blogger to fit in perfectly with their audience, in some situations positioning yourself as anything but ordinary might prove beneficial. You'll learn more about Perez Hilton's incredible success as a blogger in Chapter 14.

Whatever online personality or persona you choose to adopt, make sure that it's something that you believe in and relate to, and that it's an extension of who you really are as a person. You should be 100 percent comfortable with the online persona you create for yourself.

9. Focus on Production Quality and the Look of Your Blog

As you'll read in Chapter 13, Chris Alden, who is the President and CEO of Six Apart (the company that created and offers the TypePad and VOX blogging tools), believes that what someone blogs (or vlogs) about is far more important than the production quality or aesthetic appearance of their content. While Alden's opinion is certainly a valid one, and one that comes from one of the most knowledgeable people on the planet when it comes to blogging, the appearance of your blog *does* play an important role in how it's perceived by the public and how successful it becomes, especially if the blog is being used for professional or commercial purposes in a business situation.

The layout and design of your blog should be consistent with the online persona and reputation you're trying to develop for yourself, plus it should definitely appeal to your target audience. Chapter 5 focuses on the layout and design of a traditional blog, while Chapter 8 focuses on producing quality vlogs and podcasts, even if you have limited production skills and a tight budget.

10. Develop Innovative Ways to Market Your Blog and Generate Hype for It

The concept of "if you build it, they will come" does *not* apply to blogs and websites. Publishing online content, no matter how good it is, won't capture the attention of anyone unless you properly promote it to the appropriate audience and drive a steady flow of traffic to your blog or website.

As you'll read about in Chapter 10, there are many ways to generate traffic for a blog and strategies you can use, both in cyberspace and in the real world, to build an audience for your blog—again, even if you're on a tight budget. What you absolutely must understand is that for a blog to become successful, you must invest the time, energy, and resources necessary to promote it heavily and on an ongoing basis.

Just as with a website, registering your blog with the popular internet search engines (such as Yahoo! and Google) and utilizing search engine optimization techniques are extremely useful tools for driving traffic to a blog. Blogs can also be promoted when you become an active participant on social networking sites, like MySpace, Facebook and Twitter. There are also inexpensive ways to promote your blog using online advertising and grassroutes public relations efforts.

Regardless of your marketing budget, it's essential that you develop, implement, and manage an ongoing and organized marketing and promotional plan for your blog. This is an effort that must be maintained week after week, month after month, and year after year, if you want to build and then sustain a large audience.

Depending on who your audience is and the topic of your blog, some marketing and promotional techniques will work better than others. By tapping your own creativity, your knowledge about how well you know your audience, and your available marketing/promotional resources, be sure to adopt a multi-faceted approach to your efforts. And, most importantly, be persistent and patient.

Very few blogs become ultra-successful in a matter of days or even weeks. It could take you months or even years to develop a vast audience for your blog, even if you have a brilliant topic and take a well thought out and unique approach to your blogging efforts.

Initially, one of the best ways you can introduce your blog to the general public is to utilize search engine optimization techniques to get listed with the popular search engines, and then ensure your blog receives the best placement or positioning possible, based on keywords and well-written descriptions, headlines, and body text.

Nine Tips for Utilizing SEO to Generate Blog Traffic

While additional tips for promoting a blog are covered within Chapter 10, when it comes to search engine optimization (SEO), there are several basic techniques you can implement yourself relatively easily and with little money. Be sure to invest time to develop a good understanding of what SEO is and how it can be used. Start with some research online, as there are thousands of websites and blogs dedicated to this topic.

Warning

There are three extremely common mistakes made by bloggers when it comes to marketing a new blog. Simply by understanding what these mistakes are, you can take steps and develop strategies to avoid them, and as a result, dramatically increase your chances for achieving success. These mistakes are:

1. Not properly promoting a new blog when it's first launched.

2. Not being persistent and promoting/marketing a blog on an ongoing basis.

3. Giving up way too soon when initial marketing/promotional efforts don't generate the desired (but often unrealistic) results based on erroneous expectations.

Many search engines, including Yahoo! and Google, also offer online-based introductions to SEO and advice on how to use these strategies to obtain the best possible listings and positioning within the various search engines. If you don't want to invest the time needed to become a SEO expert, you can hire an independent company to get your blog listed with the various search engines. However, there's often a fee—one-time or ongoing—to obtain these services.

Some of the best and most basic SEO strategies include:

1. *Take full advantage of the SEO tools offered by your blogging service.* All of the popular blog hosting services offer features for helping a blogger promote

their blog and get their blog listed with the popular search engines. Take full advantage of these tools, but also take steps independently to enhance your SEO activities and the traffic to your blog.

2. *Register your blog with the search engines immediately and then periodically update or confirm your listing.* Visit the individual search engines and follow the online directions for submitting a website or blog for inclusion.

3. *Be descriptive in all of your headings and sub-headings.* Become an expert at incorporating keywords into your text, especially in your blog's main title and description, as well as within the headings and sub-headings of each blog entry. Your keywords should be extremely relevant to the topic(s) you're blogging about and should be incorporated based on what you believe would be the words or phrases someone might type into a search engine (such as Google) to find your blog or the content contained within your blog.

4. *Incorporate keywords into your main text within each blog entry.* As you're writing the main body text of each blog entry, try to use as many relevant keywords as possible. In this case, frequency of a keyword can be beneficial, as long as the frequency is used properly and in context.

5. *Create a list of highly relevant keywords or labels for each blog entry.* Almost every blog hosting service has a field somewhere on their respective blog entry creation page for creating a detailed list of keywords or labels that are relevant to a specific blog entry. Be sure to complete this field with between five and 10 relevant keywords or phrases that pertain specifically to each of your blog entries.

6. *Use keywords in your photo captions.* If your blog hosting service allows to you add special captions to your photos and images, be sure to incorporate descriptive keywords into each of your captions.

7. *Link to other topic-related websites and blogs.* Within your blog entries themselves, as well as within a separate "Links" or "Other Resources" section of your blog, be sure to list a handful of related links to blogs or websites that your audience would be interested in. At the same time, contact other bloggers or webmasters and ask them to do the same for you in order to promote your blog. The more links you have pointed to your blog from other search

engines, blogs, and websites, the better your search engine placement will be and the easier it will be for people to find and access your blog.

8. *Consider hiring an SEO specialist, at least initially, to help you properly promote your blog using search engine optimization techniques.* Obtaining good placement with the search engines, based on relevant keywords, is one of the most cost-effective and powerful ways of generating traffic to your blog, especially as you're first starting out. SEO specialists charge for their services. Freelance SEO specialists can be found on services like Guru.com and eLance.com. You can also type "SEO Specialist" into a search engine to find listings. When hiring someone, make sure you understand what services are being offered and how much you will be charged.

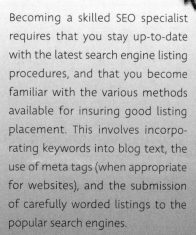

Tip

Becoming a skilled SEO specialist requires that you stay up-to-date with the latest search engine listing procedures, and that you become familiar with the various methods available for insuring good listing placement. This involves incorporating keywords into blog text, the use of meta tags (when appropriate for websites), and the submission of carefully worded listings to the popular search engines.

9. *Be patient, but persistent!* Sometimes it takes weeks to get a new blog listed with a search engine. Also, just because you get listed with Google and/ or Yahoo, or any of the other search engines, this does not guarantee you'll generate traffic to your blog. The SEO strategies you adopt should be just one part of your overall, multifaceted approach to marketing and promoting your blog. Don't forget, one of the biggest mistakes bloggers make is giving up too soon on their marketing and promotional efforts. Be patient and have realistic expectations.

There are a variety of online and in-person training programs that are designed to help you develop the necessary knowledge and skills to become an SEO and search engine marketing expert. Some of these training programs are available from:

- High Rankings (highrankings.com/home)
- Search Engine College (searchenginecollege.com)

- Search Engine Guide (searchengineguide.com)
- Search Engine Strategies (searchenginestrategies.com)
- Search Engine Workshops (searchengineworkshops.com)
- Search Marketing Expo (searchmarketingexpo.com)
- SeoBook (seobook.com/join)
- World Wide Learn (worldwidelearn.com/online-training/ search-engine-positioning.htm)

Focus on Improving Your Site's Ranking and Position

After your blog gets listed with a search engine and appears when web surfers conduct searches, it then becomes your responsibility to keep your listing up-to-date. Take whatever steps are possible to maintain and improve your listing. This is referred to as search engine optimization, because your objective is to optimize the placement or ranking of your search.

Again, this is a time-consuming process you can do yourself, or you can hire an SEO expert to handle it on your behalf, which will probably generate better results faster. If you want or need to have a listing for your site appear on the search engines quickly (as in within hours, not weeks), seriously consider using paid advertising through Yahoo!, Microsoft, and/or Google AdWords to supplement your free listings.

If you have a good-sized budget, you can also utilize display advertising and website sponsorships to ensure your message gets communicated to web surfers when they're online and actively looking for your company or its products.

Additional Search Engine Optimization Tools and Resources

To find a third-party company that specializes in submitting URL listings (for blogs and websites) to search engines, as well as search engine optimization, enter the search phrase "search engine submissions" or "search engine optimization" into any search engine, such as Yahoo! or Google. You'll discover hundreds, potentially thousands of paid services you can use, including:

- buildtraffic.com
- engineseeker.com

- godaddy.com/gdshop/traffic_blazer/landing.asp
- iclimber.com
- networksolutions.com/online-marketing/index.jsp
- seop.com
- submitasite.com
- toprankresults.com
- trafficxs.com/platinum.htm
- worldsubmit.com
- wpromote.com/quicklist/landing

What's Next?

Now that you have the knowledge and tools needed to create and publish a successful text-based blog, which can incorporate various graphic and multimedia elements, the next chapter focuses on producing video blogs (vlogs), live webcasting, and audio podcasts.

As you'll discover, producing a quality vlog or podcast requires a bit more of a time commitment, plus audio and/or video production and editing skills are required. However, for people looking to achieve fame in cyberspace, there's no better way to do this than by becoming a vlogger, hosting webcasts, or by incorporating video into your text-based blog.

Chapter 8
Vlogging (or Webcasting) Your Way to Stardom

Throughout much of this book, the term *blogging* or *blog* is used generically to encompass traditional text-based blogs, video blogs (vlogs), webcasts, and podcasts. In this chapter, however, we'll focus exclusively on vlogging and webcasting which involve producing and distributing live or pre-taped video of yourself entertaining your audience and sharing your thoughts and ideas.

As you'll discover from this chapter, vlogging and webcasting can be fun and it's a great way to become famous in cyberspace, but it also requires a lot more work than traditional blogging. In addition to creating awesome and original ideas for content, you also must possess the personality, charisma, and public speaking ability to communicate verbally with your audience. Of course, being attractive doesn't hurt either.

If you think you have what it takes to be a vlogger and/or webcaster, this chapter will explain how to produce awesome vlogs and webcasts, attract attention for your work, and distribute your videos so they can reach the largest audience possible using a variety of online services and social networking websites, including (but not limited to) YouTube, Yahoo! Video, MySpace, Facebook, BlogTV, and Stickam.

The Difference Between Blogs, Vlogs, and Webcasts

You already know that traditional blogs are comprised of primarily text and photos, but can also incorporate video clips, audio clips, multimedia elements, or widgets to enhance the content. To create a traditional blog, most bloggers register with a service, such as Blogger.com, TypePad.com, or WordPress.com, and use the online tools provided to layout and design their blog, create their content, and publish their blog.

Text-based blog entries can be created in a matter of minutes, or however long it takes you to convey your ideas and put them in writing. Vlogs, however, require you

Tip

Vlog entries tend to be relatively short in length. Three to five minutes is usually the perfect length to convey information or entertain an audience without boring them or losing their attention. As a general rule, individual vlog entries should be kept well under 10 minutes in length.

Webcasts, however, tend to be considerably longer. Webcasters who put on regularly scheduled daily or weekly live shows, for example, typically pre-determine the length for each show (between 15 minutes and one hour, for example). Longer-format webcasts tend to be interactive, allowing the webcaster to solicit live questions and comments from the audience.

to present your thoughts, ideas, opinions, and content on video. This typically involves you, the blogger, looking directly into a video camera or webcam and presenting your vlog content, just as a TV newscaster would report the news or a stand-up comedian would present their routine if they were to appear on a TV show.

Vlogs are shot on video (or recorded digitally using a computer and webcam) and can be published as part of a traditional blog or website, distributed through an online video service, such as YouTube (youtube.com) or Yahoo! Video (video.yahoo.com), or be integrated into your profile that's associated with an online social networking service (such as MySpace or Facebook). Most vloggers who are looking for fame wind up utilizing most or all of these services to distribute their vlogs to the largest audience possible.

Vlog entries are often like traditional blog entries in that they're pre-recorded and tend to focus on one or two topics at a time. With vlogs, however, not only is the content or subject matter itself important, but also how you communicate that information on video becomes essential. When it comes to vlogging, your personality, body language, appearance, and attitude all become part of the show and must be appealing to your audience. While nobody will expect your vlog to have the same professional production quality of a television show, people who watch vlogs do have expectations that you'll need to meet or surpass when it comes to basic production quality and watchability.

Once vlog entries are produced and published, they can remain online indefinitely. Most popular vloggers set up YouTube Channels and/or a separate website to showcase their vlogs, so people can gain access to all of the vlogs they've produced. Some vloggers, however, make it a habit of removing old vlog entries from the web, so only the most current ones are available to their audience. This is a personal decision and one that should be made based on what you're trying to accomplish, your audience, and your vlog's content.

Webcasts are very similar to vlogs in that they involve you standing (or sitting) directly in front of a video camera or webcam and "performing" for your audience. But a webcast is broadcast live over the internet and often allows you to interact directly with your audience, in real time, through instant text messaging or other voice or video interaction with your audience. The features and functionality available to you will depend on on the webcasting service you utilize.

Many popular webcasters maintain a regular program schedule, so their fans know how often and exactly when their shows will be online live. As these webcasts happen live, they can also be recorded and archived online so people can access them later from your website, traditional blog, through an online service

A Few Words about Podcasting

Instead of using text-based content or video, podcasts utilize audio and can be played by your audience online or downloaded and listened to on an Apple iPod or .MP3 player. Podcasting involves recording and editing your audio and making those audio files available online. In addition to publishing podcasts as part of a website or traditional blog, they can also be distributed through podcast hosting and distribution services, such as Apple's iTunes.

Because vlogging and webcasting have become inexpensive and accessible to everyone, these blogging methods have become more popular than podcasting. Plus, for audiences, watching a video tends to be more engaging and entertaining than listening to stand-alone audio.

The Apple iTunes service maintains an ever-growing library of more than 100,000 podcasts, most of which can be downloaded and listened to for free. To learn more about producing and publishing podcasts, point your web browser to apple.com/itunes/store/podcasts.html.

The Podcasting Tools website (podcasting-tools.com) is also an excellent resource for finding how-to information, as well as tools and software utilized by podcasters to produce and publish their content. Another online listing of tools, services and software of interest to podcasters can be found at the Mashable Podcaster's Toolbox website (mashable.com/2007/07/04/podcasting-toolbox).

(such as Stickam), from YouTube, or through a social networking service (such as MySpace or Facebook).

Internet Stardom Is All About Name Recognition!

Many web surfers begin to follow a traditional blog because of its content. The blog addresses a topic they are interested in and they are willing to return regularly or subscribe to the blog in order to learn more about it.

The same is true to some extent when it comes to vlogs and webcasts, but a huge component to the success of vlogs or webcasts is the vlogger/webcaster themselves. You must be able to capture the attention of your audience in order to inform or entertain them using your personality, charisma, body language, and appearance—just like a television personality. The success potential of a vlog or webcast evolves as much around you, your presentation, and your public speaking skills as it does on the topic or subject matter you're presenting.

It should come as no surprise that the most famous and popular vloggers and webcasters are "personalities" in every sense of the word. They're not just talking heads reading a pre-written script while looking into a camera or webcam. Popular vloggers and webcasters tend to stand out from the crowd, be just a bit out there, and have something unique about their personality, appearance and/or communication style that allows them to truly stand out and be memorable. Many have "star quality," just like you'd find in Hollywood.

Successful vloggers and webcasters don't just have something worthwhile, important, or entertaining to say; in many cases, they themselves are a main part of the entertainment value of the vlog or webcast. These people are able to package their content in a way that captures the attention of their audience, while always creating a demand for more content. Audience members finish watching a vlog or webcast looking forward to the next edition.

Obviously, not everyone has the personality or communication skills to become a mega-popular vlogger or webcaster—just as only a handful of people become famous television personalities or have what it takes to host a television talk show or game show, for example.

If you search YouTube, it's easy to see that there are millions of vloggers and webcasters out there trying to become famous in cyberspace or who are looking to share their knowledge or performing abilities with the world. Those who are successful manage to make a name for themselves and understand the importance of promoting themselves heavily as an online personality. These are the people who are able to obtain 50,000 to several million views of their vlogs and webcasts on a daily or weekly basis.

If you want people to watch your vlogs and/or webcasts and keep coming back for more, it's essential that you create name recognition for yourself. Each video you appear in should remind people of who you are, what you do, and where your videos can be found online.

People like Chris Crocker (mschriscrocker.com)—you know, the "Leave Britney alone" self-proclaimed crying lunatic—have become experts at making themselves stand out and be memorable with each of their vlogs. They also constantly remind people of who they are and where their latest vlogs, webcasts, or videos can be found. If you watch any of Chris Crocker's vlogs, for example, you'll notice that he mentions his own name and his website's URL multiple times. This is because becoming a successful vlogger or webcaster is all about developing strong name recognition!

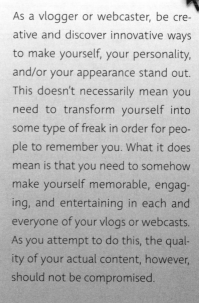

Tip

As a vlogger or webcaster, be creative and discover innovative ways to make yourself, your personality, and/or your appearance stand out. This doesn't necessarily mean you need to transform yourself into some type of freak in order for people to remember you. What it does mean is that you need to somehow make yourself memorable, engaging, and entertaining in each and everyone of your vlogs or webcasts. As you attempt to do this, the quality of your actual content, however, should not be compromised.

Producing Top-Quality Vlogs

When it comes to shooting vlogs, there are a handful of things you'll need to consider, including:

- what you'll say and the topic(s) you plan to cover
- how you'll look in the video, including your wardrobe, hair, make-up, etc.
- the background or "set" your audience will see behind you or around you
- the lighting

- the video production quality
- how you'll edit the vlog
- how and where you'll distribute the vlog.

While some vloggers have become experts at producing their vlogs and the result is something almost suitable to air on network television, many vlogs are shot in a living room, bedroom, or office, using a personal computer and a webcam. As long as what you're saying is informative and/or entertaining, and you, as the vlogger, are able to engage your audience, the production quality of the vlog won't impact your audience too much.

That being said, however, the video should be in focus. The camera shot should be steady. The audio should be clear (and free of hissing and distracting background noise). The background should not be too busy. In many cases a solid color wall or even hanging up a sheet makes a suitable background. If you do any editing, the final video should be smooth, flowing, and easy on the eyes.

Using popular video editing software on a PC or Mac, editing video has never been easier. It takes a bit of practice to get good at it, but if you focus on becoming proficient using your video editing software, you'll be able to add titles, special effects, and fades, plus edit your videos relatively quickly and with minimal effort.

Sure, you can go out an invest hundreds or even thousands of dollars on professional-quality video, audio, and lighting equipment to produce your vlogs. If your vlogs are being used to promote a company (and/or its products or services), this might be necessary to achieve the quality your customers or clients expect. However, for the average vlogger, a basic webcam connected to a PC or Mac, with the use of

Tip

Before you start producing your own vlogs, go online, visit YouTube or Yahoo! Video, for example, and watch what these services have determined to be the current most popular or most watched videos and vlogs. Pay attention to the vlogger, the production quality of the video, how the subject matter is address and packaged, and figure out why each video is so entertaining that it's become one of the most watched on the web. Once you fully understand what it takes produce an awesome blog, and you begin to understand the expectations of your potential audience, you'll have a much easier time meeting or exceeding those expectations.

off-the-shelf video editing software, will generate good enough results to get you started vlogging. You can always upgrade your production setup once your vlogs become successful.

Based on the video and computer equipment (and software) you have at your disposal, figure out what's possible from a production quality standpoint, and then strive to achieve that level of quality. On YouTube, for example, you'll find a library of free videos offering how–to tips and advice for producing YouTube videos (youtube.com/user/YouTubeHelp). Production tips for creating YouTube videos can also be found within the online-based YouTube Handbook (youtube.com/t/yt_handbook_produce#).

From a technical standpoint, YouTube (and most similar services), can accept the uploading of digital video in a wide range of formats. However, the experts at YouTube recommend the following in order to achieve the best results:

- Video format: MPEG4 (Divx, Xvid)
- Resolution: 640x480 pixels
- Audio format: MP3
- Frames per second: 30
- Maximum length: ten minutes (YouTube recommends two to three minutes)
- Maximum file size: 1 GB

Warning

It's important when posting vlogs for the public that you take steps to protect your safety. The YouTube website offers the following advice, "If you do post public videos, make sure there isn't anything in them that could help a stranger figure out who you are or where you live. Personal information, like your telephone number or home address should never be shared with other users. Watch out for things like license plate numbers on cars or images of the outside of your home which might accidentally appear in the background of a video and help a stranger to track you down. Remember, YouTube employees will never ask you for your password, e-mail address, or other account information. Don't be fooled if someone contacts you pretending to be from YouTube!"

If you plan to distribute your video via Yahoo! Video, the video file needs to meet the following specifications. Your digital video must to be less than 150 MB, in WMV, ASF, QT, MOD, MOV, MPG, 3GP, 3GP2, or AVI format, and have audio. Videos can be uploaded to Yahoo! Video by visiting this URL: video.yahoo.com/upload.

Making Your Vlogs Stand Out

The following are 20 tips (listed in no particular order) for making your vlog or webcast stand out and be more memorable, regardless of your subject matter:

1. *Be bold and be different.* Really showcase your personality and make sure you're someone who is worth watching.

2. *If your vlog is designed to convey information, as opposed to being purely for entertainment, don't just talk about a topic, delve into it and share information that people will deem useful or valuable.* Someone should walk away from watching your blog knowing something new or have their eyes opened to a different or unique point-of-view.

3. *For vlogs, edit your final production!* Don't just babble to make your vlogs longer. Remember, your audience will have a very short attention span. Say what you have to say and get on with it! Chances are, if you've recorded a ten-minute vlog, you can edit it down to five really engaging minutes (and you probably should). Once you've said what you have to say or whatever is on your mind, end the vlog. Don't keep rambling on.

4. *Focus on whatever it is that makes you and your vlog unique.* It's essential that your vlog (and you as an online personality) stand out from all others in a positive and/or entertaining way.

5. *Using your video editing software, add a few basic special effects—such as titles, fades and transitions—to your vlogs to make them more visually appealing.* Invest the time to really become proficient using whatever video editing software you have. If you're a Mac user, creating vlogs is easy using iMovie, for example. For PC users, Windows Movie Maker is a popular video editing program. These software packages are jam-packed with many useful features.

6. *Don't use the same background shot for every vlog.* Many people just sit in their bedroom, for example, point the webcam at themselves and record their vlog. This can get boring after a while for your audience. Try shooting your vlogs in different locations, unless the same background is part of what makes your vlog stand out.

7. *Use your vlog to draw people into whatever it is you're talking about.* Be engaging and when possible, get your audience emotionally involved in what you're saying. Get them to strongly agree or disagree with what's being discussed.

8. *Avoid overused clichés and topics that are so overused that it's impossible for you to say or share anything new.* For example, if after a few weeks of regular vlogging you're having trouble coming up with a topic to talk about, do not produce a vlog about having nothing to say. It's been done, it's boring to watch, and it's very predictable.

9. *Develop your own vlogging style.* This means combining your public speaking abilities, appearance, wardrobe, body language, personality, charisma, sense of humor, knowledge about your subject matter, and overall communication style and making it your own. Then, use your video editing software to enhance the visual appeal of your vlogs with expert editing and some eye-catching effects. Remember, everything relating to your video—including its production quality, the audio quality, your appearance, your background (or set), what you say, how you say it, and the length of your video—all contribute to how it will be perceived by your audience.

10. *Don't just sit (or stand) in front of a camera or webcam and read a script word-for-word.* That's boring and unoriginal! While you might want to work from a prepared outline so you don't forget to include important facts or information, be somewhat spontaneous and allow your personality to shine through in each and every video you produce.

11. *Don't rip off someone else's blogging style, look, or catch phrases.* Develop your own and be consistent.

12. *Understand who your audience is and address them at their level.* Even though you have several Ph.D.s, for example, if you start speaking like an over-educated college professor who uses terminology and language that the average viewer won't understand, you'll quickly alienate your audience. Instead, make sure everything you say is clear, easy-to-understand, and straightforward. Whenever it's necessary, simplify your content so people will be able to follow along.

13. *Encourage your viewers to take an action, voice their opinion, post their comments, and/or somehow become involved in whatever it is you're vlogging about.* Challenge or motivate your viewers to do something. Try to add some type of interactive element to your vlogs. Hosting some type of contest or quiz (with prizes) is a great way to rally viewers.

14. *Don't be afraid to be a bit controversial or go out on a limb as you present your vlogs.* Don't be afraid to fail or worry too much about what your viewers might think.

15. *Practice your public speaking skills.* If you're someone who uses the word "umm" way too much, focus on perfecting your speaking ability, and re-record your vlogs a few times until you're proud of your presentation and what you have to say is easy for your audience to understand. Also, pay attention to your body language. Understand what nervous habits you possess and practice eliminating them. It will be distracting for your audience if you're constantly playing with your hair, tapping your foot, scratching at your face, or waving your hands around wildly for no apparent reason.

16. *Remember to introduce yourself at the start of each vlog.* Keep in mind that for some of your audience members, this might be the first time they're seeing you. Later, remind your audience where they can find your latest vlogs by mentioning your website or blog address, for example. (This information can also be displayed on the screen using the title generator feature of your video editing software.)

17. *Invite special guests to be features within your vlog.* Conduct interviews and feature people in whom your audience would be interested.

18. *Don't try to be all things to all people.* Figure out who your audience is and cater specifically to that audience. Make sure your target audience will be able to relate to you. Don't try to position yourself as someone who is superior or condescending. Your audience must be able to relate well to you, as well as to your subject matter.

19. *Use proper lighting.* Lighting is as important as sound quality and contributes to your vlog's overall production quality. Make sure your lighting doesn't make

you look too pale or cover your face in shadows, for example. You don't need to spend a fortune on professional lighting gear to make the lighting look right in a video. Properly positioning a few lamps, or investing in some low-cost lighting can do wonders for how you ultimately look in your videos.

20. *Carefully monitor your use of audio effects.* If you use sound effects or music, for example, make sure the levels are appropriate, especially if you're also speaking. What you have to say should be easily heard and understandable, with as little background noise as possible. Try to record your vlogs in quiet areas, away from audio distractions like babies crying, car horns, lawn mowers, phones ringing, dogs barking, children playing, air conditioners blaring, etc.

Vlogging and Webcasting Equipment You'll Need

If you're a Mac user, just about everything you need to start vlogging (with the exception of an internet connection) came in the box with your iMac or MacBook. These computers have a built-in iSight camera and a built-in microphone for recording videos, plus they come bundled with the iMovie video editing software. You can always upgrade this equipment by purchasing a better quality video camera and microphone, and then acquiring more advanced video editing software, such as Final Cut Studio.

For PC users, to get up and running with an inexpensive vlogging setup, you'll need to purchase a webcam, microphone, and video editing software. Windows Movie Maker is an example of a basic video editing program designed for amateurs. Companies like Logitech (logitech.com) offer a wide range of optional webcams, and for under $100, you can purchase a good quality microphone that connects directly to your computer via a USB cable.

If you're looking to produce higher quality video, consider investing in a digital video camera or a camcorder that has a Firewire port, so you can easily and quickly transfer your video footage from the camera to your computer for editing. Most of the newer video cameras offer Firewire capabilities or save digital video footage directly to memory cards or DVDs that can be transferred to a computer.

When selecting video editing software, choose an application that offers basic editing functionality, plus the ability to easily add titles, special effects, transitions and fades to your footage. You also want to be able to save your edited footage in a variety of different formats and, if necessary, use data compression to make the file sizes more manageable for easy uploading to video hosting services.

Even with a good quality video camera, you'll probably want to invest in a good quality, external microphone to ensure the audio in your vlogs is the best quality possible. If your vlogs will feature just you either sitting or standing in front of the camera, a basic lapel microphone will work well. Any retailer that sells video equipment or audio equipment will have a selection of microphones to choose from, ranging in price from well under $100 to several thousand dollars, depending on their quality. Shure Pro Audio (shure.com/ProAudio/Products/WiredMicrophones/index.htm) is just one of many companies that manufacture top-quality microphones.

If you choose to invest in a professional video lighting system, the cost will range from around $300 to several thousand dollars, depending on how elaborate of a system you're looking for. Amova (home.amova.com) is just one example of a company that manufactures and distributes low-cost, but professional quality lighting equipment that can be used for video or vlog production.

Finally, consider your "set" or background. When choosing where you'll be shooting your vlogs, try to keep the background simple, so anything happening behind you won't distract your audience. Any professional photography store will sell a variety of paper and cloth backgrounds that come in solid colors and patterns. Backdrop Source (backdropsource.com) and Backdrop Outline (backdropoutlet.com) are two online companies that offer hundreds of backgrounds for sale that can be used for video production.

Distributing Your Vlogs

Once you have each edition of your vlog produced and ready to upload, the next step is deciding where you'll upload it to and how you'll make it available to your audience. While many vloggers create their own website and publish their vlogs on that site, they also distribute the videos through YouTube and Yahoo! Video (among other services), plus promote their vlogs using online social networking sites. If your goal as a vlogger is to become famous, it's important to make your vlogs accessible to as many people as possible.

By uploading your vlogs to multiple video hosting and social networking services, your vlogs will get listed with them and have a better chance of receiving prominent listings within the search engines—making them even easier to find.

If your vlogs are intended for a specific or specialized audience that you already reach via your website, posting your vlogs exclusively on your site is a good strategy. However, if building a dedicated following and becoming an online celebrity is your goal, mass distribution of your vlogs is key, as is promoting the vlogs in as many places (online and in the real world) as possible.

Promoting yourself on services like MySpace, Twitter, and Facebook is an excellent way to build a following using the profile you create. You should also interact extensively with your network of online "friends." Services like MySpace and Facebook allow you to link photos and videos to your profile.

When you upload a new vlog entry, the video hosting service you use, whether it's YouTube or Yahoo! Video, for example, will require you to enter specific information about the video. The more accurate and descriptive you are with this information, the easier it will be for people to find and watch your video.

You will be asked to describe your video by giving it a title. This title can typically be up to 80 characters in length and should include keywords and details about what your video is all about. If it's a blog entry, include your name (as the vlogger) within the title.

You'll also be asked to enter a more detailed, text-based description of your video (up to 1,000 characters). Again, be creative, straightforward, and as descriptive as possible. Entice people who will be reading the description to watch your video.

Another important part of the upload and distribution process for vlogs and videos is creating a comprehensive list of tags or keywords associated with the video. These tags should be a list of words or phrases people are most apt to use when searching for a specific video or specific content. Try to create a list of between five and 15 keywords or tags that are generally related to the topic, as well as words that are very specific. For example, if your blog is about how to train your Yorkshire Terrier puppy to sit, some of the keywords or tags you might use include:

dog, training, Yorkshire Terrier, dog trick, sit, puppy, dog training, pets, and canine. The more comprehensive your list is in terms of relevant tags, the easier it will be for someone to find your video(s).

Many video hosting sites also use predefined categories. Thus, you'll be asked to choose the most appropriate category for your video, based on its topic. Each video hosting service will offer a slightly different category list. You'll be asked to choose the primary language spoken within your video, and some of the services will ask you to set whether or not your video should be made available to the general public, or if it will be password protected so only people you authorize to view it will be able to do so.

Depending on the video hosting service, you may also be asked where the video was shot (or what location it's related to, if applicable), what date it was shot, and whether or not you'll allow people to post comments about your video (or even their own video responses).

To upload a video, ideally you want to use a high-speed internet connection. The uploading process will take between one and five minutes per megabyte, plus extra time may be required for the video hosting service to properly convert your video into a format that it's compatible with. Thanks to recent advancements in mobile blogging, many of the video hosting services now accept videos shot using a cell phone or wireless PDA that has a built-in camera.

Webcasting Strategies

From a production standpoint, many of the considerations you'll need to take into account when producing vlogs also apply, except instead of filming your content, you'll be broadcasting live over the internet, using one of many webcasting services, like Stickam (stickam.com) or BlogTV (blogtv.com), that have become popular in recent years.

Instead of keeping your content to less than ten minutes, a show that is being webcast can be any length, as long as you can keep your audience captivated and entertained. Realistically, however, a 15-, 30-, or 60-minute show, aired on a regular basis (daily or weekly), tends to work best.

Because your show is live, there is no room for mistakes. You have to be spontaneous, go with whatever happens, be able to deal well with the unpredictable, and be entertaining—all at the same time. Being able to think on your feet is essential when broadcasting live, as is the ability to communicate well with your audience without using a script that's written out for you word-for-word.

Just like being a good broadcaster or television personality, being a skilled webcaster takes plenty of practice and the right combination of poise, personality, guts, and spontaneity. Not everyone possesses these skills, and not everyone is cut out for webcasting. Before attempting to communicate with your audience using live webcasts, seriously consider producing vlogs first to develop your own style and obtain the practice you'll need to be fully comfortable in front of the camera.

Once you decide to be a webcaster, you'll need to select a webcasting service to utilize to host your shows. Make sure the service you use is easily accessible by your target audience and that it offers the features and functionality you'll need to be successful. Once you develop your following, they'll get accustomed to accessing a specific service to watch your webcast on a regular basis; you'll have a difficult time switching services and getting your audience to follow.

While you don't want to work from a script that's written out word-for-word, for each show you do you'll definitely want to create a detailed outline and plan out, minute-by-minute, what you'll do to fill the time. Remember, especially for longer format shows, interactivity with your audience works very well, so find creative ways to get your audience involved.

What's Next?

Whether you choose to create a more traditional, text-based blog or want to transform yourself into an online personality by hosting your own vlogs or webcasts, if your goal is to build a large and ever growing audience and ultimately become famous (at least in cyberspace), then the information and strategies offered in the next chapter will be particularly useful.

Chapter 9
Become Famous
as a Blogger

It's early September 2008 as this chapter is being written. Today, thousands of Hollywood's biggest stars are busy getting ready for one of the music industry's biggest events—the *MTV Video Music Awards*, which will air around the world later tonight. Yet hours before the broadcast, preparations are being made for the pre-parties, the red carpet, the actual show, and, of course, those famous after parties. All of this work goes into creating a gala Hollywood-style event that will capture the attention of the TV audience and feed their desire to experience what the entire entertainment industry is all about—hype.

Meanwhile, on the radio, the Pussycat Dolls have a huge hit, called *When I Grow Up*, that talks all about the incredible urge people have to become famous. Oh, and on TV, the top-rated shows continues to be talent competitions, like *American Idol*, *America's Next Top Model*, and *America's Got Talent*, as well as reality TV shows that exploit people in exchange for giving them 15 minutes of fame.

What does this say about our society? Well, for starters, just about everyone wants to become famous. Until recently, however, this was only possible if you landed a starring role on a TV show or in a movie, if got one of the major record labels to sign you as a recording artist, if your grandfather happened to be a billionaire which offered you the opportunity to be a socialite (like Paris Hilton), or if you somehow participated in a high-profile crime that received massive media attention. (Don't get any ideas in regard to that last option!)

> **Tip**
>
> A "cyberstar" or online celebrity is someone who achieves fame on the internet, as a blogger, vlogger, or webcaster, for example. In some cases, these people extend their fame beyond cyberspace and into the mainstream media, allowing them to become household names.

Today, however, that's all changed. Thanks to the internet, anyone who wants to become famous, and who has the creativity, willpower, and drive to make this happen, can become an online celebrity. For some, becoming famous on the internet is just the beginning. Some of the web's biggest (but not necessarily brightest) stars have gone on to become mainstream television personalities, models, and recording artists, for example.

Blogging, vlogging, and webcasting are powerful tools, capable of making everyday people famous. It's impossible to surf the web and not find people singing, dancing, voicing their opinions, complaining, and/or performing some type of outrageous antics in order to capture the public's attention.

This chapter focuses on the difference between creating, publishing, and managing a successful blog, and using that blog to transform yourself into a cyberstar. As you develop plans for your blog and brainstorm ideas for it, think carefully about what you, as a person (and blogger) want to get out of the experience.

There are millions of bloggers who opt to share their expertise and knowledge, voice their opinions, or convey information via their blog, but do this anonymously or using a pseudonym to maintain their privacy. Others don't mind using their real name, but as the blogger, they take the backseat to the blog itself and what it contains. These people often don't name their blog after themselves, nor do they do anything to stand out in the minds of their audience on a personal level. Instead, it's their content that makes their blog popular.

Of course, there's another group altogether that use their blog as a showcase for themselves. Their goal is to become famous, and their blog is simply a potential launching pad for that success. These people often name their blog after themselves, put a heavy emphasis on utilizing photos and/or video featuring them, and they go out of their way to stand out from the crowd as a unique online personality.

As you personally take on the role of blogger, vlogger, or webcaster, you must make the decision about how you'll position and promote yourself and how much attention you hope to receive for yourself. Only then can you design and manage your blog appropriately to achieve that objective. Someone who wants to become an online celebrity will need to take a vastly different approach with their blog than someone who hopes to remain anonymous (yet still have a popular and successful blog).

Blogging: An Alternative to Starring on Reality TV

The biggest difference between reality TV shows and blogging is that you can become a famous blogger without signing outrageous contracts with TV show producers that allow the television networks to exploit you for the entertainment of their viewers. Instead, you can exploit yourself, for your own benefit, in order to achieve fame on the internet and potentially beyond.

Whether you take the reality TV approach or the blogging approach to become famous, you'll need to make yourself stand out as a true personality—utilizing your looks, personality, intelligence (or lack of it), mannerisms, creativity, sense of humor, whit, passion, communication skills, and need to be the center of attention. Becoming a cyberstar is not for the shy, timid, or introverted.

Just as reality TV puts everyday people in outrageous, ridiculous, and/or extraordinary circumstances to see how they'll react (while TV audiences watch), if you choose to become an online celebrity, you may need to put yourself in crazy situations to help make yourself stand out, be unique, and capture the attention of web surfers.

Of course, if your blog is more serious in nature, you can rely on its topic or subject matter and your ability to communicate well with your audience to launch you into cyber stardom, but chances are, this will also require you to demonstrate an extremely outgoing and strong personality, as well as strong and sometimes controversial opinions in order to get noticed.

Personal Name Recognition Versus Blog Popularity

The main thing to understand as a blogger is that you can have a hugely successful and popular blog, without becoming famous or well known yourself. You can focus on your blog's subject matter exclusively and cater to your audience's wants and needs, without putting yourself in the spotlight or making yourself the center of attention.

However, if your goal is, in fact, to become famous, this process becomes all about developing strong name recognition for yourself and requires really putting yourself out there. You, not necessarily your blog, need to be the star, which means your blog becomes more of a launching pad or platform from which you'll derive your fame.

Step one in becoming famous as a blogger is to name your blog after yourself. While subject matter of the blog can be about anything whatsoever, each of

Tip

In mainstream media, Paris Hilton is the perfect example of a personality who is famous, but for no particular reason. In addition to being known because she is rich and blond, she developed her own catch phrase and she goes around saying "That's hot." On the web, Chris Crocker and Perez Hilton are outrageous examples of personalities—not just bloggers.

your blog entries should convey information, but also focus on your personal thoughts, your opinions, and what's on your mind. As much as you want your audience to benefit somehow from the content of your blog, you also want them to learn your name—and remember it!

Step two for becoming a famous blogger is to reinforce the name recognition you're trying to build with plenty of photos, videos, and other visual content that focuses on you.

Step three in the process involves positioning and showcasing yourself as an online personality—not just a boring, run-of-the-mill blogger. Whether on TV, in the tabloids, or on the internet, personalities must stand out from the crowd, be unique, and have the type of personality that attracts people to them. It's as much about attitude as it is about looks and intelligence.

It also doesn't hurt to come up with a catch phrase for yourself that people will come to associate with you. This might be the way you open or end your vlogs, or something you say at least once during each vlog.

There are many ways to set yourself apart on the web, in terms of developing your unique personality and persona. You can dress differently, dye your hair an unusual color, showcase a quirky personality or sense of humor, focus on being extremely controversial, be extremely entertain and engaging, and/or put yourself in unusual situations that capture the attention of your audience.

People are often intrigued, mesmerized, and entertained by personalities. They want to follow their every move and are constantly wondering what they'll say or do next. While they may not have other recognizable talents (such as acting or singing abilities or extreme intelligence or intellect), personalities are outgoing, spontaneous, and appear fearless. They become famous for who they are, not for what they do or what actual accomplishments they've achieved.

Contrary to popular belief, becoming a famous online personality will take a lot of hard work and planning. (Yes, planning.) Once you've created yourself, so to speak, you'll then need to work extremely hard to be a constant self-promoter—on the web and potentially in the mainstream media. Within the entertainment industry, the constant craving for publicity of any type is referred to being a "media whore," which is usually a requirement for becoming famous online or in the real world—at least initially.

Becoming famous—on the web and/or in the real world—requires that people learn and remember your name. You become a brand onto yourself that needs to be heavily promoted and marketed, in much the same way a company, like Apple, Nike, FedEx, Coca-Cola, Disney, American Express, or Honda would promote its name and brand. As a personality, you become just like a product that needs to appeal to an audience.

Unfortunately, there are no rules for becoming famous on the web. Everyone goes about this in their own way, using their own strategies and focusing on their own personal attributes. One thing is for sure, however—creativity and being fearless are essential! You can't be afraid of what other people might think of you or how you'll be perceived by people outside of your target audience.

You can't freak out when negative things are said about you or when you're harshly criticized for no apparent reason. Instead, you need to adopt the philosophy that any publicity is good publicity and that anytime anyone is talking or gossiping about you, whether it's good or bad, they're still focusing on you and helping to build your name recognition.

While this advice is suitable for someone looking to become the next Chris Crocker, for example, it's important to understand that it is possible to become famous on the web and be well respected at the same time for your

Tip

Just as a major company would create a detailed marketing, promotions, and public relations plan to promote itself and its products/services, as an up-and-coming personality, consider developing a marketing plan for yourself and your blog.

Figure out how you'll creatively use your blog, the mainstream media, personal appearances, and other activities to promote yourself and build name recognition and popularity for yourself (or the persona you create as a blogger).

Figure out what makes you unique, likeable, or able to attract attention, and develop plans to exploit those areas in a way that helps you achieve your objectives.

Tip

No matter how hard you work to become famous, it often requires the assistance of the mainstream media, plus good timing and a bit of luck.

accomplishments, intelligence, education and for your positive contributions to society. There are plenty of bloggers who become well known for raising money and being active with well-respected charities, or for sharing important information that somehow enriches the lives of others.

When it comes to seeking fame via the internet, there are many paths to follow and approaches you can take that will lead to the notoriety you seek, but it will impact how people perceive you. It's important to determine how you want to be perceived and then take steps to pursue those goals.

Warning

Once you place yourself into a certain category as you begin to pursue your online fame and your reputation begins to form, keep mind that it's extremely easy to utterly destroy a positive reputation with one wrong move or mistake. At the same time, it's extremely difficult (and sometimes impossible) to repair a destroyed reputation or dramatically improve a bad reputation if people have little or no respect for you. If you want to be famous, but carry with you a respectable reputation and be known as someone that people love (as opposed to love to hate), you'll need to work toward this and formulate a plan for achieving it.

Communicating with Your Fans

As you develop your fan base, it's important to stay in touch with your fans on an ongoing, and if possible, somewhat personalized basis (at least initially). Encourage interactivity via your blog by convincing people to post comments, for example. You can also host contests, pose challenges, or somehow rally your fans to focus on some type of cause, or to participate in a specific activity.

If you're not comfortable hosting a live webcast, give your fans the opportunity to get to know you better (and interact with you directly) by participating in online (text-based) chats. You can add chat functionality to your blog using a widget. Set aside an hour per week, for example, to participate in a chat. Throughout the week, advertise exactly when you'll be online chatting live.

You might also opt to encourage people to e-mail you directly. Responding to e-mails individually will get time consuming after a while, but it's a great way to start building a fan base on a grassroots level.

Assuming your blog focuses on a specific topic and has a somewhat targeted audience, schedule in-person appearances when and where the people in your audience might get together, such as a trade show or some type of event. At these events, have something to giveaway that promotes you and your website. You can also offer to give lectures or make appearances, and/or or teach workshops/classes as a way to get your name out there.

Taking advantage of the latest technologies to communicate directly (or indirectly) with your fans is another strategy. For example, you can have your fans sign up to receive text messages from you on their cell phone, which you can send on a regular basis. Or, you can set up a voice mail service that allows your fans to call you, hear pre-recorded messages, and then leave their own message that can be heard by you and your other fans. Creating an online newsletter (that gets e-mailed to your fans), and/or publishing eBooks that help to promote yourself and your message is another way to draw in new fans and maintain your fan base.

Becoming an online celebrity can be a full-time gig. After all, to achieve the notoriety and fame you're seeking will require you to build, maintain, and constantly grow your fan base. Yet another way to do this is to become extremely active on the online social networking sites (including, but not limited to MySpace, Facebook, and Twitter). Many online celebrities maintain a presence on all of the popular social networking sites, while also maintaining their own website and blog.

The more online fame you achieve, the more important it is to regularly update your blog and demonstrate an online presence. The more of a personal approach you take when it comes to branding yourself and building your fan base, the easier it will be for you.

> **Tip**
>
> SayNow (saynow.com) is a service that allows celebrities, musicians, comedians, athletes, community leaders, and bloggers stay in close contact with their fans through voice mail messages and even live conference calls. The service currently has more than two million "fans" registered. This service offers a variety of services bloggers and online celebrities can utilize to build and stay in contact with their fans.

Tip

When trying to build a fan base, one way to reach new people in a positive way is to truly inspire them. If people appreciate who you are, what you do, and what message(s) you're conveying within your blog, for example, they're more apt to follow you over the long term. Fans are a great resource for obtaining more fans, so inspire them to promote you through word-of-mouth advertising and by posting "bulletins" about you to all of their online friends.

Remember, your online persona/personality should be consistent with the content of your blog and appealing to your target audience. It should also remain consistent over time. Once you establish yourself and people respect you as an expert in your field, for example, focus on building a solid and positive reputation for yourself.

What's Next?

While this chapter focused on how to transform yourself from an ordinary web surfer and run-of-the-mill blogger into an online celebrity, the next chapter focuses on many of the ways you can (and should) promote your blog in order to drive traffic to it. The more popular your blog becomes, the easier it will be for you to achieve fame.

Chapter 10
Driving Traffic
to Your Blog

I f you're looking to create a blog that you'll share only with a handful of friends, coworkers, and/or family members, the main time investment in your blog will be creating the content for it. However, if your goal is to get hundreds and thousands of web surfers to visit your blog, it's going to take a considerable effort on your part to promote it and drive a constant flow of traffic to it.

For most bloggers, even ones who are already famous, the biggest challenge is attracting traffic to their blog. This chapter focuses on proven strategies you can use to promote your blog. Your goal as you use these and other promotional tactics should be to make yourself and your blog stand out—be unique, be creative, and most importantly, figure out what your audience wants and give it to them.

While some of the strategies offered in this chapter are one-time activities, the majority of them need to be done on an ongoing basis. Few of these strategies, however, will generate instant results. In other words, be persistent, be patient, and be proactive. Also, don't just adopt one or two of these strategies and assume you'll generate all of the traffic you desire. It will be necessary to invest considerable time to implement at least several of these and other promotional strategies simultaneously.

Yes, promoting your blog can be a time consuming process, but it doesn't have to be an expensive one. In fact, most of strategies offered in this chapter are free, or cost very little money to implement. Although, if you

Tip

Depending on your audience and the topic of your blog, some of the strategies discussed within this chapter will work better than others in terms of generating traffic. As you launch and manage your promotional efforts, track the results carefully to determine where your visitors are coming from and which strategies are working. It will probably be necessary to fine-tune your various promotional activities as you strive to improve the results being generated.

have a promotional budget available, hiring experts to help you with search engine optimization (SEO), and in creating a paid online advertising campaign would be money well spent, assuming you hire experienced people capable of generating the results you desire. Hiring experts will also make generating traffic to your blog a faster process.

Most bloggers, however, take a grassroots approach to their marketing efforts—they do what they can themselves, when they can, and they allow the traffic to their blog build up at a slow but steady pace.

Monitoring Your Blog's Traffic

As you invest your time (and possibly your money) toward marketing and promoting your blog, it's essential that you monitor the results of your efforts so you can determine what works well, what strategies need fine-tuning, and which are a waste of time.

If your blog hosting service doesn't automatically allow you to generate detailed and real-time traffic reports, consider registering with an independent service that offers this information. (You may be required to pay a low monthly or annual fee for this service.)

A few companies that offer real-time blog traffic reports include:

- BlogTracker (tracker.icerocket.com/index.php)
- GoDaddy Traffic Facts (godaddy.com/gdshop/hosting/stats_Landing.asp)
- Google Analytics (google.com/analytics)
- GoStats (gostats.com)
- Site Meter (sitemeter.com)
- Site Traffic Report (sitetrafficreport.org)
- Stat Counter (statcounter.com)

16 Free Ways to Generate Traffic for Your Blog and Build a Following

Just as there are no rules when it comes to creating a blog that will attract attention, there are no guaranteed methods to promote a blog that will generate a desired level of traffic to it. Realistically, reaching your traffic goals could take months (or longer) and will require you to successfully implement at least several of the following promotional strategies.

The following are 16 proven blog promotional strategies that you can begin implementing immediately. These strategies are not listed in any particular order, so don't assume that the first strategies listed will work better than the ones at the end of the list. The results you generate using each strategy will be unique based on your blog and your efforts.

Again, make sure your blog hosting services allows you to track traffic to your blog so you can more easily determine which of your efforts work best. Obviously, you ultimately want to invest the majority of your time on the promotional efforts that are generating the best results.

Warning

One of the biggest mistakes bloggers make is launching their blog with unrealistic expectations about how long it will take to generate traffic to their blog and how much time is necessary to make their promotional efforts actually work. Make sure your goals and expectations are realistic, especially if you're new to blogging and you don't already have experience marketing and promoting websites and blogs.

1. Register Your Blog with the Search Engines

When more than 80 percent of all web surfers want to find something online, whether it's a tidbit of information, a particular website, or some type of specialized content, the place they typically begin (if they don't already know the URL address for the website or blog they're looking for) is at a search engine, such as Google or Yahoo!

There are hundreds of search engines and web directories available to web surfers. The most popular are Google and Yahoo!, along with MSN.com, ASK.com, AOLSearch.com, and AltaVista.com.

Your goal as a blogger is to first get your blog's URL listed with each of the major search engines, and then work toward optimizing your listing so it receives the best ranking and placement possible.

After performing a Google or Yahoo! search, for example, a typical web surfer will visit the first listing, and maybe the second and/or third. But all subsequent listings will be ignored. This is why earning a top placement or ranking with each

Tip

When it comes to hiring a company to help with your blog's search engine optimization, there are hundreds of choices. You'll want to compare prices, as well as services offered. For example, will the submission service simply get your blog listed with the search engines, or will it take added steps to earn you excellent placement or a top ranking? Will the service evaluate your blog to make sure its content and design (and HTML programming) will generate the best results with the search engines? Also, you'll need to determine if the service will keep your listing up-to-date on an ongoing basis, and whether or not this will cost extra.

Tip

It's important to understand that the listing submission process is different for each search engine and web directory. Then once you've completed the process, it will be necessary to update your listing periodically in order to maintain and hopefully improve your ranking or position.

search engine is essential for driving traffic to your site.

The first step is to register your blog with each of the major search engines. This can be done, one at a time, by manually visiting each search engine and completing a new website recommendation form. This process is time consuming and often confusing. An alternative is to pay a third-party submission service, such as GoDaddy.com's Traffic Blazer, to register your site with hundreds of the popular search engines simultaneously.

The following information will help you get your blog listed with the popular search engines. Keep in mind, it could take several weeks for your listing to appear, so be patient!

List Your Site with the Popular Search Engines

As soon as your blog is published (posted on the web), you'll want to begin the process of listing it with the search engines and web directories. Depending on which blog hosting service you use, this might automatically be done for you, however, it never hurts to supplement whatever is done on your behalf with your own SEO efforts.

Why list your blog with the search engines? The answer is simple. Most web surfers begin their search for specific content from a search engine. They enter in keywords or phrases, and then they follow the first few links provided by the search engine in order to reach the blogs or websites that potentially interest them.

When listing your site with some of the search engines and web directories, the process will be as simply as entering the URL address of your site, as well as its title. The listing and submission process for other search engines, however, is much more in-depth and must be done correctly. In some cases, your site will need to get approved by a human before it gets listed.

The following links can be used to submit a listing for your new blog on some of the most popular search engines and web directories:

- Google (google.com/addurl)

- Yahoo! (siteexplorer.search.yahoo.com/submit)

- MSN Live Search (search.msn.com/docs/submit.aspx)

- AltaVista (altavista.com/addurl/default)

Tip

While it's not necessary to get listed on every single search engine, your goal should be to obtain highly ranked listings on the most trafficked and most popular search engines, such as Yahoo! and Google, in order to potentially reach the most number of people.

Focus on Improving Your Site's Ranking and Position

After your blog gets listed with a search engine and appears when searches are conducted by surfers, it then becomes your responsibility to keep your listing up-to-date and take whatever steps are possible to maintain and improve your listing. This is referred to as search engine optimization (SEO), because your objective is to optimize the placement or ranking of your search.

Again, this is a time consuming process you can do yourself, or you can hire a SEO expert to handle it on your behalf, which will probably generate better results faster.

Tip

A comprehensive introduction to search engine marketing and search engine submissions can be found at the Search Engine Watch website (searchenginewatch.com/show-Page.html?page=webmasters).

Tip

Getting your blog listed with the popular search engines is a cost-effective and powerful way to driving qualified traffic to your blog. It should be a priority when it comes to planning and then implementing your overall marketing, advertising, promotional, and public relations efforts.

Utilize Search Engine Optimization Tools and Resources

To find a third-party company that specializes in submitting URL listings to search engines, as well as search engine optimization, enter the search phrase "search engine submissions" or "search engine optimization" into any search engine, such as Yahoo! or Google. You'll discover hundreds, potentially thousands of paid services you can use, including:

- buildtraffic.com/indexnew.shtml
- engineseeker.com
- godaddy.com/gdshop/traffic_blazer/landing.asp
- iclimber.com
- networksolutions.com/online-marketing/index.jsp
- seop.com
- submitasite.com
- toprankresults.com
- trafficxs.com/platinum.htm
- worldsubmit.com
- wpromote.com/quicklist/landing

2. Tell Your Friends, Relatives, and Coworkers

This may seem like common sense (and it should), but one of the best ways to quickly start generating traffic to your blog is to simply ask your friends, coworkers, and relatives to check it out and offer their feedback. Then, if they like what they see (and/or hear), ask these people to help you spread the word about your blog to their friends.

In addition to simply telling your friends, relatives, and coworkers about your blog, consider following up your conversation with a short and upbeat e-mail that includes your blog's URL as a hyperlink, so all the reader needs to do is click their mouse to access it.

If you go through your personal phone book or database of e-mail addresses for contacts, you should easily find lots of people with whom you have some type of relationship. Invite these people to visit your blog.

As you create your list of people to contact, don't forget about friends and acquaintances you know through your house of worship, health club, country club, golf club, PTA, who are fellow members of a professional association, or who you know through another type of club membership that's associated with your hobby or special interest(s). If any of these clubs, associations, or organizations have a newsletter or website, ask that information about your blog be listed, assuming the content of your blog is appropriate.

You'll quickly discover that word-of-mouth advertising is an extremely powerful promotional tool, plus it's free and works very quickly.

3. Get Involved with Online Social Networking

Online social networking has become a way for people to meet in cyberspace, communicate, share ideas, and network. In addition to MySpace (myspace.com) and Facebook (facebook.com), for example, which are designed more for entertainment or non-professional purposes, there are also online social networking services, like LinkedIn (linkedin.com), that cater to business professionals.

One of the best ways to generate traffic to a blog is to become active on one or more of the social networking sites. Develop an online presence on these sites and utilize the networking functionality offered to help you cost-effectively promote yourself and your blog. Be sure to list your blog within your profile, plus consider posting regular bulletins to your online "friends" that announces when new content to your blog is added.

When creating your online profile after registering with a social networking service (like MySpace or Facebook), be sure to incorporate a list of special interests within your profile that relate to your blog, plus list your blog's URL. You want people who are scanning random profiles (based on keywords or interests, for example), to find your profile, learn about you, and become interested in visiting your blog as a result of information listed within your profile. Adding photos of

Tip

In addition to joining and becoming active on the more mainstream social networking services (such as Facebook and MySpace), look for a services that cater to special interests or industries that relate directly to the content of your blog. This will make it easier to reach your target audience.

yourself to your profile also helps people feel like they know you better.

Online social networking services are free to join. Keep in mind, however, social online networking services do not allow members to blatantly advertise their businesses (unless you pay to advertise on the service), so don't harass your online contacts ("friends") with constant spam messages or other communications that can be construed as blatant commercial advertising. Focus on offering a more subtle exchange of information and ideas, which is what these services were designed to promote. As you "exchange ideas," be sure to mention your blog and its URL.

Once you've registered with one or more social networking services, become an active participant in online communities and discussions that relate to your blog's topic. Plus, try to acquire as many "friends" as possible so you can post messages or bulletins to reach these people in the future. Use the member search feature to find people in your blog's target audience or who share a common interest and request to become friends with them.

Most people, before accepting a new friend (especially if it's a request from a stranger) will review that person's online profile. If your profile is appealing, they'll accept your friend's request, plus learn about your blog at the same time. Over time, it's not uncommon for popular bloggers to acquire 25,000 to 100,000 MySpace or Facebook friends, for example.

4. Participate in Live Online Chats and Webcasts

Especially if you're a vlogger, one way to more quickly establish yourself as an online personality is to participate in live, online chats or webcasts that are hosted through social networking sites, such as Stickcam (stickcam.com), BlogTV (blogtv. com), Mogulus (mogulus.com), or Broadcaster (broadcaster.com).

In addition to starring in live online webcasts, you can post your vlogs and other multimedia content on these sites as part of your profile, plus use this online presence as a promotional tool to tell people about your blog and link people to it.

It's not uncommon for popular bloggers to attract hundreds of people to their live online webcasts or chats. This provides for an interactive forum that allows people to get to know you. Participating in this type of promotional effort isn't for everyone. You must be comfortable interacting with strangers via a live webcam, plus be entertaining and interesting at the same time. In other words, you'll need to showcase yourself as an online personality—not just as a blogger.

Before deciding to host your own live, online webcasts, take the time to participate in or watch events hosted by other vloggers and online personalities who have already achieved a high level of popularity. This will help you discover what will be required of you, plus help you more easily address the expectations of your audience.

5. Add Keywords When Creating Blog Content

In addition to having your blog listed with the search engines, many blog hosting services automatically get the search engines to list individual blog entries. For this to help you generate traffic to your blog, it's essential that you incorporate SEO techniques into your blog content.

As you're creating your headlines, sub-headings, and text-based content, incorporate keywords and phrases into your blog that you know people will use to search for your content. If your blog is about tennis, for example, the keyword "tennis" should appear as often as possible, but within proper context.

Also, it's an excellent strategy to incorporate your full name (as the blogger) and your blog's main title into your blog entries often, but as appropriate, in order to improve not just your chances of getting listed with the search engines, but to receive the best possible placement.

Most of the blog hosting services also request that for each blog entry, the blogger provide a list of labels or keywords that are associated with that blog entry. Be sure to list between five and 10 relevant keywords for each entry to make it easier for web surfers to find what they're looking for, plus assist the search engines is properly categorizing and ranking your blog.

While it's important to incorporate keywords into your main blog copy, it's absolutely essential that your overall blog description (which is a short paragraph about your blog) incorporate as many keywords as possible. If you're using Blogger.com to create and host your blog, for example, your blog's description can be a maximum of 500 characters.

6. Register Your Blog with Online Blog Directories and Blogging Communities

In addition to the popular search engines, such as Google and Yahoo!, there are many online-based blog directories and online communities for bloggers. Invest the time necessary to get your blog listed with these directories. In some cases, this might require you to include a link within your blog to the blog directory.

Your blog hosting services probably has its own blog directory, which you should opt to be listed with. However, you'll need to manually register to get your blog listed with other blog directories.

A few of the more popular and comprehensive blog directories:

- Best of the Web Blogs (blogs.botw.org)
- Blog Catalog (blogcatalog.com)
- Blog Hub (bloghub.com)
- Blog Listing (bloglisting.net)
- Blog Search Engine (blogsearchengine.com)
- Blog Universe (bloguniverse.com)
- Bloggeries (bloggeries.com)
- Bloggernity (bloggernity.com)
- Globe of Blogs (globeofblogs.com)
- Super Blog Directory (superblogdirectory.com)

To find additional online-based blog directories to list your blog with, type the search phrase "blog directories" into any search engine, such as Google. It will be necessary for you to complete a separate online questionnaire to get your blog listed with each directory. (It'll save you time if you cut and paste your blog's one paragraph description.) Once you get listed with each directory, view your listing at least once per month and update it as needed.

Whenever possible, create an online profile for yourself (as the blogger) as part of your blog directory listing. Include information about yourself, your expertise on the topic(s) you're blogging about, and a photo. Of course, you should also use the profile to promote your blog—again using appropriate and relevant keywords.

7. Tap Into the Power of YouTube

If you're a vlogger, there's no better way to distribute your video content then through YouTube. Create your own YouTube Channel and encourage people to subscribe to it. Even if you don't consider yourself to be a vlogger, you can create a single vlog and post it on YouTube (and other similar services), which can serve as a video-based promotion and invitation to the general public to visit your traditional, text-based blog.

More information about how to become a successful vlogger and utilize YouTube can be found within Chapter 8.

8. Position Yourself as an Expert to the Media and Utilize Public Relations Efforts

If you're an expert in a specific field (or about a specific topic) and your blog relates to your area of expertise, let the media know about you and your blog, and make yourself available to be interviewed for news stories, human interest stories, and features. Also, contact talk radio stations and try to get yourself booked as a guest.

The best way to make yourself known to the media is to create a press kit focusing on yourself and distribute it to relevant media people—reporters, journalists, editors, producers, etc.—that cover your area of expertise. This involves utilizing well-established public relations practices and techniques.

A press kit is typically comprised of press releases, a bio, a photo, recent press clippings, and other information—all formatted in a very specific way—to quickly educate a journalist/reporter about who you are and why you could be a good source for them. Of course, the various elements of your press kit (including your bio and press releases) should contain your contact information, including your full name, blog URL, phone number (home, work and cell), and e-mail address. Your press kit should quickly describe your credentials and position you as the ideal person to interview for news stories or articles that relate to your field of expertise.

The best way to create a press kit that will get attention is to hire a public relations professional or consultant. Not only is it important to use these tools to capture the attention of the journalist/reporter, but also the content of your press kit needs to be formatted perfectly and presented in a way that will get the journalist's attention.

Understand that reporters, journalists, editors, and producers typically work under very tight deadlines, but they're always in need of interesting, well-informed, and credible sources to interview and/or profile. It's important that when you pinpoint which media outlets and specific reporters, journalists, editors, producers to contact, that you target only people who cover your area of expertise and that you don't harass them with too many mailings, e-mails, or phone messages.

If you blog about local politics in your city, for example, contact the media professionals at local and regional newspapers, magazines, television stations, and radio stations that cover local politics and send them your press kit. Do this around election time when they're more apt to cover local politics and require experts to interview.

If your blog covers politics, don't waste time approaching the local sports reporter or other journalists that don't cover a relevant beat. One of the best ways to generate positive publicity for yourself and your blog is to build long-term and professional relationships with reporters, journalists, editors, and producers.

You'll discover that if you can get featured in the media, your credibility will instantly increase, as will traffic to your blog. Most currently mega-popular bloggers built at least some of their success and audience from publicity generated in the mainstream media—not just in cyberspace.

Using public relations strategies, your goal is to work with reporters, writers, editors, and journalists and try to convince them to include information about you, your company (if applicable), and your blog within their editorial content.

When you use public relations, you provide reporters, writers, editors, and journalists with the information they need to include within their articles or stories. However, you have absolutely no control over what's actually written or said about you or your blog. You run the risk that details will be misrepresented or that important details will be left out.

The benefit to public relations, however, is that when you, your company, and/or your blog are featured within the editorial content of various mainstream media outlets, it doesn't cost you a penny, and the results can be extremely beneficial in terms of generating new traffic to your blog.

The easier you make it for reporters, writers, editors, and journalists to include information about you, your company, and/or your blog within their articles, features, reviews, or segments, for example, the better your chances are of receiving the free media coverage you're seeking.

Like advertising, planning, and executing an effective public relations campaign takes skill, creativity, experience, and the ability to capture

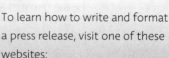

Tip

To learn how to write and format a press release, visit one of these websites:

- publicityinsider.com/release.asp
- press-release-writing.com/10_essential_tips.htm
- internetbasedmoms.com/press-releases
- wikihow.com/Write-a-Press-Release

the attention of reporters, writers, editors, and journalists in a positive way. If done correctly, being featured in a single newspaper or magazine article, or on a radio or television program, can easily generate a better response than spending tens of thousands of dollars in paid advertising. Plus, once the publicity starts to appear in the media, you'll find it much easier to generate additional coverage. You'll probably notice a snowball effect.

The best way to begin trying to generate free publicity is to write a well-written press release about yourself and your blog. Again, this press release must adhere to a standard press release format, contain some type of newsworthy message, be well-written, and contain all of the information reporters, writers, editors, and journalists need to know. Answer the questions who, what, where, when, why, and how. A typical press release is double spaced and fits on one or two pages.

Sample Press Release

On the following page is a sample press release that fashion designer Kiel James Patrick (who is interviewed in Chapter 14) created and distributed to the mainstream media in order to announce his autumn '08 product line and the launch of his blog, *KJP Life*. As you review this release, notice the way it is formatted. Utilizing the correct formatting for a press release is essential if you want it to get noticed.

Kiel James Patrick Expands KJP Bracelet™ Line
For Autumn With "Toggelash Falls" Collection
KielJamesPatrick.com

For Immediate Release

Contact: [Insert Name]
[Insert Phone Number]
[Insert E-mail Address]

Cranston, Rhode Island—September 12, 2008—Kiel James Patrick, the 25-year-old fashion designer and veteran fashion model who created and launched the popular KJP Bracelets™ earlier this year, has expanded the product line for the fall with a collection of new bracelets that are now available exclusively from the company's website (KielJamesPatrick.com) and from a select group of upscale boutiques.

"This intricate new autumn line embodies the essence of all that is classic, chic, and stylish," explained Patrick. "We've seamlessly combined traditional designs, with luxurious silks, tweeds, and other fine and vintage fabrics to create these new bracelets. The "Toggelash Falls' collection' bestows an artful elegance to its wearer."

Like all of the handcrafted KJP Bracelets™, these new designs incorporate vintage and recycled fabrics and clasp around the wearer's wrist using a custom-designed bronze button that displays the KJP logo. The interior of each band is lined with Kiel James Patrick's signature plaid fabric.

The KJP Bracelets™ in the new "Toggelash Falls" collection are priced starting at $42 each and represent the newest all-American accessory that has fashion-focused males and females alike clamoring to wrap around their wrists. "The bracelets are stylish and custom-designed to reflect the wearer's unique personality," added Patrick.

Additional information about the KJP Bracelets™ can be found on the company's website (kieljamespatrick.com). This month, in conjunction with the bracelets being featured on MTV, Kiel launched KJP Life (kjplife.blogspot.com), a personal and company blog which offers a forum for him to interact directly with his customers and fans.

Kiel James Patrick is currently available for interviews and product samples from the new "Toggelash Falls" collection of KJP Bracelets™ are available upon request by calling (XXX) XXX-XXXX (Kiel@KielJamesPatrick.com).

#

Compile Your Customized Media List

After your press materials are created, the next step is to compile a list of specific reporters, writers, editors, and journalists, based on their "beats," or the topics they typically report on or write about.

There are several ways to track down the right people to send your press materials to at various mainstream media outlets, but first, you need to create a list of media outlets you want to target in hopes of generating publicity. Next, contact each media outlet and obtain the name, title, address, phone number, and e-mail address for the appropriate reporter, writer, editor, or journalist at that media outlet. An alternative is to purchase a comprehensive media directory that lists this information.

Bacon's Media Directories (866.639.5087/us.cision.com/products_services/bacons_media_directories_2008.asp) publishes a comprehensive listing of all newspapers, magazines, radio stations, and television stations, along with contacts at each media outlet. The printed directories are updated annually; however, a complete media database is also available online for a fee.

Several other companies offer similar directories and databases. The reference section of a public library may be a good resource for this information. These directories include:

- The Gebbie Press All-In-One Media Directory, (845) 255-7560, gebbie.com
- Media Contacts Pro, (800) 351-1383, mediacontactspro.com/products.php
- Burrelles/Luce, (800) 368-8070, burrellsluce.com/MediaContacts

To save money compiling your media list, consider visiting a large newsstand, looking through all of the newspapers and magazines, and then checking the masthead of each appropriate publication for the proper contact details. You can also review the ending credits of television talk shows and news programs, to find the

Tip

Once your press release is written, to save time and potentially money, you can pay a press release distribution service, such as PR Newswire (prnewswire.com), to distribute it electronically, via fax, or by U.S. Mail to the media outlets or media contacts you desire. Within hours, thousands of reporters, writers, editors, and journalists could have information about you, your company and your products waiting within their in-box.

Tip

In addition to creating printed copies of your press materials that can be mailed to targeted reporters, writers, editors, and journalists, you'll also want to create a "Press," "Press Room," or "Media" area within your blog that contains these materials and makes them available for downloading by members of the media.

name of the show's guest or talent booker, plus contact news and talk radio stations to find the names of producers or guest bookers.

Mastering the art of working with the media to generate free publicity for yourself, your company, and your blog can be an extremely cost effective way to promote your blog, plus build a positive reputation on a local, regional, national, or even international level, but on a shoestring budget.

You'll find that once you start generating positive publicity, that other media outlets will eventually start coming to you in order to feature you, your company or your products within their editorial coverage.

Often, the best time to approach the media to generate publicity is when a relevant news story is currently being covered, or if your blog's topic (and your area of expertise) directly relates to a specific event. In general, you'll get more attention from the media if you approach them on a Tuesday, Wednesday, or Thursday, and you avoid contacting them when they're under a tight deadline.

9. Obtain Links to Your Blog on Other People's Blogs and Websites

Obtaining links to your blog from other websites and blogs helps you in two ways. First, it tells people about your blog that might not already know about it. Plus, the search engines pay attention to how many links from outside sources you have to your blog. If you have many established links to your blog from other blogs and websites, this will help to improve you positioning or ranking with the search engines.

To get your blog listed on other blogs and websites, simply make contact with other bloggers or webmasters and propose a link swap. In other words, if they post a link to your blog, within your blog, you'll post a link to theirs. This method works best if you pinpoint websites and blogs that target the same audience as your blog or that cover a similar topic, but that are not necessarily in direct competition with you.

BlogUpp! (blogupp.com) is a unique blog cross-promotion tool that can help any blogger obtain free advertising on other blogs within the network, in exchange for displaying ads for other participating blogs within your blog. It's a powerful tool for generating free traffic.

10. Offer an "E-mail This Post" Feature with Each Blog Entry

Once you start generating traffic to your blog, use those visitors to help you generate more traffic. There are several ways to do this. One of the easiest is to incorporate an "E-mail This Post" or "E-mail a Friend" icon within each blog entry that allows a visitor to quickly forward a blog entry that interests them to a friend via e-mail. This helps to get the word out about your blog, better distribute your content, and it takes only seconds for a visitor to your blog to use.

If your blog hosting service doesn't offer this feature, find a third-party widget you can add that offers this functionality. For example, the AddThis.com website (addthis.com) allows you to add "E-mail a Friend" functionality to a blog. You can also obtain this functionality by visiting the Softpedia website and downloading the "Send" script which can be incorporated into your blog entries (webscripts. softpedia.com/script/Modules/Drupal-Modules/Send-46724.html).

11. Get Your Blog Entries Listed on Digg and Reddit

Digg (digg.com) and Reddit (reddit.com) are two extremely popular services that offer an ever-evolving listing of links to articles, blog entries, and news stories that web surfers nominate. The more votes an article, blog entry, or news story receives, the higher up on the Digg or Reddit list it goes.

If you manage to get one of your blog entries listed high up on either Digg or Reddit, you're virtually guaranteed thousands of new visitors to your blog. These services are free to join, and you can easily add functionality to your blog that allows your visitors to nominate specific blog entries for inclusion on Digg or Reddit's lists of what's popular on the web at any given moment.

Digg and Reddit work in a very similar way. According to Digg's website, "Digg is a place for people to discover and share content from anywhere on the web. From the biggest online destinations to the most obscure blog, Digg surfaces the best stuff as voted on by our users. You won't find editors at Digg — we're here to provide a place where people can collectively determine the value of content and we're changing the way people consume information online. Everything on Digg — from news

Tip

To discover how to add functionality that allows your blog's visitors to submit your blog entries to Digg, point your web browser to: digg.com/tools/integrate. To add functionality that allows your blog's visitors to easily submit your blog entries to Reddit, point your web browser to: reddit.com/buttons/.

to videos to images to Podcasts — is submitted by our community (that would be you). Once something is submitted, other people see it and Digg what they like best. If your submission rocks and receives enough Diggs, it is promoted to the front page for the millions of our visitors to see. Because Digg is all about sharing and discovery, there's a conversation that happens around the content. We're here to promote that conversation and provide tools for our community to discuss the topics that they're passionate about. By looking at information through the lens of the collective community on Digg, you'll always find something interesting and unique."

12. Utilize RSS Feeds To Syndicate Your Content

RSS Feeds utilize web-based technology that allows your blog content to automatically be picked up and distributed by third-party RSS readers. Your blog's content can be subscribed to by your visitors and viewed using their RSS reader. Being able to distribute your blog content via an RSS feed makes it easy for a greater number of people to access it. For more information about how to utilize this web-based technology that's quickly growing in popularity, especially among bloggers (and people who read blogs), visit the WhatIsRSS website (WhatIsRSS.com).

Many of the blog hosting services, including Blogger.com, automatically offer the ability to distribute blog content through RSS feeds. According to the Blogger.com website, "Syndication means that when you publish your blog, Blogger automatically generates a machine-readable representation of your blog that can be picked up and displayed on other websites and information aggregation tools. Special pieces of software, called Newsreaders or Aggregators, can scan these feeds, automatically letting you know when the sites [blogs] have updated. One reason to syndicate your site is to gain a wider audience by attracting aggregator users."

If someone already has a custom My Yahoo! or iGoogle home page, for example, the RSS feed from your blog could automatically appear on their page (if the user subscribes to your feed), meaning they'd be able to read all of your latest blog entries, without physically having to visit your blog. Using this same technology, webmasters can also publish blog content on their websites.

13. Post New Blog Entries Regularly and Notify People When New Content Is Added

Once you get new people to access your blog, you want them to return often and become a regular follower. To do this, as the blogger, you need to continuously post new and interesting content. Encourage your visitors to subscribe to your blog via an RSS feed, or join your e-mail mailing list to be automatically notified when new content is added to your blog. This is functionality your blog hosting service might provide, or it can be added by incorporating a specialized widget to your blog.

To keep people interested in your blog, however, it's essential that you live up to whatever promises you make to create new content. For example, if you promote that new content will be posted on a daily or weekly basis, you need to diligently post your new content.

14. Leave Constructive Comments and Feedback On Other People's Blogs

Most blogs and web message boards encourage people to leave feedback and post related comments. As a blogger, you can visit other blogs and websites and post your own constructive comments or feedback, but within your message (or comment), include details about your own blog, including its URL.

Find blogs and websites that have large followings, such as those hosted by major newspapers or television stations. Post comments related to major news stories and/or stories that related to your blog's primary topic. Another way to create a following by posting comments is to write reviews of books related to your blog's topic and post them on Amazon.com and BN.com, for example. On these sites, comments related to bestselling books are read by thousands of people.

15. Add Your Blog URL to Your E-mail Signature

If you're like most people, you probably send and receive dozens or hundreds of personal and work-related e-mails each day. One subtle way to promote your blog

Tip

If you work for a company that you don't own, be sure to ask permission from your boss before adding your blog information to the e-mail signature of your work-related e-mail correspondence. If, however, your blog is work related, adding your blog info to your e-mail signature as you communicate with your clients and customers is a great way to drive traffic to your blog and communicate more effectively with those with whom you do business.

is to include a one-line description of it (and link) within the e-mail signature of your outgoing e-mails.

16. Add Links to Your Blog from Your Personal or Company Website

If you already have a successful personal or company website, one of the best ways to drive traffic to your blog is to heavily promote it directly on the your existing website. This can be done in several ways. You can add banner ads to your website so people can instantly access your blog. Or, you can add your blog to the main menu of your site. You could also incorporate the RSS feed of your blog directly to one of the main pages of your site.

Depending on your website, you might want to incorporate your blog directly into the site, or opt to keep the website and blog totally separate.

Run Paid Ads with Google AdWords and Similar Services

It used to be that the most cost-effective, quickest and easiest ways to drive traffic to a website was to utilize online banner ads (display ads). These ads could be purchased to appear on websites that catered to the same audience or demographic the advertiser was attempting to reach. These days, however, banner ads are not typically the best or most cost-effective way to promote a blog (or a website).

Whenever you visit one of the popular search engines, as well as many other types of websites, including blogs, you'll often notice short, text-based ads displayed on the page that are directly relevant to what you're searching for, or to the content on the site you're currently visiting. For example, if you've done a search about Yorkshire Terrier puppies, the paid, text-based ads you'll see displayed will relate directly to dogs and/or Yorkshire Terriers.

These text-based ads are paid for by advertisers using one of several services, including:

- Yahoo! Search Engine Marketing, (866) 747-7327, sem.smallbusiness.yahoo. com/searchenginemarketing

- Google AdWords, adwords.google.com

- Microsoft AdCenter, advertising.microsoft.com/search-advertising

Search Engine Marketing has a number of benefits to the advertiser, including:

- It's extremely inexpensive to launch a Search Engine Marketing ad campaign. The initial investment is typically under $50, plus you have 100 percent control over your daily ad spending. Once you set your budget, you pay only for the actual clicks to your site, not the impressions (people who see your ad).

- You can create and launch a fully customized Search Engine Marketing campaign in just minutes and start seeing results within hours.

- The success of your campaign will depend on your ability to select appropriate and relevant keywords that are being used by web surfers to find specific content on the web.

- You can track the success of your campaign in real-time, using online-based tools provided by Yahoo!, Google and/or Microsoft when you use their respective services.

- Your ad campaign can be expanded as you begin to achieve success, or it can be modified or cancelled in minutes (not weeks or months), to address changes in your overall marketing campaign or your company's objectives.

How to Launch a Paid Search Engine Marketing Ad Campaign

The first step to launching a Search Engine Marketing campaign is to choose the service or services you'll use, such as Yahoo! Small Business' Search Engine Marketing, Google AdWords, or Microsoft AdCenter. If you opt to use Google AdWords, for example, your ads will appear on Google, whenever someone enters a search phrase that matches the keywords you select in your ad (providing you're willing to pay the going rate for that ad to be displayed—a concept that will be explained shortly).

In addition to Google AdWords ads being displayed through Google's own search engine site, the company has partnered with thousands of other websites and blog operators that also display context-sensitive ads through the AdWords service. This is referred to as Google AdWords' content network, and it includes About.com, Lycos.com, FoodNetwork.com, The New York Times On The Web, InfoSpace, Business.com, HowStuffWorks.com, and literally thousands of other sites from around the world, plus many blogs hosted by Blogger.com (and potentially other blog hosting services.)

In fact, according to Google, "The Google content network reaches 75 percent of unique internet users in more than 20 languages and over 100 counties. As a result, if you advertise on both the Google search network and the Google content network, you have the potential to reach three of every four unique internet users on Earth."

Yahoo!, Microsoft, and Google have similar content networks that allow targeted, text-based ads to be displayed on a wide range of websites well beyond each company's primary search engine or web directory.

As you compare the Search Engine Marketing programs offered by companies like Google, Yahoo!, and Microsoft, not only will you want to compare rates, you'll also want to determine if each respective company's content network will help you reach your company's own target audience.

Once you choose which company or companies you'd like to advertise with, the process of launching your campaign involves a few basic steps, including:

- Set up an account with the Search Engine Marketing company you'd like to work with. This will require the use of a credit card, debit card, or PayPal account. You'll need to pay a deposit of about $50 to get started. (The deposit amount will vary among the various services.)

- Create a detailed list of keywords that relate directly to your blog. These keywords can include industry jargon, your blog's main topic, product names, your name, your company's name, and any other keywords you deem relevant.

- Create a text-based ad. Each ad includes a headline, a short body, and a URL that links directly to your website.

- Decide on how much you'd like to spend on your campaign each day. Part of this decision includes deciding how much you're willing to pay each time someone sees your ad and clicks on it in order to reach your website. With this type of advertising, you do not pay for the number of impressions the ad receives. You only pay each time someone actually clicks on the link to visit your website. Based on the keywords you select, you'll be competing with other companies running ads with similar keywords. Using a complex formula that takes into account how much you're willing to pay-per-click, your ad(s) placement, and the frequency each is displayed will be determined. The more you are willing to pay per-click, especially for popular keywords, the better your ad placement will be and the more frequently it will be viewed by web surfers actively using those same keywords to find what they're currently looking for online. When you launch your campaign, you must set a maximum cost-per-click, as well as your total daily spending limit, which can be as little as $10 per day.

- As you create your Search Engine Marketing campaign, in addition to setting your own list of keywords, you can also determine who will see your ad(s) based on geographic location.

- To help you create a comprehensive and effective list of keywords, the Search Engine Marketing services (operated by Yahoo!, Google, and Microsoft, among others) offer a set of online-based tools to assist you in creating your ad's keyword list and forecast how many impressions your ad will ultimately receive, based on your ad budget.

- Once your ad campaign is running, you can utilize online-based tools to keep tabs on the number of overall impressions, click-thrus, ad placement, ad positioning, and related costs. This tracking is done in real-time, so you'll know instantly if your campaign is working.

As you create your Search Engine Marketing campaign to promote your blog using one of these fee-based services, you'll come across a handful of advertising-related terms, including:

- **Click-Through-Rate (CTR).** This refers to the number of clicks your blog receives (as a result of someone clicking on an ad) divided by the total number of impressions (views) the ad received.

- **Cost-Per-Click (CPC).** This number refers to the total cost of running the ad campaign, divided by the number of clicks to your blog that are received. The goal is for this number to be as low as possible. For example, if you pay $100 for a campaign that generates 10 hits, your CPC is $10 each. However, if that same $100 campaign generates 1,000 hits, your CPS is just $ .10 each.

- **Display URL.** This is the URL for your blog that's actually displayed in your Search Engine Marketing ad. In reality, you can have the ad link to any URL or any HTML page within your domain. If the Display URL is SampleBlog.com, in reality, the link could lead a surfer to SampleBlog.com/NewPost.htm.

- **Keyword.** This is a specific word or phrase that relates to a product, company, or any content within your blog that you're looking to advertise or promote. When using Search Engine Marketing, when someone uses the search phrase that matches your keyword, your text-based ad could be displayed.

A complete glossary of terms can be found at Yahoo!'s website (signup13. marketingsolutions.yahoo.com/signupui/signup/glossary.do). Understanding these terms will help you better utilize the advertising tools that are at your disposal.

The Anatomy of a Search Engine Marketing Ad

Some of the reasons why text-based Search Engine Marketing ads work so well are because the ads that appear for each web surfer are always directly relevant to the topic they're actively seeking. The ads are also very short and to the point, plus they serve as links directly to blogs or websites that have the content the surfer is looking for at that very moment.

From the advertiser's standpoint, this type of advertising can be extremely targeted by region and/or by keywords. These ads can quickly and efficiently prequalify a potential blog visitor and attract them to your blog at the precise moment they're looking for the content it offers.

In addition to ensuring your ads get the best possible placement on the search engine websites, as well as throughout the appropriate websites within the Search

Engine Marketing company's content network, it's your responsibility as the advertiser to create a short, text-based ad that quickly captures the reader's attention and generates enough excitement for them to click on your link.

Creating an effective Search Engine Marketing ad takes creativity. What you say in your ad must be relevant, appealing, and attention getting. However, you have relatively little space to accomplish this rather significant task.

Regardless of whether you use Yahoo Search Engine Marketing, Google AdWords, Microsoft AdCenter, or another service, the anatomy of the ad that web surfers actually see will be basically the same. Every ad will be comprised of the following components:

- **Title.** This can be up to 40 characters long. It should be brief, but attention getting.

- **Description.** This portion of your ad can only be 70 characters long, so again brevity is essential, but what you say must make an impact and appeal directly to your target audience. When possible, incorporate one or more of your keywords into the ad itself (in both the title and the description). Two goals of your ad should be to announce that your blog offers the information the surfer is looking for, and then to somehow differentiate your blog from the competition.

- **Display URL.** This is the blog address that will be displayed within the ad. The actual link, however, can lead to a different URL, such as a blog, website, or a sub-page within your domain. Ideally, the link should take the surfer directly to the main page of your blog, if that's what you're promoting—not your website's Home Page.

From your perspective as the advertiser, it's easy to create and utilize a handful of different ads that run simultaneously that incorporate different headlines and messages and that will appeal to slightly different target audiences, but that ultimately lead to the same place—your blog. It's common for bloggers to simultaneously run several different campaigns and use different content and different keywords on each.

As you create your ads and each overall campaign, you'll need to create a list of relevant keywords that perfectly describe your blog. Who ultimately sees your ad will depend heavily on the keywords associated with each ad. Ideally, the key-words you utilize should also correspond very closely to the content of your blog. Each keyword can be a single word or a phrase that's up to 100 characters long. The web surfers who see your ad, however, don't actually see your keyword list.

The service you use will help you select appropriate keywords if you're having trouble compiling your list. Most of the services allow advertisers to associate up to 50 unique keywords or phrases with each of their ads. As you create your keyword list, you do not have to use multiple variations of a single word (such as "widget" and "widgets"). Just make sure each word is spelled correctly.

Setting Your Search Engine Marketing Budget

One of the best things about Search Engine Marketing campaigns is that they can be created and launched using a very low initial budget. At least initially, you'll probably want to experiment with a few different ad variations and keyword lists until you create an ad that has a low Cost-Per-Click and high Click-Through-Rate. Once you've formulated one or more ads that are generating appealing results, this is when you should begin investing hundreds or thousands of dollars into that a campaign. Spending thousands on a campaign that ultimately generates poor results will waste your money and not generate the traffic to your blog that you want and need.

Utilizing Online Display (Paid) Advertising to Promote Your Blog

Online display advertising allows you to purchase ad space on other websites that potentially appeal to your target audience. Your ads can utilize text, graphics, animation, sound, and even video to convey your marketing message. Unlike tra-ditional print ads, however, someone who sees your online display ad can simply click on the ad and be transferred to your blog or website in seconds.

Running online display ads on popular websites costs significantly more than utilizing short, text-based Search Engine Marketing ads. What your ad says and the visual elements used to convey the message (the overall look of the ad) are equally important. Thus, in addition to spending more to display your ads, you'll probably want to hire a professional advertising agency or graphic artist to design the ads themselves to ensure they look professional and are visually appealing.

Depending on where you want your online display ads to appear, the size requirements, ad content specifications, and how much you pay will vary dramatically. In addition to choosing appropriate websites to advertise on, you'll need to select the exact placement of your ad on each website's page. Online real estate has value, based on the potential number of people who will be seeing your ad, and the physical size of your display ad (which is measured in pixels).

In general, the more people who will potentially be seeing your ad, the higher the ad rates will be. Depending on the website, however, you may have to pay based on overall impressions (the number of people who simply see

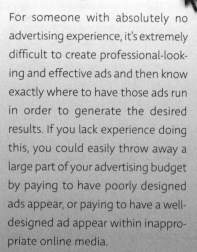

Warning

For someone with absolutely no advertising experience, it's extremely difficult to create professional-looking and effective ads and then know exactly where to have those ads run in order to generate the desired results. If you lack experience doing this, you could easily throw away a large part of your advertising budget by paying to have poorly designed ads appear, or paying to have a well-designed ad appear within inappropriate online media.

your ad), or you may only be responsible for paying a pre-determined fee only when people click on your ad. Another alternative is to pay a commission when a website offers a referral that results in a sale. The payment terms will typically be created by the website on which you'll be advertising.

As the advertiser, your main objective after creating a display ad that expertly conveys your message in a visually appealing way, is to find the perfect websites to advertise on. These should be sites that directly appeal to your target audience. Ideally, you want your ad(s) to be seen at precisely the moment someone is looking for information or content that's available within your blog.

The best way to find websites to advertise on is to put yourself in your target customer's shoes and begin surfing the web in search of sites that offer content that's appealing. Next, determine if those sites accept display advertising, and then request advertising information. Sites that accept display ads will typically have a link on the Home Page that says, "Advertise Here" or "Advertising Information."

Creating, launching, and managing a successful online display ad campaign requires specific skills. Instead of throwing away money on misguided advertising

Tip

Another powerful promotional tool is to host some type of weekly or monthly contest or prize giveaway. This will encourage people to visit your blog to sign up, and then return often to re-enter. People love the opportunity to win stuff.

experiments, if online display advertising is going to be part of your overall advertising, marketing, public relations, and promotional efforts for your business, consider hiring an experienced advertising agency to help you. You'll pay a bit more initially, but being able to utilize the experience and expertise of a trained advertising professional will ultimately generate much better results and save you money in the long run.

Create and Distribute Special Business Cards or Promotional Materials

If you have a way to approach people in the real world who would be interested in your blog, one way to tell them about it is through the use of promotional materials, such as custom-printed business cards, bookmarks, postcards, brochures, or other items that feature details about your blog, including its URL.

For example, if you're a doctor with a successful medical practice and you have a blog that offers medical information your patients would be interested in, you could have a special business card or postcard printed that announces the blog, which you can personally hand to each patient. This same strategy works if you operate a retail business or consulting business, for example.

Using a graphics program, you can layout and design customized promotional materials. Because the cost of full-color printing is now so affordable, printing up thousands of full-color business cards, bookmarks or postcards, for example, will cost between $25 and $150.

Companies like PrintRunner (printrunner.com) and VistaPrint (vistaprint.com) allow you to order custom-printed promotional materials online and have them shipped to you within a week. These companies even offer templates to help you more easily create professional looking promotional materials on your computer using popular PC or Mac software.

Depending on your budget, you could also have custom-printed pens, balloons, or even M&Ms candies (mymms.com/customprint/) imprinted with your blog's title and URL. The item(s) you use as promotional tools for your blog should appeal to and be appropriate for your blog's target audience.

Don't Forget to Focus on Your Personal Security

Let's face it, there are a lot of crazy people in the world. By publishing a blog, you're in essence making yourself a public figure and could attract some level of local, regional, national, or international fame and recognition. Especially if your blog content is controversial, you're bound to come across people who don't agree with you and who are angered by your blog's content.

As a blogger, take proper precautions to protect yourself in cyberspace and in the real world. For example, never distribute online (or within your blog) your home address, phone number, Social Security number, credit card information, or any other information about yourself that could be used to track you down.

Also, never agree to meet strangers who originally make contact with you online, unless you're able to confirm their identity. Even then, only agree to meet in a very public place, and don't attend the meeting alone.

When you register with the various online social networks, do not complete the portions of the online profile questionnaire that request your personal contact information (aside from an e-mail address). If your blog has no relevance to your employment, don't reveal where you work or what company you work for.

How much personal information about yourself you opt to share with followers of your blog is entirely up to you, but for your own safety and security, refrain from revealing too much in the way of personal information. While it's

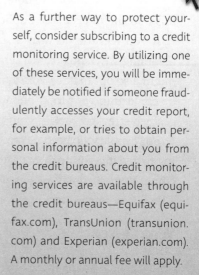

Tip

As a further way to protect yourself, consider subscribing to a credit monitoring service. By utilizing one of these services, you will be immediately be notified if someone fraudulently accesses your credit report, for example, or tries to obtain personal information about you from the credit bureaus. Credit monitoring services are available through the credit bureaus—Equifax (equifax.com), TransUnion (transunion.com) and Experian (experian.com). A monthly or annual fee will apply.

The LifeLock identity theft prevention service (lifelock.com) is also a worthwhile investment for all Americans, whether you're a public figure, blogger or everyday person looking to protect their identity and credit rating. The cost of this service is about $10 per month.

doubtful some crazy stranger will ever show up at your door, some bloggers do experience problems with cyber-stalkers. If you are ever threatened by someone as a result of being a blogger, contact the appropriate authorities immediately.

One option you have as a blogger is to create a fake name for yourself or to post your blogs anonymously. While you'll need to use your real name to establish the blog with the blog hosting service, you don't need to reveal it to the people who visit your blog.

As an added protection, if you register your own domain name for your blog, consider paying a bit extra to the domain name registrar you use to have your identity kept secret. This is similar to having an unlisted phone number. Otherwise, it's very easy for someone to determine who a domain name is registered to, because this information is made public by the domain name registrars.

If you feel the need to distribute a mailing address via your blog, consider obtaining a P.O. Box from a service that is not required to reveal your identity. You might also opt to have your home phone number turned into an unlisted number by contacting your local phone company, and obtain an e-mail address that can't easily be tracked back to your home address.

For people who become famous bloggers, one of the potential drawbacks is having to give up your privacy. However, utilizing just a bit of common sense when it comes to protecting yourself, your identity, and your personal information will go a long way toward keeping you safe as a blogger.

What's Next?

For many bloggers, simply creating, publishing, and then promoting their blog is enough. Becoming "famous" as a blogger isn't high on their priorities list, nor is generating revenue from the blog. However, if one of your goals is to earn money from blogging, the next chapter will explain some of the most popular ways bloggers just like you are earning an income simply by operating a successful blog.

As you'll discover from Chapter 11, while few people actually get rich as bloggers, it is possible to generate revenue once you begin attracting a significant level of traffic to your blog.

Chapter 11
How to Get Rich
from Blogging

O kay, the title of this chapter may be a bit misleading, at least for some of you soon-to-be bloggers out there. In reality, unless your blog generates thousands or even tens of thousands (or more) visits per week, chances are you won't be able to get really rich by generating revenue directly from your blog.

However, even with a modest level of traffic, you can potentially generate a steady revenue stream using a variety of different strategies, many of which are discussed in this chapter. The more creative you are in terms of utilizing these money-making strategies, the more successful you'll be, especially if you're able to target a specialized audience.

A blog can be used as a powerful marketing and promotional tool for your company's products or services, and provide an easy and cost-effective way for you to communicate with your customers and clients, while at the same time boosting their loyalty and potentially generating repeat business. So while a company's blog might not be a direct revenue producer, it can be a tool for increasing business and increasing sales.

For blogs created by individuals that are not affiliated with a company but that targets a specific audience, several potential direct revenue generating opportunities exist. However, not everyone creates a blog with the goal of transforming it into a moneymaking venture. In some cases, displaying ads or utilizing some of the revenue generating strategies discussed within this chapter may be totally inappropriate for your audience or for the blog you'll be creating.

If, however, you're creating a blog that will cater to a specific target audience and you'd like to be financially rewarded for your blogging efforts, there are easy ways of earning money by taking advantage of "pay-per-click" advertising opportunities. This involves displaying short, text-based, context-sensitive ads within your blog's content, or by displaying graphic-based banner ads or other advertising content.

Warning

Until your blog is well established and regularly attracts a significant audience, it will be difficult, if not impossible, to generate any type of serious revenue, regardless of what strategies you put into place.

Your ability to generate revenue from a blog stems from your ability to reach many web surfers on a steady basis. After all, when it comes to displaying ads, you'll be compensated either on a "pay-per-click" basis or for overall impressions (each time a visitor to your blog sees an ad).

Even if you'll be selling products or services directly from your blog or soliciting donations from visitors, only a small percentage of visitors to your blog will realistically make a purchase or give money, so your blog's revenue generating potential will be based mainly on the level of traffic it attracts.

Incorporate Text-Based, Context-Sensitive Ads Into Your Blog

Perhaps the quickest and easiest way to begin generating revenue from your blog is to register for and participate in the Google's AdSense program. Once your blog has been published, set up a free online account (visit google.com/adsense/login/en_US/) and you'll be able to choose how and where small, text-based, context-sensitive ads will appear within your blog.

Once your AdSense account is set up, the service automatically examines the content of your blog entries and delivers text or image ads that are directly relevant to your audience and your blog's subject matter. Because these ads are perfectly matched to your content, this dramatically increases the chance of your visitors clicking on the ads, which is how you'll generate revenue.

As the blogger, AdSense allows you to fully customize the size and appearance of the ads to be displayed so that they match the overall look and design of your blog. All of the necessary HTML programming to add this functionality to your blog is created for you. If you use Blogger.com (also a service of Google), the ads can be automatically added to your blog. Otherwise the process requires a simple cutting and pasting of supplied HTML code within your blog.

On signing up for AdSense, all of the advertisers are managed by Google and the AdSense service, which maintains strict content guidelines. However, you have the ability to filter out ads you don't want displayed within your blog.

AdSense pays its bloggers both on a pay-per-click (CPC) and cost-per-thousand impressions (CPM) basis, depending on the advertiser and your blog's traffic. As you get started, you'll earn revenue each time someone visiting your blog clicks on one of the ads displayed through the AdSense service. How much you earn per-click, however, varies based on a wide range of criteria, including how much the advertiser is willing to pay to appear within blogs and websites featuring topic-specific content.

As a blogger, to increase the chance that a visitor to your blog will click on one or more ads, it's best to intersperse ads between blog entries, as well as display them along the left and/or right column (also referred to as the sidebars within your blog), depending on your blog's format. Also, choose a bold color to display each ad's headline to draw more attention to the ads, but match the background color of the ad to your main blog page.

To determine what will work best in terms of generating the highest click-through rates possible (in order to generate the most revenue from the ads you're display-ing), don't over-saturate your blog with ads, or you will take too much attention away from your blog's main content, which is why people are visiting your blog in the first place. Also, try experimenting with different ad sizes, shapes and placement within your blog to determine which get the best response from your specific audience.

After you join the AdSense service, be sure to take advantage of the various tutorials offered by Google to help you generate the best results from participating in this program. Google publishes an informative and official AdSense blog, which offers strategies and information designed to help bloggers and webmasters fully utilize the AdSense service to generate revenue. To access or subscribe to this blog, visit adsense. blogspot.com.

While Google's AdSense works with all of the blog hosting services (or blogs created from scratch that are hosted as part of a website),

Tip

Google AdSense experts have deter-mined that displaying wider format ads within a blog (which are hori-zontally displayed banners) tend to generate a better click-through response than vertically displayed ads, because the horizontal ads are easier to read. The most success-ful ad formats through AdSense are: 336x280 Large Rectangle and 300x250 Medium Rectangle, as well as the 160x600 Wide Skyscraper. You can see samples of the various ad sizes and how they'd potentially look within your blog when you access the AdSense website.

Tip

Instead of displaying ads within your blog, the Blogvertise service (blogsvertise.com) will pay bloggers to incorporate specific mentions of products, companies, and/or services directly into their blog entries as part of their content. The blogger gets paid between $4 and $25 for each mention. While this can be a good way to generate money from your blog, it could negatively impact your credibility as a blogger if your audience discovers you're accepting money for writing about specific topics or endorsing specific companies, products, or services.

some of the blog hosting services have created their own advertising programs that work in a very similar way to AdSense. Which service you use is a personal decision, however, you can display ads from multiple services within your blog if you choose to.

Become an Affiliate for Well-Known Companies and Showcase Their Display Ads

Another way bloggers generate revenue from their blog is to become an affiliate for a specific advertiser or become a member of an affiliate program, such as LinkShare (linkshare.com), Google Affiliate Network (google.com/ads/affiliatenetwork), or Commission Junction (commissionjunction.com).

If you visit almost any eCommerce website operated by a large company, chances are that company offers an affiliate program to help drive traffic to their website. As a web publisher (blogger), you can join an affiliate program and agree to display graphic (banner or button) ads from participating companies within your blog, in exchange for compensation.

Some companies offer their affiliates (bloggers and webmasters who display their ads) a flat-fee when a blog's visitor simply clicks on an ad. Others, however, pay the blogger a commission based on the total value of whatever the web surfer purchases after clicking on the ad. This option allows the blogger to earn some serious cash if the web surfer buys a high-ticket item. Yet another alternative is that the blogger gets paid a pre-determined flat fee every time someone clicks on an ad and makes an actual purchase from the company's website.

When you sign up with an individual affiliate, which is free of charge to do, how you will be compensated for displaying the company's ads will be outlined in detail. As the blogger, you'll then be able to choose from a handful of pre-created ads in various sizes that you can easily incorporate into and display anywhere within your blog.

When choosing which affiliate programs to join and what ads to display, focus on companies you know are of interest to your blog's primary audience. Typically, if you visit a specific company's website and request to join its affiliate program, your blog will have to be approved by that company, plus, as the blogger, you'll need to agree to the affiliate program's terms and conditions.

By joining a service like LinkShare, Google Affiliate Network, or Commission Junction as a blogger, you will have access to literally hundreds of affiliate programs operated by well-known companies. You can then work with as many participating companies as you'd like (once you're approved by each), yet all of your blog's traffic, commissions, and revenues will be calculated and tracked by one company (LinkShare, Google Affiliate Network or Commission Junction, for example).

LinkShare, Google Affiliate Network, and/or Commission Junction facilitates the relationships between you (the blogger) and the advertisers by providing full report-generating functionality, managing the links and ads, tracking results and commissions, and sending out the payments on a regular basis to the affiliates (you the blogger). For the blogger, there is no charge to join any affiliate programs, plus you can determine which advertisers you'd like to deal with, and then have total control over where ads are displayed within your blog.

Joining appropriate affiliate programs allow you (the blogger) to display ads from well-established, name-brand, well-known companies and earn money from displaying these ads. These ads can help give your blog credibility (because you can capitalize on the name recognition of the companies whose ads you are displaying), plus if you match up your blog's content with relevant ads from specific

> **Tip**
>
> LinkShare, Google Affiliate Network, and Commission Junction are affiliate program operators that each have hundreds of high-profile, brandname companies working with them as advertisers. When you join any or all of these services, you can pick and choose from many different companies that are directly relevant to your blog's content (or audience), but at the same time, be sure to choose affiliate programs that pay the highest commissions.

Tip

If you visit Jason Rich's Travel Blog (JasonRichTravel.com), for example, you'll see AdSense text-based ads displayed between most of the individual blog entries. Along the right sidebar of the blog are display ads and banners that are from companies that participate in the affiliate programs offered by LinkShare and Commission Junction. Each of these display ads offers a different compensation plan for the blogger, but was handpicked to appeal directly to the blog's target audience (in this case leisure and business travelers). You'll notice that the ads that are displayed are all for travel-related products or services that someone reading Jason Rich's Travel Blog might be interested in at the same time they're reading the blog entries.

advertisers, the chances of a visitor clicking on the ad (and you generating some revenue) increases dramatically.

For example, Jason Rich's Travel Blog (JasonRichTravel.com), features an entry about how to buy luggage. This blog's audience is made up of leisure and business travelers. Within this particular blog entry are specific tips for selecting quality luggage and recommendations for companies that manufacture the highest-quality luggage. In conjunction with this blog entry, ads for companies like Tumi Luggage are displayed. So, if someone clicks on that ad and winds up purchasing luggage, according to the affiliate agreement, a commission of between nine and 11 percent of the total sale is paid.

One feature that the affiliate program services, like LinkShare, Google Affiliate Network, and Commission Junction offer is real-time report generating, so you can access detailed information about how well specific ads are doing within your blog, quickly calculate how much you're earning, and obtain HTML code or links to different ads from the advertisers you've chosen to work with.

Many advertisers who participate in affiliate programs offer both online display ads (banners and buttons in various sizes and shapes), but also offer smaller text-based ads, and other types of links you can incorporate into your blog's content. As a blogger, you must determine if you want banner and display ads scattered throughout your blog's content. If you believe larger format or graphics-based ads will distract your viewers and detract from your blog's content, but you still want to generate money from your blog, consider displaying only smaller, text-based (AdSense) ads, or building text-based product links into the actual content of your blog. For example, if you mention the title of the book, that title can be set as a hyperlink that transfers the reader directly to Amazon. com to order the book if they click on it, allowing you to earn a commission as an Amazon.com affiliate.

Ultimately, to earn the most money possible on an ongoing basis by participating in affiliate programs, as the blogger you must pick and choose the best advertisers to work with, select the most appropriate and attention-getting ads from those advertisers, and strategically place those ads within your blog's content to encourage your blog's visitors to click on them. As you'll discover, the size and placement of the ads, as well as their relevancy and how well known the advertiser is, will all impact your click-through rate, so plan on experimenting once your blog is published and you begin displaying ads.

Sell Your Own Display Advertising Space

If you're successful as a blogger and your blog begins to generate a substantial and ongoing level of traffic (in the tens of thousands or millions of unique visitors per day or week), you could potentially generate higher revenue by selling your own ad space directly to online advertisers, and charge top-dollar per thousand impressions, for example, if your blog reaches a specialized or targeted audience.

Most online advertisers won't even consider working directly with a blogger to buy online ad space within a blog unless the blogger can demonstrate a truly enormous level of traffic. A blogger like Perez Hilton (see Chapter 14), for example, has achieved the level of success where he can profitably sell ads directly to advertisers who want to reach his vast worldwide audience.

Once you reach this level of success and there's a demand by advertisers for their ads to appear within your blog, you'll need to develop an information kit for advertisers and advertising agencies and provide the information they'd need to buy advertising space. At this point, you'll easily be able to hire the services of advertising experts to help you properly sell your blog's ad space for the highest prices possible.

Sell Products or Services Directly or Link to an eCommerce Site

Another way bloggers can earn money from blogging is by incorporating some type of eCommerce elements to their blog and directly selling products or services

Tip

PayPal (storefront.paypallabs.com/authenticate/review) has developed a free widget that can be incorporated into a blog that allows bloggers to create a mini storefront within their blog and sell products directly from it. This widget is relatively easy to set up and is an effective way to add eCommerce functionality to a basic blog. You must have an active PayPal account to utilize this widget within your blog, plus have items to sell.

from it. For example, within the blog, you can describe a product or service, offer reviews or tips, and then include a "Buy" icon so your blog's visitors can order the product/service from you on the spot and pay using a major credit card or via a PayPal or Google Checkout account.

Some of the blog hosting services offer eCommerce functionality that you can incorporate directly into your blog. You can also include specialized widgets that offer eCommerce functionality or allow you to link to a specific eBay auction, for example.

If you plan to sell products or services directly through your blog, become familiar with how to operate an online business. My book *Click Starts: Design and Launch Your E-Commerce Business in a Week* (Entrepreneur Press) is an excellent source of information for designing, launching, and managing an online-based business.

Create and Sell Official Merchandise Related to Your Blog

Once some bloggers have built up a dedicated following, many have supplemented their income by selling official, custom-designed T-shirts or other products that relate to their blog. Perez Hilton and Chris Crocker, along with countless other bloggers, continue to do this. For no upfront investment, you can create and sell custom printed T-shirts and other products that you design using a service like CafePress.com (cafepress.com).

CafePress allows you to create a free online store to sell the products (T-shirts, etc.) that you design. This online store can be linked directly to your blog.

Solicit Sponsorships for Your Blog

If your blog is educational or focuses on some type of charitable cause, one way to earn income from it is to solicit one or more corporate sponsors. These sponsors would pay a monthly or annual fee (which you can set) to be associated with your blog and/or your overall cause.

An excellent example of this is the Where the Hell Is Matt? website/blog (wherethehellismatt.com), which features the Dancing 2008 video. Matt's travel expenses and internet video production costs are being paid for by Stride gum (stridegum. com), in much the same way a company would sponsor programming on a public radio or public television station.

Stride gum became a sponsor of Matt's blog/website after his first internet dance videos (filmed in 2005 and 2006) went viral and were seen by millions of web surfers worldwide. Matt's concept was simple. He traveled around the world (initially to 39 countries on all seven continents) and filmed himself dancing in well-known public places. These dancing clips were edited together and combined with music to create an extremely powerful and entertaining video that subtly promotes world unity.

Should you choose to solicit sponsorships for your blog, you will need to define clearly what each sponsor will receive, such as display ads or promotional mentioned within your blog, for their investment. This type of financial arrangement will work extremely well if you, as the blogger, begin to receive a lot of national media attention for your blog, or your blog builds a huge audience. This national attention would allow your sponsor(s) to receive positive publicity and brand name recognition in a way that isn't blatant advertising.

Some successful bloggers are able to hire themselves out as paid spokespeople for small- to medium-sized companies that wish to utilize the popularity of online celebrities in order to better appeal to their audience. If, in addition to a regular blog audience of several hundred thousand people, you also have an online friends list of 300,000 or more on MySpace or Facebook, you have a fan base (audience) that companies may want to tap into by paying you to be their

> **Warning!**
>
> If you opt to charge for premium content, one ongoing challenge you'll have is the need to prevent piracy of your content and keep hackers from distributing unauthorized passwords to your premium content without paying for it. This is functionality you may have to hire a programmer to add to your blog, since it's not typically offered through the popular online blog hosting services.

spokesperson or to assist them with their own promotional/advertising efforts. Find companies that might want to reach your audience and approach them with some unique promotional ideas that involve you as a spokesperson or host of an event.

Offer a Membership with Members-Only Privileges and Offers

For bloggers who are able to generate a strong following and offer unique content that visitors perceive to be valuable, another revenue generation strategy is to charge a monthly or annual membership fee for people to access certain areas of your blog or specific (premium) content. This password-protected area of your blog would need to offer members-only privileges and/or content that your audience would deem worthy of actually paying for.

One scenario in which this revenue strategy could work is if an author or expert published a free blog, but then offered extended excerpts from a best-selling book or exclusive videos of them lecturing as premium content that people could pay for and access via the web. Perhaps the expert would guarantee their paid subscribers direct access to them via live chats or through e-mail. The premium content, however, would need to be something of interest to the blog's audience and not available elsewhere.

The problem with this revenue-generating scenario is that there is so much information and content available for free on the internet, in libraries, on radio, on television, and in other forms of media, that it's extremely challenging to get people to pay extra for online content. However, there are certainly situations where people are willing to pay for online content, especially if it's in the form of valuable audio, video, or multimedia information that's unique or exclusive.

How much you can charge for premium content through a blog will vary greatly, based on the type of content being offered, the topic, and the intended audience. Access to premium blog content could be paid for online (through your blog) using a major credit card, PayPal, or Google Checkout, for example. Once someone pays for access, they'd automatically be e-mailed a unique username and password that would grant them access to the premium content for a pre-determined period of time.

Solicit Donations Using ChipIn!

If you have a personal blog or a blog that promotes a charitable cause and you want to solicit voluntary donations from your blog's visitors, one very easy way to do this is by adding the ChipIn! widget (chipin. com) to your blog.

After visiting the ChipIn! website and registering for a free account, you can create a customized ChipIn! widget for your blog that explains what you're trying to raise money for and how much money you're hoping to raise. This widget will prominently display a "ChipIn" icon so people can instantly donate any amount of money they wish to you using the PayPal service.

To use the ChipIn! service as a blogger, you must already have an established PayPal account, so you can electronically receive the funds donated to you. This widget works with any blog hosting service, and can also be added to a profile within the popular online social networks, such as MySpace and Facebook.

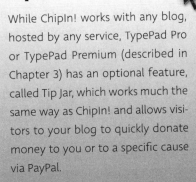

Tip

While ChipIn! works with any blog, hosted by any service, TypePad Pro or TypePad Premium (described in Chapter 3) has an optional feature, called Tip Jar, which works much the same way as ChipIn! and allows visitors to your blog to quickly donate money to you or to a specific cause via PayPal.

Once you've customized your ChipIn! Widget from the company's website, you'll be provided with the appropriate HTML code which you can simply cut and paste into the appropriate area of your blog. The whole process takes just minutes.

Of course, how well the ChipIn! widget works to help you earn the money you're soliciting will depend greatly on how well you promote your cause and motivate your blog's visitors to donate money. Sure, this widget can be used to raise money for charities, but it can also be used to raise money for personal reasons.

Use Your Blog as a Promotional Tool for Your Company

One way that companies use blogs is as a promotional and marketing tool for its product(s) and/or service(s). The blog can link to a separate but related eCommerce website, where someone can actually make their online purchases.

Taking this approach allows the blog to have its autonomy and be used to build customer loyalty by developing a relationship with customers, without bombarding them with hardcore sales messages or ads. Instead, the blog can offer customer testimonials, answers to common questions, how-to articles (directly related to the product/service), and other information or content the potential buyers will find informative, valuable, and relevant.

Creating an online community around your product/service via a blog that also offers live chat capabilities and messaging/commenting functionality to encourage interactivity, for example (which is possible using widgets), is a great way to promote a company and its products or services, while at the same time building a company's credibility and reputation.

Again, a blog can be integrated within a company's website or eCommerce site (accessible through a menu option or banner link), or be kept totally separate, although links between the blog and site can easily be established. If you're creating a blog for a company, it's important to clearly define the blog's goals and objectives, and then add the appropriate content and functionality to the blog so that it properly caters to your (potential) customers and clients.

Land a Job as a Professional Online Community Moderator

Once you prove yourself as a blogger, you might be able to land a paying job contributing to a company's blog (as an editor or columnist), or get yourself hired as an online community moderator—someone who reviews all comments and communications happening within an online community and ensures that all of the content remains suitable for the audience and stays within the guidelines created by the company operating the online community or online chat room, for example.

Many companies are discovering the need to host a blog or online community, but don't have the in-house staff to create and manage this type of online presence. Thus, they look to hire experienced bloggers who know how to create and manage content and interact with online users. If you love blogging and interacting with web surfers in cyberspace, this could be an excellent part or full-time career opportunity to pursue.

What's Next?

Becoming a successful blogger will require a bit of a learning curve and some experimentation as you become proficient using the tools offered by your blog hosting service and start creating content designed to appeal to your audience. As you begin to acquire the skills and experience necessary to achieve your blogging goals, chances are you'll encounter a few challenges and make a few mistakes. If and when this happens, don't get discouraged.

When it comes to blogging, persistence is as essential as creativity. The next chapter explains some of the most common mistakes bloggers make as they're learning the skills required to be a successful blogger; it also explains how to avoid making these mistakes.

Later, by reading the in-depth interviews with well-known and successful bloggers, you'll be able to learn directly from their experiences, tap their knowledge, and discover their secrets for creating, publishing, and managing a successful blog.

Chapter 12
The Top Ten Biggest Blogging Mistakes

So far, you've learned all about what it takes to create, publish, and manage a successful blog, and potentially become famous and/or generate a respectable income in the process. You already know there's a ton of competition for your blog out there in cyberspace, and if you want your blog to stand out, it needs to offer something unique or special that your target audience wants, needs, or will appreciate.

While much of this book has focused on the things you should do in order to make your blog successful, this chapter focuses on some of the biggest mistakes bloggers make and offers strategies for avoiding them.

Some of the mistakes described here may seem like common sense things to avoid, especially after reading the first 11 chapters. However, they've been included in this chapter because newcomers to blogging make them all too often. When it comes to blogging, utilizing creativity combined with common sense often goes a long way toward achieving success.

That being said, let's take a closer look at some of the most common mistakes bloggers make. Listed here, in no particular order, are the top ten most common mistakes bloggers typically make. While making one or more of these mistakes probably won't be catastrophic or impact the long-term success of your blog (assuming you quickly identify the mistake and correct it), it'll save you time, money, and aggravation if you avoid these mistakes altogether.

> **Tip**
>
> One of the best ways to learn about some of the pitfalls you might encounter as you attempt to create, publish, and manage your blog is to communicate with fellow bloggers. There are many online communities dedicated to bloggers and blogging. You should also become an avid reader of other popular blogs to see firsthand what works and what doesn't.

1. Having Unrealistic Expectations

It's true, creating, publishing, and managing a blog isn't that complicated of a process. With basic knowledge (acquired from this book), and with just average web surfing skills, most people can get a blog published on the web within a few hours.

However, just publishing a blog and adding new content to it is only part of the overall equation for success. Most bloggers don't initially realize how much time and effort is actually required to promote their blog and generate traffic to it. Contrary to popular belief, simply publishing your blog will not automatically drive web surfers to it.

If you want hundreds, thousands of even millions of people to access your blog, you need to understand the following realities:

- Building up a significant audience for your blog is going to take weeks, perhaps months—not minutes or hours.

- You will need to invest time, effort, and creativity to properly promote your blog to its intended audience in order to drive traffic to it. (See Chapter 10 for ideas about how to do this.)

- If you don't somehow differentiate what your blog offers from the millions of other blogs already on the web, people will not be interested in yours. You might get them to visit your blog once, but they won't return again and again. Repeat visits to your blog are essential if you want to develop a strong following for it.

- Once you pick a topic to blog about, you must continue to publish original, relevant, informative, and/or entertaining content that will be of interest to your audience. This content needs to be created and published on an ongoing basis.

- As you begin promoting your blog, you need to continue your efforts, otherwise you'll stop generating new traffic to your blog and the level of new traffic will drop off quickly. Your blog promotion efforts should be multifaceted and ongoing.

- It takes time for a blog to become popular, even if it's being properly promoted. Don't expect overnight success. Just getting your blog listed with the popular search engines, for example, could take several weeks. One of the biggest mistakes first-time bloggers make is giving up too quickly. Be persistent and stay motivated. Unless you're willing to spend thousands or tens of thousands of dollars to initially advertise your blog, or you already have an established audience for it (and a way to reach that audience quickly to tell them about your blog), it will not generate a lot of traffic at first, so have realistic expectations.

- Unless you happen to get invited to be a guest on a national television show, your blog gets featured prominently in a network television news story, or one of your blog entries happens to reach the front page of Digg or Reddit, for example, you, as the blogger, will not become famous overnight. Becoming a true online celebrity doesn't just take time and amazing amount of creativity, it also required a bit of luck and good timing. (Chapter 9 focuses on what it takes to become famous as a blogger.)

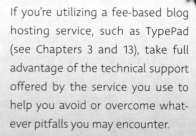

Tip

If you're utilizing a fee-based blog hosting service, such as TypePad (see Chapters 3 and 13), take full advantage of the technical support offered by the service you use to help you avoid or overcome whatever pitfalls you may encounter.

If you're using a free blog hosting service, take advantage of the online-based support databases and FAQ (frequently asked questions) documents that are offered.

If you'll be operating a business-oriented blog or you have funds to invest in your blog's development, consider hiring a professional blog design service that can help you design and launch your blog and avoid the most common mistakes people often make.

- If you're hoping to become a millionaire as a blogger or you think this is the perfect get-rich-quick scheme, think again! If your blog is able to attract a significant and steady flow of traffic (in the thousands of tens of thousands of visits per day or week), and you utilize some of the revenue generating strategies covered in Chapter 11, you should be able to earn some money from blogging, but realistically, most people don't get rich just from their blog, and if they do, it's a process that takes a long, long time. If you're looking for overnight riches, you have a better shot at winning the lottery.

2. Not Targeting the Appropriate Audience with Your Content

One challenge many bloggers encounter, at least initially, is creating content within their blog that will appeal to their target audience. It's also essential to maintain consistency and continuity, while staying on topic.

When choosing an overall topic to blog about, make sure there's plenty to cover and that what you have to say will be interesting, non-repetitive and appropriate for your audience. Showcase yourself as someone who is extremely knowledgeable about the topic, as well as credible. It's perfectly okay to have strong opinions and share them, as long as you're able to support your position in an intelligent way (to help maintain your credibility).

Write in a way that caters to your audience's education level, interests, and personality. If you alienate your intended audience, they will abandon your blog.

3. Creating Unoriginal or Uninteresting Content

While you probably won't be able to come up with a topic that's never been blogged about before, you can put a unique or unusual twist to your blog's content in order to make it interesting, compelling, informative and/or entertaining. Another common mistake bloggers make is simply repacking or reiterating information that's already readily available on the web and in the mainstream media.

If you don't have an original or different way to package and communicate what you intend to blog about, choose another topic or you'll have a very difficult time building up an audience and generating traffic to your blog. Depending on your topic, simply incorporating a bit of your own personality and writing style into the blog may be enough to set it apart from others.

Just like web surfers, people who read blogs have a very limited attention span. If a blog entry doesn't capture their attention within a few seconds, that visitor will surf elsewhere.

One common mistake is simply lifting pre-created and generic content about a topic from other sources, adding a bunch of relevant ads to the blog, and then hoping large numbers of people will click on those ads so you can generate revenue. Blog readers and web surfers have become too savvy to fall for that get-rich quick approach sometimes used by bloggers. Don't bother creating a generic blog that's search engine optimized based on specific key-words for the sole purpose of generating click-through ad revenue. If your blog's content is generic and unoriginal, people won't stay long enough to click on your ads.

4. Disclosing Too Much Personal Information

When you become a blogger who generates a good level of traffic to their blog, you automatically become something of a public figure or online celebrity, at least on some scale. While you might not become a household name across America, you could easily become well known within specific circles. That being said, many bloggers make the mistake of disclosing too much personal information about themselves.

Some of the problems bloggers can encounter include: identity theft, being stalked, or having threats made against them. Before disclosing too much information about yourself within your

Warning!

Thanks to the internet, private information about people is very easy to obtain. For example, if you know someone's full name and what city they live in, obtaining a listed phone number takes seconds. With a phone number, obtaining a home address is a very quick process, and with a home address, savvy people can acquire all sorts of additional personal or private information about an individual. If you become a "famous" blogger, transfer your home phone number to an unlisted number by contacting your local phone company, and use an e-mail address and domain URL that can't easily be tracked back to you.

blog, consider the possible ramifications. Think about how that information could be used and whether or not you want that information out there. This might include stories about your past (skeletons in your closet), as well as details about where you live, where you work, your phone number(s), and what kind of car your drive.

While you probably won't personally to get to know the people who access your blog, as someone reads or accesses your blog on a regular basis, they'll often feel as if they've gotten to know you and may begin to consider themselves a close and personal friend. This is the same problem celebrities, professional athletes, politicians, and other public figures sometimes face.

As a general rule, refrain from disclosing your home address and phone number, a personal e-mail address that can be tracked to your home or work address, or any other personal details that could potentially put you at risk. Most bloggers never have a problem with stalkers, threats, or identity theft, but for those few that do, it can be a scary and difficult experience—not just for you, but for your family and coworkers as well.

5. Creating Your Blog So It's Not Web Surfer Friendly

Offering compelling and original content within your blog if your visitors can't easily access it is pointless. As you're designing the look of your blog, make sure its interface is easy-to-navigate, intuitive, and that the content people want to access is never more than a click or two away.

To make navigation easier, within your blog's main page, display a list of keywords or a directory of entry topics/headlines. Also, offer a search feature within your blog. Be sure to focus on the visual appeal of the content as well. The color scheme you use should be easy on the eyes, the font(s) and typestyle(s) should be easy-to-read, and you'll want to make excellent use of white space.

If you opt to incorporate widgets into your blog, choose applications and functionality that are useful and that won't confuse your blog's visitors or that are irrelevant. Remember, at least some of the people visiting your blog might be extremely interested in your topic, but they might not be savvy web surfers.

Especially if your blog is being created from scratch, make sure it's fully compatible with all of the popular web browsers, including older and current editions of each browser. If you're blog requires the very latest browser plug-ins to access content, but most people don't yet have that new plug-in, it'll be difficult, if not impossible, for people to properly experience your blog.

If you're utilizing a popular blog hosting service, take advantage of one of the professionally designed blog templates that are offered. This will help you properly format your blog and will automatically provide the features and functionality web surfers (blog readers) want and need, without you having to make too many decisions or have any programming skills.

6. Adding Too Much Clutter to Your Blog's Format

Using a combination of text, photos, graphics, animations, widgets, video and audio, it's very easy for a blog to become too cluttered with content and ads. As you design and write your blog, focus on utilizing white space. As you generate text, for example, use short paragraphs and sentences that are easy to read. Avoid long paragraphs of text or mixing and matching too many fonts/typestyles within a sentence or paragraph.

If you want people to respond to ads featured within your blog, position them so they're visible, but don't overpopulate each page of your blog with too many ads or too much content. If a visitor perceives your blog features too many ads and too little useful content, they'll simply surf elsewhere.

Likewise, if your blog features too many widgets that offer irrelevant or trivial content that doesn't contribute to your visitor's experience in a positive way, they'll simply surf elsewhere. There's a very fine line between having enough bells and whistles to make your blog look impressive, without oversaturating it. Only you can judge what's appropriate for your blog, based on the topic and your intended audience, as well as the goals you have for the blog.

Tip

When creating an extra long blog entry that includes a vast amount of text, break up the text into several parts, so that no more than 300 to 500 words appears on the screen at any given time. It's perfectly acceptable to have a Part 1, Part 2, and a Part 3 to a blog entry, assuming each part is easy to find and access. If your content is easy to read, it'll be much easier to capture the attention of your audience and keep it. Plus, if you're displaying ads, you can generate more impressions for each ad if those ads appear on multiple screens as someone is reading a particularly compelling or entertaining blog entry that's split into multiple parts.

7. Purposefully Misrepresenting Information as Fact, When It's Pure Fiction

When blogging, having strong personal opinions and sharing them is not only allowable, it's encouraged. After all, giving everyday people an open forum to communicate with others is what blogging is all about.

However, as a responsible blogger, it's important to make is very clear when you're stating an opinion versus sharing documented facts or statistics, for example. It's all too easy to use powerful language and mislead people by misrepresenting opinions or ideas as facts, for example.

Among news journalists and reporters working for newspapers, magazines, radio, and television, for example, mixing facts with opinion is not considered ethical, unless that journalist is doing an editorial. Otherwise, it's considered biased and irresponsible journalism.

As a blogger, you are not obligated to uphold the standards of professional journalism, but if you want to build and maintain credibility as a blogger, it's a good strategy to make it clear when your blog contains ideas and opinions, versus documented facts and statistics. Listing sources for facts or statistics, or attributing information in the form of direct quotes from other people (such as experts on a topic, for example) is recommended.

People often believe what they see or read and don't always bother to determine if the source of the information is credible. In other words, some people would just as soon gather their insight into world news or politics from John Doe's blog as they would from CNN.com. Whether your blog caters to entertainment-seeking web surfers or data-crunching academics, it's up to you as a blogger to decide if you can live up to the responsibility of distributing credible information, or if you'd rather misrepresent the content of your blog and disguise opinions and ideas as facts. Remember, your personal credibility and the credibility of your blog is on the line.

8. Not Properly Promoting Your Blog To Generate Traffic

Many people who first get into blogging will spend hours designing their blog and writing their first few blog entries, insuring that everything winds up looking perfect and exactly how they envisioned it. These bloggers are extremely proud of their accomplishment when their blog actually goes online, but quickly become disappointed and frustrated when thousands of people don't access their blog within a few hours or days after it first gets published.

Yes, you want to invest the necessary time, effort, and resources to create the absolute best blog possible, and be able to showcase your very best work to the world, but if no one knows about your blog, there's no way they'll ever access it.

At the same time you're creating and launching your blog, formulate and launch comprehensive promotional efforts that will drive traffic to the blog. This might mean simply telling your close friends, family members, and coworkers about the vacation blog you've just published after returning from your honeymoon, or it could mean developing and implementing a national or worldwide campaign designed to drive thousands of people to your blog each day.

Keep in mind, regardless of what promotional efforts you initiate, your expectations for initial traffic to your blog should be realistic, or you're setting yourself up for a disappointment. As you've read numerous times throughout this book, generating a steady flow of traffic to a blog takes time, effort, persistence, and patience.

9. Violating Copyright and Trademark Laws with Your Not-So-Original Content

While it's true that a blog is an open forum for you to communicate with the world on your own terms, certain laws pertaining to copyrights, trademarks, defamation, and liability, for example, still apply.

As a general rule, never publish content that you don't own the rights to—text, graphics, images (photographs), music, audio records, or video. You can, in most cases, however, post links to YouTube videos produced by other people, or embed that footage into your blog with proper credit.

In terms of libel and defamation, use common sense. It's often OK to post your own comments or thoughts (positive or negative) about a celebrity, politician, or a public figure, but different rules apply if you spread false information about private citizens, such as your next-door neighbor or your boss.

When it comes to adhering to copyright, trademark, defamation, and/or libel laws, it's always better to err on the side of caution and avoid publishing content in your blog that could lead to lawsuits. If what you plan to publish falls into a gray area, for example, or you're not sure whether or not your freedom of speech rights apply, consult with an attorney before adding that content to your blog.

Realistically, if your blog is only read by a small number of people, even if you do violate a copyright law, for example, you probably won't get caught. Or, if you do get caught, you'll simply be asked to remove the content in question. However, if you become an online celebrity and start getting a lot of attention for yourself and your blog, your blog's content will be more carefully scrutinized and you're much more apt to get caught and held responsible for breaking any laws. It's best to just be responsible about what you publish, from the beginning.

You'll find that your fellow bloggers are very protective of their original content, as are webmasters. So if you try stealing someone else's content without permission (plagiarizing it), even if this doesn't lead to lawsuits, it could easily destroy your reputation and lead to other complications which will be frustrating and time consuming to resolve.

There are laws in place that allow for the fair use of certain types of copyrighted content. If you opt to use content that doesn't belong to you, determine if "fair use" applies, or if you need to obtain written permission from that content's copyright owner before using it. For more information about this, visit copyright.gov.

10. Not Taking Into Account How Your Blog Will Impact Your Personal and Professional Life Outside of Cyberspace

Some bloggers protect themselves and the strong or controversial comments, ideas or statements they publish by creating their blog and posting their content anonymously. If, however, you opt to use your real name and include details about yourself within your blog, people will hold you personally responsible for whatever content you create and publish. This can have a detrimental impact on your personal and professional life, not to mention your reputation as a blogger.

Always assume that your blog's content will be accessible and will be read by your family, friends, and coworkers, as well as people living in your community, who attend your house of worship, and who belong to the same clubs or associations as you. If you publish negative comments that people might not agree with or that are offensive, you will most likely be held accountable by those around you, whether or not these people comprise your blog's target audience.

Bloggers often make the mistake of badmouthing their boss, a college professor, or someone they know, believing that the person they've blogged about will never find out. Never make this assumption! When you publish content on the web, unless it's encrypted and password protected, chances are anyone from almost anywhere in the world will be able to access it—including your current boss or the human resources person deciding whether or not to hire you for the job for which you've applied.

If you publish content that is highly controversial, think about how the people around you will react to your blog and how it will impact your personal and professional reputation outside of cyberspace. Also, consider how a tarnished reputation could impact your spouse and kids.

Assuming your blog takes off in a big way, you could develop a following that's as large as a major daily newspaper's readership, or as big as the audience of a

"Fair Use" of Copyrighted Material

The following text is an excerpt from the U.S. Copyright Office's website (copyright.gov/fls/fl102.html) that explains "fair use."

One of the rights accorded to the owner of copyright is the right to reproduce or to authorize others to reproduce the work in copies or phonorecords. This right is subject to certain limitations found in sections 107 through 118 of the Copyright Act (title 17, U. S. Code).

One of the more important limitations is the doctrine of 'fair use.' Although fair use was not mentioned in the previous copyright law, the doctrine has developed through a substantial number of court decisions over the years. This doctrine has been codified in section 107 of the copyright law.

Section 107 contains a list of the various purposes for which the reproduction of a particular work may be considered 'fair,' such as criticism, comment, news reporting, teaching, scholarship, and research. Section 107 also sets out four factors to be considered in determining whether or not a particular use is fair:

1. the purpose and character of the use, including whether such use is of commercial nature or is for nonprofit educational purposes;
2. the nature of the copyrighted work;
3. amount and substantiality of the portion used in relation to the copyrighted work as a whole; and
4. the effect of the use upon the potential market for or value of the copyrighted work.

The distinction between 'fair use' and infringement may be unclear and not easily defined. There is no specific number of words, lines, or notes that may safely be taken without permission. Acknowledging the source of the copyrighted material does not substitute for obtaining permission.

The 1961 Report of the Register of Copyrights on the General Revision of the U.S. Copyright Law cites examples of activities that courts have regarded as fair use: 'quotation of excerpts in a review or criticism for purposes of illustration or comment; quotation of short passages in a scholarly or technical work, for illustration or clarification of the author's observations; use in a parody of some of the content of the work parodied; summary of an address or article, with brief quotations, in a news report; reproduction by a library of a portion of a work to replace part of a damaged copy; reproduction by a teacher or student of a small part of a work to illustrate a lesson; reproduction of a work in legislative or judicial proceedings or reports; incidental and fortuitous reproduction, in a newsreel or broadcast, of a work located in the scene of an event being reported.'

Copyright protects the particular way an author has expressed himself; it does not extend to any ideas, systems, or factual information conveyed in the work.

The safest course is always to get permission from the copyright owner before using copyrighted material. The Copyright Office cannot give this permission.

When it is impracticable to obtain permission, use of copyrighted material should be avoided unless the doctrine of 'fair use' would clearly apply to the situation. The Copyright Office can neither determine if a certain use may be considered "fair" nor advise on possible copyright violations. If there is any doubt, it is advisable to consult an attorney.

regional or national television show. When this happens, you become a public figure and will be held to different standards than private citizens.

Discovering fame—whether it's for 15 minutes or ongoing—will impact your personal and professional life in many different ways. It's important to be prepared for those changes and challenges in order to properly deal with them as they occur. Inside, you may feel like the person you've always been, but in terms of how the public perceives you, you will be known by many more people and your thoughts, actions, and even your appearance, will be scrutinized.

There is a price to fame. Before pursuing it, make sure you're able and willing to pay that price and are willing to give up your privacy. Otherwise, while your blog might become incredibly successful, the changes in your personal and professional life could be catastrophic—just ask any celebrity who has wound up in rehab or in bankruptcy court.

What's Next?

So far, you've read all about how to create, publish, manage, and promote a blog, but you haven't yet been exposed to any real world blogging experience. To help you prepare yourself to become a successful blogger, Chapters 13 and 14 feature in-depth, exclusive interviews with a handful of high-profile blogging experts who share their own personal thoughts, insights, and advice about blogging.

These interviews offer you that chance to learn from people who have already achieved tremendous success as bloggers and who have overcome all of the common pitfalls and challenges associated with blogging. These people have discovered how to successfully create captivating and original blog content, plus promote their blog to the masses.

Chapter 13 focuses on interviews with blogging experts who represent blog hosting and blog design services, including Google's Blogger.com. In Chapter 14, you'll read interviews with people from all walks of life and of different ages who have achieved fame and, in some cases, fortune as bloggers.

Chapter 13
Blogging Experts Share Their Wisdom

Sometimes the best way to learn something new is directly from an "expert," who has knowledge and proven proficiency, and who is willing to offer you advice based on their firsthand experiences.

Also, it's always good to learn from other peoples' mistakes, so you don't have to repeat those mistakes yourself. At the same time, studying and emulating what others have done to achieve their success is also a sound strategy.

Well, as someone who is new to blogging, what better way to learn about becoming a successful blogger than from people who have already proven themselves to be experts? What you are about to read in this chapter and the next are people's personal opinions. You're free to agree or disagree with the advice that's offered from these experts, but it's being provided to give you additional knowledge and insight into the world of blogging.

Even if you don't know any successful bloggers or blogging experts when you can call or turn to for personalized guidance and advice, this chapter features interviews with four blogging specialists who share extremely valuable information about on how to achieve success as a newbie blogger.

From Taj Campbell and Chris Alden, you'll learn all about how to utilize a blog hosting service, such as Blogger.com, TypePad.com, or VOX.com, and then discover what it takes to create, manage, publish, and promote a successful blog.

In the interview with Josh Mullineaux, you'll learn why it might be beneficial for you

> **Tip**
>
> The people interviewed within this chapter all represent companies that offer some type of service to bloggers. The next chapter offers in-depth and exclusive interviews with some of the world's best-known bloggers, including Perez Hilton and Chris Crocker.

to hire a professional blog designer to help you initially design and launch your blog, especially if the blog will be used to promote an established business or its products/services.

While a professional blog designer charges a fee for their work, you're guaranteed to wind up with a blog that's highly functional, visually appealing, that looks totally unique (because it will be designed from scratch, not from a template), and that will appeal to your audience.

While several chapters of this book focus on how bloggers should utilize online social networking services, like MySpace and Facebook, to help promote a blog and to build awareness for themselves, in her interview, Catherine Brown talks about how businesses can and should utilize online social networking to better communicate with their customers and clients.

Taj Campbell

Product Manager, Blogger.com (Google)

Website: blogger.com

Back in August 1999, a small start-up company called Pyra Labs was created by three friends who had a passion for blogging. This was before blogging was really all that popular. The company offered tools for everyday people to create their own blogs. The services offered ultimately evolved into Blogger.com. As more and more people jumped on the blogging bandwagon, Blogger.com's base of users began to expand dramatically, from the thousands to the hundreds of thousands. This is when the folks at Google took notice and ultimately acquired the company. Today, Blogger.com is one of the most popular services for creating, managing, and publishing blog content. It is one of the most popular blog hosting services in the world. It provides bloggers with all of the online-based tools and resources needed for just about anyone to create, publish and manage a traditional text-based blog that can also incorporate photos, graphics, audio clips, video clips and other types of multimedia and interactive content.

Aside from offering a robust, yet extremely easy-to-use set of blogging tools and resources, one reason by Blogger.com appeals to so many bloggers is that all of the services offered are 100 percent free. In fact, Blogger.com even offers the tools needed to help bloggers generate revenue from their blog, as opposed to spending money hosting and managing it.

Because Blogger.com is now part of Google, the service is compatible with many of Google's other online-based applications and tools, including AdSense, YouTube, and Picasa, plus it's compatible with a wide range of third-party tools and widgets that allow bloggers to fine-tune and customize their blog, all without needing any programming knowledge or skills.

In this interview, Taj Campbell, a product manager for Google's Blogger.com, offers his advice on how to best use Blogger.com, or any blog hosting service, to create the best blog possible and to make your blog truly stand out. More information about Blogger.com and its services can be found in Chapter 3.

Q: *In your opinion, what sets Blogger.com apart from the other blog hosting services on the web?*

TC: We took an already existing service and then enhanced it when Google took it over. The service underwent a major resign in 2005. It is now a dynamic publishing tool that allows users to interact with the content they access. Our Blogger.com service also now fully interacts with other Google products and services, which is a big thing that differentiates what we offer. This allows us to offer a more comprehensive experience for bloggers and people accessing the blogs, and we're able to do it all, essentially for free. Going forward, you'll see even more integration with the Google Apps world.

Q: *What would you say makes a successful blog?*

TC: That really depends how you want to define 'successful.' If a successful blog to you is based on how much revenue it generates, that success will depend on the level of traffic you can drive to your blog. Some people judge their success by how much of an interactive community they're able to create around their blog and how much it appeals to their audience.

I would say a blog is successful if it's able to show a steady growth in traffic over time. I believe a successful blog is one that gets new people visiting it based on word-of-mouth advertising and based on a large number of outside links from other sites that promote the blog. If a blog has a lot of repeat visitors, plus a lot of interaction amongst its visitors, these are signs of a successful blog.

Being able to create good quality new content on an ongoing basis is also a sign of a successful blog and blogger. A successful blog stays on topic and its content remains cohesive.

Q: *If someone wants to start a blog, what tips can you share to help him or her get started?*

TC: Most people can figure out pretty easily how to create their initial blog and add a few entries to it. What some people can't figure out as readily is how to tell people that their blog exists so they can drive traffic to it. I recommend building as many relationships as possible with other bloggers and website operators who can share links to your blog. Also, make your blog content available through RSS readers. We have discovered that more and more web surfers prefer to subscribe to a blog and automatically receive content updates, as opposed to having to visit a blog's URL on a regular basis.

The best way to generate return traffic to your blog and to help it achieve success is to keep adding new and original content to it on a regular basis.

Q: *How important is the topic someone chooses to blog about?*

TC: More and more blogs are differentiating themselves and catering to a very specific market by focusing on a niche topic. This is something that newspapers, magazines, and other forms of media can't really do that well. Whatever topic you choose to blog about, it's essential that you cater to a specific audience with your blog and that you understand who that audience is. Out of the tens of millions of blogs that Blogger.com hosts, many of the ones that become the most popular cover very specialized to niche topics that you don't see covered in other places.

I see lots and lots of successful blogs that cover specific or specialized areas of knitting, cooking and grilling, for example. What topic you blog about doesn't really matter as long as your blog stays cohesive and focused on a topic, and that your content caters to a specific audience that you truly understand.

Q: *How important is it for a blog to be unique in order for it to stand out?*

TC: As important as it is to offer unique content, I think it's more important to really focus on developing a community around your blog. By this, I mean getting visitors to your blog to become active by posting comments, for example. What makes blogging so attractive these days is that a blog no longer just features static content. A blogger can really build a relationship with their audience, and that's important. Visitors should feel welcome to contribute to a discussion and feel like they're part of an online community based around your blog and its subject matter. I believe a blog's uniqueness can come from the blogging community that's created, not just from the content created by the blogger.

Q: *How important is a blog's main title and URL in terms of its overall ability to become successful?*

TC: If you're relying on search engines to help drive traffic to your site, its main title and its URL [website address] are important. However, once people know how to find your blog, having a relevant and catchy title is less essential.

When someone creates and publishes a blog using Blogger.com, they're given a free URL that incorporates 'BlogSpot' in the URL. However, bloggers can easily register their own custom domain name, for a small annual fee, which might be easier to promote and easier for visitors to remember.

Q: *When someone creates a blog using a service like Blogger.com, they must select a template for their blog's design. How important is this selection?*

TC: The appearance of your blog is extremely important. Its appearance will be based on which template you select and how you customize that template. In the near future, I'd like to see Blogger.com add even more template choices than what we already offer. Blogging is a means of self-expression that goes well beyond the text and photos you add to your blog. You can express yourself using color, design elements, and graphics, for example, using our Layout Editor.

Ideally, when someone visits your blog, they should feel like they're visiting something that's unique. Really investing the time and effort to fully customize your blog's appearance by personalizing the template you choose is a great way to enhance its uniqueness.

When choosing which blog hosting service you'll utilize for your blog, take a close look at the layout and design options that are offered and figure out how much you'll be able to customize the look of your blog, without needing any programming knowledge. A blog publishing platform should offer a lot of control over customization of the templates and the blog's appearance.

Aside from the customization capabilities and functions available using the Blogger Layout Editor, if you are familiar with HTML and Java, you can fully customize every aspect of your blog's appearance, which is something most other services don't offer. To really tap the customization capabilities offered through Blogger.com, there is a bit of a learning curve. Because our service is so popular, however, there are many outside sources for templates, plus professional designers who can be hired that specialize in blog customization using Blogger.com compatible templates.

Q: *When a blogger wants to add functionality or more interactivity to their blog, the easiest way to do this is using widgets. What are some of the most popular widgets that are compatible with Blogger.com?*

TC: A new widget, called The Blog List, offers blog roll functionality that's dynamic. What this means is that when someone is visiting one blog that focuses on a specific topic, using a blog roll, they can immediately access additional blogs that focus on the same or a similar topic. Also, for people who want to earn money from their blog, the AdSense widget is very popular.

To make it easier for visitors to a blog to follow along as new content is created, adding a 'Subscribe' widget allows visits to be alerted when new content to a blog is added. For the blogger, using this feature can dramatically increase repeat traffic to the blog.

Lately, I've also seen people making creative use of photo slides shows within their blogs. Again, this is functionality available using widgets. I believe the best widgets to add are ones that drive traffic around and help visitors find and access additional topic-related content.

Q: *How easy is it to start generating revenue from a blog?*

TC: Adding the functionality to begin generating an income is very easy using Blogger.com, for example. However, you'll only begin to see income if you're able to drive a steady flow of traffic to your blog. Using a simple widget, you can utilize Google's AdSense service to begin displaying ads that will generate revenue for you when your visitors click on those ads. [Additional information about AdSense can be found in Chapter 11.]

Once a blog is established and has a strong flow of traffic, it's common for bloggers to affiliate themselves with additional ad networks outside of AdSense. Participating in affiliate programs and displaying larger, graphic-based ads from advertisers that are relevant to your blog is certainly a popular route to follow if you want to earn money from your blog. Make sure the ads you display, however, are of interest to your audience and relate to the topic of your blog.

Q: *What would you say are some of the biggest challenges bloggers face as they're trying to get their blog established in cyberspace?*

TC: There are two really big challenges. The first is growing an audience for your blog. There are people who are comfortable writing for no one, but most people who create a blog do so with the intention of other people accessing it.

The other big barrier to entry is people initially figuring out what they want to write about. Even once they establish their topic, when they're faced with a blank new blog entry screen, it's intimidating for them to start writing to create entries. I recommend choosing a topic area in advance and when you do this, at the same time, create a list of potential blog entry topics, and then keep adding to this list as time goes on. Brainstorming new blogging ideas is sometimes one of the hardest parts for a new blogger.

Another thing people can do is link their blog content and develop blogging ideas based on other activities they're doing online, particularly on the online social networking sites. If you already use Twitter, for example, you can expand those one-line entries about what you're doing into full-length blog entries if you're just a little bit creative.

Q: *These days, creating just a text-based blog seems outdated. Is this the case?*

TC: Because adding multimedia content, like video, to a blog has become so easy, it's also become popular. As a result, I think an ever-growing percentage of people who read blogs expect more elaborate content than just text. However, this will depend on your blog's topic and its intended audience. When you have an opportunity to add a photo or video that makes sense, I recommend adding it.

One thing you can do to help you gauge what types of content is appropriate for your blog is to reach out to your audience and solicit feedback. You can do this by asking them to post comments, or you can use a widget to incorporate a poll or survey into your blog's content. Soliciting feedback is also a great way to build a relationship with your audience.

Q: *What are some of the biggest mistakes you see bloggers make on a regular basis?*

TC: People give up on their blog much too easily. If they don't immediately see a huge audience visiting their blog, they abandon their blog much too soon. Building up an audience takes time and persistence. Bloggers need to be extremely proactive in terms of driving traffic to their blog in creative ways. This is an ongoing process and an extremely important one that can't be ignored.

Once you start publishing your blog, keep it up by adding new content and promoting it. Be patient, but persistent and you will start to see a growth in traffic over time.

Q: *Do you have any other advice for creating content that's compelling?*

TC: One approach is to be controversial, but this isn't a requirement. It is acceptable and very common for bloggers to have strong opinions and to attract visitors that share their point-of-view or who strongly oppose their point-of-view. There is, however, a lot of room to share the creative things you do, without being controversial. I think most bloggers will have better luck picking a topic that really interests them, and then catering their content to an audience that shares the same interest, even if the interest is a hobby, such as knitting, cooking, or fishing.

Q: *If a blogger's goal is to become an online celebrity, what advice can you share?*

TC: You can become a famous blogger simply by creating a fun, informative, or interesting interactive community around your blog. You do not need to be full of yourself or extremely outrageous to get attention. The great thing about blogging is that distribution of content has become very easy and it's not too difficult to create a name and a reputation for yourself.

Q: *What are some of the newest trends in blogging that you see growing in the future?*

TC: We're going to see a huge growth in mobile blogging, now that more and more people are using cell phones and wireless PDAs that connect to the internet and that have keyboards and cameras built into them. Bloggers will be able to blog more easily about random events that happen in their lives, because they'll literally be able to post a blog entry from just about anywhere.

I also think people will be able to incorporate a lot more different types of media content into their blogs, like digital photos or short video clips shot using their cell phone. Adding this content will become even easier.

Q: *One rule of thumb for web design is to make a web page interesting so that it captures the attention of a visitor in just a few seconds. Does this rule also apply to blogs?*

TC: Web surfers have very short attention spans, and the rule definitely applies to blogs as well. Within seconds of accessing a blog, viewers should know why they are there, what's being offered to them, why the blog is unique, and why the content is of interest to them. Otherwise, they'll surf elsewhere.

Below the main title of the blog, which should explain what the blog is all about, I believe a short, text-based description of the blog should be displayed. This should offer a one- to three-sentence summary of the blog's purpose and who it'll appeal to. This way, someone can determine if the blog is of interest to him or her in a matter of seconds. How the blog looks, in terms of its layout and design, will also impact a visitor's initial impression of the blog.

In addition to the main title and the text-based description, near the top of the main blog page, I recommend incorporating something visually interesting that'll attract a visitor's attention. A compelling photograph or very catchy headlines for blog entries can often do the trick. When you're trying to attract new visitors, that initial first impression you make is extremely important.

Q: *In your opinion, what's the most outrageous blog you've seen?*

TC: If you mean outrageous in a creative and positive way, I'd have to say Post Secret (postsecret.blogspot.com) is a blog that stands out in my mind. The blogger, Frank Warren, started a community where people send him anonymous postcards to a P.O. box that reveal very personal secrets about themselves. Every Sunday morning, Frank posts the best, funniest, or most revealing postcards he receives that week for everyone to read. A lot of very interesting content and a whole online community has been created around these anonymous postcards. Through the publication of four different books based around this content, and with the help of visitors to his blog, Frank has raised over $500,000 for a suicide prevention organization. [As of September 2008, this blog has received over 180,307,060 hits from web surfers around the world.]

Q: *Do you have any other advice for someone looking to create a blog?*

TC: Check out Blogger.com. We've streamlined the experience to make creating and publishing a blog as quickly and easy as possible. The service is available in more than 40 languages and we have a powerful set of features. If you're thinking about starting a blog, just give it a try. There's very low risk involved. I think you'll see that blogging can be a lot of fun once you get started.

Chris Alden

CEO/Chairman, Six Apart (TypePad and VOX)

Phone: (415) 344-0056

Website: TypePad.com, VOX.com and SixApart.com

Six Apart Ltd. provides award-winning blogging software and services that have changed the way millions of individuals, organizations, and corporations connect and communicate across the world every day. Founded in 2002, San Francisco-based Six Apart has become a global company that continues to lead in the blogging and software media industry with the Movable Type publishing platform, the TypePad hosted blogging service, and VOX, a free blogging service.

The company's flagship product and service is TypePad, which is a fee-based, full-featured, online blogging and hosting services that offers an extremely powerful, yet easy-to-use set of blogging tools and services. Like Blogger.com, for example, TypePad uses a point, click and publish interface that requires no programming knowledge whatsoever.

Because TypePad is a fee-based service, in addition to offering a broad range of tools for creating, publishing, managing, and promoting a blog, the service also offers telephone and online-based technical support for bloggers, plus advanced blogging features that are unique to TypePad. For example, instead of offering just a handful of blog templates someone can choose from when initially creating their blog, TypePad offers a database containing more than 1,000 professionally designed templates that can be fully customized.

In keeping up with all of the latest technologies and blogging trends, TypePad also offers cutting-edge tools for mobile blogging, as well as tools for analyzing and measuring blog traffic. The ability to record and publish audio podcasts is also included with the TypePad service, as are widgets that allow bloggers to quickly and easily add connectivity, interactivity, and additional functionality to their blog.

The basic TypePad service is priced starting at $4.95 per month (or $49.50 per year). There's also a TypePad Plus ($8.95 per month/$89.50 per year), TypePad Pro ($14.95 per month/$149.50 per year), TypePad Premium ($29.95 per month/$299.50 per year), and Business Class ($89.95 per month/$899.50 per year) service, each of which offers greater functionality and more powerful tools for a blogger to utilize.

For someone who is first starting out with blogging and isn't sure if they're ready to make a financial investment in launching their blog, Six Apart also offers its VOX.com blog hosting service, which is a scaled-down, yet still highly functional version of TypePad. Anyone can sign up and launch a blog using VOX.com for free.

As the CEO and Chairman of Six Apart, not only is Chris Alden an expert blogger himself, he has the opportunity to work firsthand with many of the world's other most successful bloggers. In this interview, Alden shares his own advice on what it takes to become a successful blogger and offers tips for avoiding some of the most common pitfalls inexperienced bloggers often encounter.

Q: *How did you personally get involved in the blogging business?*

CA: I have been involved in the publishing business since 1993. I co-founded Red Herring Communications, which was a technology business magazine, internet property, and conference business. In 2002, I started blogging, and then in 2003, I started a company, called Rojo, which made it very easy for people to read blogs. Later, in 2006, Rojo was acquired by Six Apart, which is how I joined this company. I have been around media and technology since before the commercialization of the internet. I have witnessed firsthand how media publishing has been transformed by new media and internet technologies, including blogging.

Q: *What is unique about Six Apart and the blogging services it offers directly to bloggers?*

CA: There are many steps involved with creating, publishing, managing, promoting, and generating revenue from a blog. Six Apart is different from our competition, because we're the only company that has features and programs in place to help bloggers do all of these things. In the blogging world, there are blog publishing tool venders, blog hosting services, design services, and blog revenue generation programs. We offer all of this, and more.

TypePad.com is a fee-based hosted blogging service which has become one of the most popular in the world, and our VOX.com service is a hosted blogging service that is free. In addition these services, we have a full customer support team and many programs in place that can help bloggers create and publish their blog, overcome challenges, drive traffic to their blog, and generate revenue from it.

We also offer professional blog design services, so bloggers can tell us exactly what they want built, and we'll build it for them. Our media team can help drive traffic to your blog and generate revenue from your blog by selling advertising for you on your blog. Many of these services are included with a paid subscription to TypePad account.

Q: *What are some of the main differences between TypePad and VOX, from a blogger's standpoint?*

CA: TypePad is the preferred choice for people who are really dedicated to their blog. People who want full design control over their blog, or who wish to display ads on their blog in order to generate revenue will prefer TypePad. It is the most customizable and most powerful hosted blogging platform available. For bloggers who are trying to transform their hobby of blogging into a part-time or full-time career, for example, or for companies to create a business-oriented blog, TypePad offers the right tools and functionality.

VOX is for people who are blogging for social reasons. They want to connect with a neighborhood of friends, and they want to share photos, for example, with their friends and family. This service is for people who blog as a hobby, not as a career.

We have millions of bloggers around the world using our tools. The blogs that we power reach well over 100 million people, and includes some of the most trafficked blogs and web properties in the world.

Q: *Why do you think blogging has become so popular in recent years?*

CA: Blogging offers a fundamental way for people to communicate. Media is a one to many format due to the constraints of the economics. It's always been expensive for ordinary people to print and publish a newspaper, magazine, or book, for example, in order to reach the masses. Blogging suddenly represented a way for anyone to become a publisher and to reach a large audience of people. One core desire people have is the urge to communicate. It's at the core of human nature. People want to have a voice and an identity, and use it to converse with other people.

Q: *What are some of the major trends in blogging that you see happening?*

CA: Blogging has become much more social in recent years. In the past, a blogger would post a blog and other people would read it. Today, bloggers can post their content, and then their audience can respond by posting their own comments, which creates an interactive forum or community around the blog itself. Another major trend has been the evolution of social networks, like Facebook, Friendster and MySpace. These services allow people to communicate on a peer-to-peer basis.

Today, many blogs have become micro social networks. A lot of bloggers are evolving from just being publishers to being online community leaders.

Q: *What tips can you offer in regard to how someone should get started if they want to become a blogger?*

CA: The first thing is to determine if you're really dedicated to blogging and want to really pursue it, or if you just want to experiment with blogging. If you're dedicated to the idea of publishing a blog, open a TypePad account. This gives you access to our online-based tools and our support team. We will help you through every step of the blogging process and really reduce the learning curve. When you use TypePad, you don't need to figure out anything on your own. We're here to help you.

Because our design tools are so robust and we have over a thousand templates, it's easy to create a blog that is perfectly suitable for whatever it is you want to do. The real key to blogging is to pick something that you are passionate about. Most blogging success stories are created by people who start blogging about something they love. They enjoy the process of blogging and for them, the journey is the reward. In this situation, the fame and fortune associated with a successful blog will often follow.

Write the blog you would want to read. I think that's the most important rule when creating a blog. From a design standpoint, pick a template and look for your blog that most closely matches your sensibility. The design you choose will be your online representation for what you're creating. If your blog is aesthetically pleasing to you, it will probably send the right message to your readers.

Each of our professionally designed templates has already taken into account the best positioning for headers, sidebars and columns, for example. For the blogger, our templates are designed to be highly functional and accessible. So the trick is to choose a design that's right for you.

Q: *How important is it for a blogger to add multimedia content to create a successful blog?*

CA: It's not so much what type of content you use in your blog, whether it's text, photos, graphics, audio, or video. What your primary objective should be is to create good content using the resources you have available. There are so many blogs that are phenomenally popular and they're just comprised of text, and maybe a few photos. There are also many extremely successful blogs that utilize video, for example. If video is something that lends itself well with what you're trying to accomplish in terms of how you communicate using your blog, by all means, use video. The content you use, however, should really connect with the core concept of what your blog is trying to be. I would not impose artificial rules on what type of content you should or shouldn't use within your blog. Instead, I would do what feels right for whatever it is you're trying to accomplish with each new blog entry you create.

Q: *How can widgets best be used to add functionality to a blog, without having to do any programming?*

CA: TypePad has a built in widget feature and offers the largest selection of add-on widgets than any other blogging platform. To use a widget requires no programming whatsoever. The key with widgets is to determine whether the functionality of a particular widget will add any real value to the overall experience of your blog. You know your audience better than anyone else, or you should. Blogging is a very individualist activity. Every blog is different, which is what makes this opportunity so powerful. Choose widgets that give your blog the features and functionality you want your blog to have, without over saturating it with irrelevant content.

Q: *In your opinion, once someone launches a blog, what is the best way to start driving traffic to it?*

CA: Create content that is compelling and that is ideally unique. Post new content often, and engage with the rest of the blogosphere. Make a point to link to other blogs and websites that are interesting to you. A lot of blogs also generate traffic through the search engines. Getting linked to by lots of other blogs and websites, however, is one of the keys toward not just building traffic, but also improving your search engine placement.

The biggest piece of advice I can offer to new bloggers is to be persistent. This is why the journey needs to be the reward. If your sole goal is to have a lot of traffic in your blog's first few weeks or you're looking to get rich quickly, you're just not going to be successful. There are a lot of cases where a blog is obscure for a long time before it becomes widely popular. Perseverance is the best key to success when it comes to blogging.

As you're writing your blog's main description and brainstorming a title, and then again as you write blog entries, put yourself into the mindset of someone who will be using the search engines to find your blog based on its content. Incorporate keywords that are very relevant and well thought out. If your blog is about how to make a great meatloaf, think about what someone who is looking for a meatloaf recipe would do when they access a search engine, such as Google. Use those phrases in your titles and in your copy.

Go to Google and try looking for a good meatloaf recipe, if that's your blog's topic or subject matter, and see what comes up based on different keywords or search phrases you use. See what other blogs and websites are doing, and how they're using keywords to build traffic.

Q: *Blogger.com works seamlessly with AdSense, for example, if someone wants to start generating revenue from their blog. What does TypePad offer so bloggers can earn income from their efforts?*

CA: TypePad also has a comprehensive advertising program and is fully compatible with AdSense and the various affiliate programs, like Commission Junction, that link advertisers with bloggers and website operators. Once you're accepted into our advertising program, we will provide you with the content needed to displays ads on your blog, and you will be paid for doing this. We offer a very straightforward program. The more traffic your blog receives, the more money you can earn.

TypePad also has partnerships with Amazon.com and eBay.com, for example, which make it easy to add product specific links within your blog's content. If someone makes a purchase, you receive a commission. If you're looking to earn money from your blog using affiliate programs, think carefully about what types of products or services your audience would most be interested in, and then find companies that have an affiliate program in place so you can display their advertising in exchange for sales commissions.

Another option is to sell your own products or service directly from your blog. It is possible to add eCommerce functionality relatively easily to a blog using widgets. By blogging about your own products or services, and also selling them online, you can create compelling content that will interest your potential customers. Thus, a blog can become a much more powerful selling and marketing tool than an eCommerce website that offers no value-added content.

Don't focus too soon on how you can make money from your blog. Instead, your initial focus should be on how you can create something that's really valuable to your audience. If you're successful in creating a blog that transforms into a prosperous and heavily populated online community, for example, it will be much easier to incorporate revenue-generating strategies later.

Q: *Mobile blogging has become a very popular trend recently. What functionality does TypePad offer to facilitate this?*

CA: TypePad has custom-created mobile blogging software for Apple's iPhone and several other cell phone and wireless PDA platforms, including BlackBerries and Windows Mobile devices. I think mobile blogging is a very viable way for people to update and maintain their blog.

Today, almost any mobile device can be used for adding text or photos to an existing blog. It's also possible to manage comments and do other blog maintenance from a mobile device. We've made the mobile blogging process very simple. We've also developed ways to make it easier for anyone to access and read blogs using wireless mobile technology.

Currently, we're also developing technologies that will make it easy to integrate a blog with the online social networks. We see this convergence of blogging and online social networking as a fast-growing trend in blogging. We also see a lot of people experimenting with video and webcasting in conjunction with their blogs.

When it comes to producing video content, production value is something to consider. However, the quality of the content is far more important. A highly produced video will always look better than an amateur video, but the video editing programs available for basic PCs and Macs, anyone can create well-produced amateur videos with relative ease. Plus, if the video content is very interesting to your audience, you can usually get away with a lower production value. Sometimes, an over-produced video could come off to your audience as inauthentic. It all depends on the subject matter and the audience.

Q: *What are some of the biggest mistakes you've seen bloggers make?*

CA: One of the biggest mistakes is having unrealistic expectations. There's an expression that states, 'It takes a lot of time and effort to create an overnight success.' This is definitely true for blogging. Go into blogging for the right reasons and have realistic expectations in terms of how long the whole process takes, especially when it comes to generating traffic.

Also, I recommend reading lots of other blogs to see what really works and what doesn't. Don't just throw up one or two blog entries and a lot of advertising widgets designed to make you money and expect you'll be successful.

Q: *Which blogs have caught your attention as being really amazing?*

CA: Some of my favorite blogs include The Huffington Post (huffingtonpost.com/theblog), BoingBoing (boingboing.net), Serious Eats (seriouseats.com), and Talking Points Memo (talkingpointsmemo.com).

Josh Mullineaux

Director of Marketing, Unique Blog Designs, LLC

Phone: (870) 619-4550

Website: uniqueblogdesigns.com

Let's face it, you may consider yourself to be an awesome writer and written communicator who has a tremendous amount to say about a particular topic, but when it comes to layout and design, and developing an easy-to-navigate user interface for a blog or website, you might be utterly clueless. Yet, you understand the importance of creating and designing a blog that is visually appealing, professional looking, and highly functional.

To compensate for your lack of graphic design or website design knowledge, skill, and experience, especially if you're planning to launch a blog for a company (or to promote a product or service), you might consider hiring a professional blog designer. Offering similar services as a website designer, a blog designer can work with you to create a unique and fully-customized blog that perfectly caters to your audience.

Instead of relying on a blog template (which could easily result in your blog looking like many others), hiring a professional blog designer or blog design firm would result in your blog being totally unique in its appearance, plus give you the ability to custom-tailor its functionality specifically to meet your needs.

Josh Mullineaux represents a small but growing blog design firm called Unique Blog Designs, LLC. The company employs a team of highly skilled and experienced bloggers, designers, and programmers who work closely with their clients to create totally customized blogs.

The company launched in August 2007, but has already attracted a fast-growing list of more than 200 clients, including individual bloggers and companies of all sizes. In this interview, Josh Mullineaux, the company's director of marketing, shares advice on how and why a blogger (or company interested in launching a blog) might want to hire a professional blog designer. He also offers a handful of extremely useful tips and strategies to bloggers who are interested in designing and managing their own blog.

Q: *What types of services does Unique Blog Designs, LLC offer?*

JM: We have been in the website design services business since 2003. Based on the number of requests we started to receive from clients for blog design, we launched this business. With more than 16,000 new blogs started every single day, we saw an opportunity for creating custom blog designs for individuals and businesses.

Q: *If someone opts to hire a professional blog designer, what steps are involved to work with someone?*

JM: We would spend time speaking with the client about their plans for the blog. We'll ask a lot of questions about what they envision it to look like, what their approach will be, what colors they like, who their audience will be, and what type of functionality will be needed. Once we know basically what they're looking for, we can offer them one of our three different blog design packages. Our basic design package includes one blog layout for a single page. Our more elaborate packages include a home page, logo design, and other services.

When creating a blog, we utilize the WordPress service and functionality. That's our specialty. Once we create an overall look for a blog, we'll fine-tune the design and get it ready to publish. Our turn around time for creating a blog design from scratch is between five and eight weeks, but this varies based on a client's needs.

For business blogs, in addition to hiring a professional blog designer, I also recommend hiring a blog consultation service that can help you create content targeted specifically to your audience.

Q: *Why do you think blogging has become so popular and so many people are getting into it?*

JM: Blogging is a very social activity. It allows individuals and businesses to potentially connect to tons of people from around the world. Blogging gives anyone the opportunity to share his or her thoughts in a public forum.

Thanks to services like Blogger.com, TypePad.com, and WordPress.com, it's very easy for anyone to publish a blog, even with no technical knowledge or programming skills. It's much easier and quicker to publish a blog than it is to design, publish and launch a website, for example.

Q: *All the blog hosting services offer professionally designed blog templates that anyone can use and fully customize. With this resource available, why would a blogger need to hire a blog designer to create the design for their blog?*

JM: If someone is first trying out blogging, I would recommend choosing a free template to get started. There are a lot of really nice, professional-looking templates out there. Our service is ideal for an individual or company that wants their blog to have a very distinct look and feel. A unique looking blog that offers customized functionality is good for branding.

The thing about templates is that they are not exclusive. While you can customize the template to some extent, your blog will still look very similar to all of the other blogs that also utilize that same template. So if you want something that's totally unique and that stands out, a custom designed blog is your main option.

Unique Blog Designs spends a lot of time creating very personalized and customized blog designs for our clients. Our goal is to ensure that our clients' blogs don't look like other blogs on the web. We also study the web surfing habits of people and create designs that focus on how people most commonly view and navigate around blogs. For example, we have spent a lot of time studying the eye movements of web surfers, so we know how and where to position content on a page to optimize the layout.

All of our packages are full blog design solutions. We add all of the widgets and functionality to your blog, plus we offer the support you need through-out the process. This reduces the learning curve many bloggers go through. When we're done with our design process, you simply need to add your content, and you're ready to publish. For our clients, we design the blogs appearance and layout. We don't create the content.

Q: *What tips can you offer to someone deciding on the layout and design for their blog?*

JM: The first thing you want to do is get on the web and check out your competi-tors' blogs and websites. See firsthand what they're doing and how they're doing it. This research will prove extremely valuable. Try to develop an under-standing about why they're doing whatever it is they're doing. Ascertain from these other sites and blogs what you like and don't like. Focus on elements such as the color scheme, the layout, and the ease of navigation.

Try to gather as much information as you can about blog design philosophies. This will help you develop a better understanding of what your blog will need to incorporate. There are many free resources on the web for bloggers, including how-to articles, forums that allow bloggers to exchange informa-tion, and online tools that are useful to bloggers for creating or enhancing their blog design. I recommend fully utilizing these free services.

Whether you hire a blog designer or choose to do the design work yourself, first develop an understanding of exactly what you want, and what you envi-sion your blog should look like.

Q: *What are some of the biggest misconceptions bloggers often have when they first get started?*

JM: People don't realize how much work is really involved in creating a highly successful blog. They see it's really easy to publish a basic blog, but they don't take into account how challenging it is to create really unique and quality content on an ongoing basis, while at the same time, promoting the blog to drive traffic to it. This can be a highly involved process and their initial expectations are not always realistic.

Q: *What tips can you provide in regard to actually creating original blog content?*

JM: This is a very personal process that everyone approaches differently. By default, if you're writing your own content, your own personality will be automatically incorporated into it, so that provides some level of uniqueness. Focus on what you're interested in and what you think your audience will want.

If you're not comfortable as a writer, consider hiring a freelance writer or editor to help you out, at least initially, to create content for your blog, especially if the quality of the content is important and the blog is business or work-related.

Q: *Do you have any advice for generating traffic to a new blog?*

JM: First, look at all of the ways traffic can be driven to a blog: through word-of-mouth, search engines, advertising, links from other blogs, and through the online social networking sites. Focus your energies on making the best use possible of these various traffic-generating approaches. We've determined that search engines can provide the most stable flow of new traffic, but getting yourself established and listed with the search engines can be a time-consuming process onto itself.

If you'll be using search engine optimization efforts to drive traffic to your blog, really research your keywords and put a lot of thought into this process. I also recommend becoming active in the blogosphere and generating links to your blog from other blogs and websites. Don't give up on your blog if you don't immediately start to generate a lot of traffic to it. Building traffic can be a gradual process.

Q: *Is there a blogging trend that you see growing?*

JM: I see more and more website operators adding blogs to their existing sites, whether it's a personal website, a company or corporate website, or an eCommerce website. Not only does a blog allow you to build an online interactive community, but it also can dramatically help with your website's search engine optimization efforts if done correctly.

Catherine Brown

Director of Business Social Networking, Dotster, Inc.

Phone: (360) 449-5900

Website: dotster.com

Millions of web surfers have literally become addicted to online social networks like MySpace, Facebook, and Twitter as a way to meet new people and interact with their friends, family, and coworkers. Many bloggers have learned how to tap these services as powerful promotional tools for themselves and their blogs.

While these online social networks initially appealed primarily to young people, they're quickly growing in popularity among people of all ages, and can be used by companies of all sizes as a way to interact effectively with customers and clients.

Helping companies of all sizes and in all industries learn how to utilize online social networking and online-based communities is the goal of Dotster, Inc., which is based in Vancouver, Washington.

In addition to developing a specialty in helping companies become proficient utilizing online social networking to better reach their clients, Dotster is also one of the world's largest domain name registrars, plus it offers website/blog hosting services, search engine optimization services, and other fee-based services of interest to website and blog operators.

In her interview, Catherine Brown shares advice to company owners about the power of tapping into online social networking as a way to more cost-effectively interact with customers and clients.

Q: *How did the whole social networking phenomenon begin and who primarily does it appeal to?*

CB: It started with the youth market, with the growth in popularity of MySpace and Facebook, but as the technology started to mature and people began to see how successful these sites are, businesses started to take notice. Today, online social networking sites appeal to people of all ages and are being taken seriously as a promotional, advertising, and marketing tool by companies in many different industries.

When appropriate, companies are advertising on the popular online social networking sites, like MySpace and Facebook, to reach their target demographic. For business professionals, LinkedIn is an example of an online social networking services that specifically targets a business audience. Smaller online social networks also sometimes target specialty or niche audiences that are appealing to advertisers.

In addition to advertising, companies are using online social networking technology to better communicate with their customers and clients. In cases where a company creates its own online social network, this is typically referred to as a 'user community' that is custom created for a specific company and for a specific purpose.

Q: *What does Dotster, Inc. do for its clients to help these companies utilize online social networking?*

CB: We help companies utilize existing online social networks as an advertising tool, but we also help them create, from scratch, their own online communities. Through these communities, companies can better interact with the clients or customers to promote their products, handle support issues, and improve their customer service. Any company that currently targets high school or college students really needs to utilize online social networks as a marketing and promotional tool. Within a few years, as this technology becomes more and more appealing to adults, it will also become essential for any company that has a customer base to tap into online social networking.

We recommend that our clients closely look at who their customers are and determine their online habits to figure out if tapping into online social networking is currently viable as a marketing or promotional tool.

Q: *What are the steps involved in helping a company create its own online community?*

CB: We create the online community from scratch, so it can be completely branded around the company, a product, or a service. We can add whatever features and functionality the client wants, and choose a format that best caters to the client's customers. For example, we can create online forums or chat rooms, so people can communicate with each other, as well as with representatives from the client company. We can also offer blogging functionality, or use the online community to distribute training or how-to videos. Once the site is launched, we help our clients create and launch a special marketing campaign to generate traffic to it.

Once a client comes to us with the desire to create an online community, the process of designing and ultimately launching it can take anywhere from a few weeks to several months, depending on the complexity of the online community and the goals of the client. Currently, the majority of our clients are very customer service-oriented, and include high-end food and wine companies, health care companies, and media companies, including magazine publishers.

Q: *So when you help a company launch its own online community, is this just a glorified website for advertising?*

CB: No, not at all. The purpose of these communities is to encourage communication with clients or customers. We encourage our clients to incorporate as much value-added content as possible, and use only very low-key advertising within the community. It's a much softer-sell approach that's used for building customer loyalty. It can also be used to reduce customer service or support costs by making available interactive online content. The online forum can also include a blog, for example.

Dotster has people on staff who can work with your company to create new and compelling content, as well as design an online community or blogs you'll be using to communicate with your customers. We also recommend that you look to your customers for ideas on the types of content they'd appreciate.

Q: *What are some of the ways a company can promote its company or blog, for example, using the existing online social networking sites, like MySpace and Facebook?*

CB: Companies can advertise on these sites and reach very targeted audiences. They can also become active in the various special interest forums and sub-tlety promote their company through posting messages or comments, or by participating in online chats. There's a fine line between offering value-added material that your customers will appreciate and making a community too commercial, however.

Q: *What is a major concern that a company should have when launching its own online community?*

CB: You want to make sure that you have someone in place to serve as the community's moderator to ensure all of the content that goes online is suitable. You also need to make sure that if you're going to invest the resources and funds to create an online community, that you properly promote it in order to drive the right traffic to it. This is a much easier process if you already have a customer base.

Once you have people visiting your online community, whether it's to read your company's blog, obtain support, gather information related to a specific topic, or to learn about your products, you want them to become return visitors. This requires that you keep your content fresh by publishing new content on a regular basis.

Q: *What type of financial investment is a company looking at to hire Dotster, Inc. to create an online community?*

CB: Our basic service starts at $900, with a $199 per month fee. For larger online communities that require more features and more customization, the prices are higher, and are quoted on an client-by-client basis. The basic service includes the design and launch of blogs, forums, galleries, and other functionality, for example. What we create will ultimately have all of the functionality of any other online social network, but it will be completely branded for the client. The client will not need to have anyone on staff who knows how to program. We offer all of the tools needed for a client to maintain their community and add content, without the need for programming.

Q: *What should companies understand about the popularity of online social networks?*

CB: Not only are we seeing the popularity of the existing online social networking sites growing very quickly, we're seeing new sites and services launch on a regular basis. As this technology matures and becomes more mainstream, and the early adopters, who were high school and college students get older, participating in online social networking will continue to be a growing part of people's everyday lives, regardless of their age.

What's Next?

In an effort to save the best for last, Chapter 14 features in-depth and exclusive interviews with some of the world's most famous and successful bloggers.

Now that you know all about what it takes to create, publish, manage, and promote a successful blog, you can acquire some additional knowledge from the firsthand experiences of people like Perez Hilton and Chris Crocker, plus discover directly from them (in their own words) what it took to become successful and then maintain their success.

Chapter 14
Cyberstars Reveal
Their Secrets to Success

For some bloggers with the dream of becoming famous, it takes months or even years of hard work, persistence, a tremendous amount of creativity, careful planning, expert skills as a self-promoter and marketer, plus the guts to share their lives with potentially millions of strangers in order to achieve success and truly stand out from the millions of other bloggers in cyberspace.

More and more bloggers who have achieved success online and who have become extremely well known in cyberspace have also made the transition to mainstream media. Some have landed roles on popular television shows or in major motion pictures, while others have been awarded recording contracts by major record labels, or have leveraged their online fame to become bestselling authors or public speakers.

Achieving success as a blogger and becoming famous in cyberspace could be a stepping stone to launching a new career, or at the very least, provide you with fame and a steady income as a result of your blogging efforts.

Realistically, not everyone has what it takes to become a huge online star. Even if your blog does generate a large level of traffic on a consistent basis, as the blogger, you might become well known among your blog's followers, but making that transition to becoming a household name in the real world is another thing altogether.

If you have the ambition to become the next big cyberstar, you'll want to discover the secrets of success from those who have pioneered the path before you. In this chapter, you'll meet a handful of well-known bloggers and celebrities who utilize blogging. You will have the opportunity to learn from their success and read, in their own words, what it took to achieve it.

Perez Hilton

Entertainment Gossip Blogger
and Personality

Blog URL/Website: perezhilton.com

If you're planning to become a blogger, but you don't know the name Perez Hilton, the first thing you need to do is more research about blogging. Perez Hilton is one of the world's most famous bloggers. His self-titled blog features entertainment industry and celebrity gossip, and it receives more than nine million views every single day. That's almost a bigger daily audience than *Entertainment Tonight, Access Hollywood, E! News Daily,* and *Extra* combined.

Perez Hilton has gone from blogger to being one of the most influential entertainment and celebrity gossip columnists in Hollywood.

Perez is an online celebrity who has made the transition to mainstream celebrity. It's almost impossible to read any entertainment magazine or watch an entertainment TV news program and not see Perez or hear about him. He's become a powerful force in the entertainment industry. What he says in his blog can make or break careers.

Tip

Among his many accomplishment as a blogger, Perez was named the number one web celebrity for 2007 by *Forbes* magazine, and has recently been named as one of the 15 most influential Hispanics in the U.S. by *People in Espanol.* In February 2008, eMarketer identified PerezHilton.com as one of the top five websites for college-aged women. He even beat out MySpace!

Having a successful blog has also allowed Perez to write the bestselling book, *Red Carpet Suicide: A Survival Guide on Keeping Up With the Hiltons,* which was published in January 2009. He's also been featured on literally dozens of television shows, and in 2008, had a starring role in the film *Another Gay Sequel: Gays Gone Wild* (TLA Releasing).

Perez Hilton grew up in Miami, Florida, but currently lives and works in Los Angeles.

Q: *How did you get started blogging?*

PH: I didn't start my blog looking for fame or fortune. I started it for fun, as a hobby. Everything else sort of happened by accident. I still find it funny that I am working on the internet, because I consider myself to be a tech-idiot. When I started reading blogs years ago, most of them were personal blogs created by individuals. What I did differently was that I was one of the first people to discuss celebrity news and gossip on the internet, as opposed to blogging about myself.

Back then, nobody was covering celebrity news the way I was. I updated my blog multiple times throughout the day, everyday. Even the mainstream entertainment magazines didn't have websites or blogs back then, so I was pretty much alone in what I was doing.

When I started my blog, I did it for fun. I never thought anyone except for a group of my friends would be reading it. In fact, I wasn't even sure my friends would read it. I have been very surprised and lucky about everything that's happened.

Q: *How old were you when you started blogging?*

PH: I created my blog when I was 26. That was about four years ago, in 2004. Now, on average, my blog receives more than nine million page views per day.

Q: *What did you do to promote your blog and yourself to create such a huge audience?*

PH: Absolutely nothing. I was one of the very first bloggers doing what I was doing, and when you're the first at anything, you always have an advantage over everyone else that comes along after you. If I weren't one of the first people to start the celebrity blog trend, I would almost definitely get lost in the shuffle. These days, there are thousands of celebrity gossip blogs out there.

Aside from a bit of luck, the key to my success is that I work very hard. I have always worked harder than anyone I know. Even now that I am successful, I still work harder than anyone I know. I don't allow myself to become lazy, nor do I take my success for granted. I work really hard because I really love what I do. I also love working for myself.

Q: *How much time do you spend working each day?*

PH: I'd say that I work at least 16 hours per day, everyday. At this point, I have a small staff helping me. My staff includes my mother and sister, along with an assistant.

Q: *What made you start blogging about entertainment gossip, as opposed to some other topic?*

PH: That was what I wanted to write about. I didn't want to write about myself, because I thought my own life was boring. Celebrities are crazy and a lot more fun to discuss. When I started blogging, the big celebrity news was Brad Pitt and Angelina Jolie's relationship. I actually coined the phrase Brangelina.

Q: *How do you make your blogging approach different from everyone else?*

PH: I am just being me. That's why I don't view any other blogs as competition, because none of them can mimic my own unique style and personality. The website is a reflection of my interests and personality.

Q: *On a daily basis, how do you choose the content for your blog when there are so many juicy entertainment stories out there to choose from?*

PH: It all depends on what interests me that day. I am my own reader. If I enjoy reading about something, or I think a story is interesting, I incorporate it into my blog. I look for stories that are shocking or crazy. I look for stories that I think will be engaging and make people want to post comments or forward the blog entry to their friends.

Q: *On a day-to-day basis, what is the most challenging part of your job?*

PH: I don't get enough sleep. The only challenge I face is that I have to make time to sleep. I love what I do, so I don't find any aspect of my work challenging. On any given day, I never have to say, 'Gee, I have nothing to write about.' It's always the exact opposite. There's an incredible amount of potential material for me to blog about. I literally have to force myself to get at least five hours of sleep each night.

Q: *In addition to becoming one of the most widely read bloggers on the internet, you have become a celebrity in your own right. How do you deal with your own fame?*

PH: I still don't consider myself to be a celebrity. I classify myself as more of a personality or entertainer. I am well read by others, and I appreciate that. As a person, however, I am no different than I was before I started this. One of the most fun things for me about being famous is that not everyone likes me, and I think that's a really good thing. It helps to keep me grounded. The fame I have achieved as a blogger is what it is. In Hollywood, there are actually restaurants and hotels, for example, that I am banned from entering, just because of who I am and what I write about on the internet.

I am happy when I am quoted in the mainstream media, because each time someone new reads my name, that's a potential new person who will visit my blog. And, at the end of the day, it's all about my blog and building its audience.

Q: *What don't people know about Perez Hilton that you would like them to know?*

PH: There is a lot that people don't know about Perez Hilton, and I don't really care if they know more about me or not. I think the biggest misconception people have about me is that I am like a one-dimensional cartoon character in real-life. I'm not! I describe myself as musical. That's the first word that comes to my mind.

Q: *What advice can you share with someone who wants to start a blog?*

PH: Ask yourself why you want to start a blog. If you're starting a blog to become famous, you really need to adopt a gimmick. It's really important to stand out and to do something a very different way.

Also, choose your subject wisely. Once you start blogging about something, you can't all of a sudden change your topic. What matters most is your content. The better your content, the more readers you'll get.

Expect to put in long hours, for a long time, before you become rich or famous as a blogger. I didn't earn a penny from my blog for well over a year. When it did start to become popular, I made a little bit of money displaying Google Ads. It took a long time before I started to earn a decent income from this.

Q: *While you were growing your blog, what did you do to attract your audience?*

PH: I didn't have to do too much to promote my blog. Because I was one of the only people doing this when I got started, I eventually received coverage in the mainstream media, and that is what really allowed my blog and my own popularity to grow. It was the mainstream media that really promoted me and the blog.

Q: *At this point in your career, what is the most rewarding aspect of your work?*

PH: For me, the most rewarding aspect of my work is that I am able to take care of my entire family. I was able to move them out to Los Angeles from Miami and I now spend a lot of quality time with them.

While people perceive that I now have a lot of power in the entertainment industry, I don't view myself as having any power at all. I don't like that word and I don't use it. I use the word 'opportunity.' That's what I have. I don't have mind control powers over my readers. I don't control them or look down upon them. I respect them and they don't always agree with me. My readers are smart, sophisticated and have a good sense of humor. I share, and through the blog, my readers have the opportunity to receive and be receptive to that content.

Q: *From a layout and design standpoint, what advice can you offer to other bloggers?*

PH: I think ease of use is important. Keep your blog design simple. Sometimes, less is more. Make sure your blog isn't straining on someone's eyes. Choose a color scheme that is aesthetically pleasing.

When I started my blog, I used a template from Blogger.com that I hardly modified at all for the first six months. At the time, that was enough to get me featured on national television. Initially, I put little thought into my blog's layout and design. Today, with so much competition out there, I think the design of a blog and how it looks is much more important.

Q: *What advice can you offer about incorporating photos into a blog?*

PH: I would advise bloggers to make sure you have permission to use whatever photos you incorporate into your blog. That was a mistake I learned the hard way when I first started out. It's much easier to pay for photos and to have permission to use them, then it is to fight lawsuits against you for copyright infringement. When I first started blogging, I was ignorant and didn't even know I was violating copyright laws by using photos without permission or without paying for them. That was a learning experience for me. I started my blog for fun, but when I became a big boy on the internet, I had to start playing by big boy rules.

Q: *Have you ever had any regrets about anything you've written in a blog? Do you think you've ever crossed the line?*

PH: No, never. I've said some pretty crazy things, but I never regret anything. I don't always say what's on my mind, however. Sometimes, I will exaggerate something to get more of a reaction from readers. There have been stories that I've blogged about that I as a person didn't think were a big deal, but online, Perez Hilton made a huge deal out of the story because it would be good for the website. For example, I am not a prude. Far from it. But, sometimes it's fun to act prudish to get a rise or reaction out of people reading the blog.

Q: *As the world's most famous blogger, what blogs do you read on a regular basis?*

PH: I don't have time to read any other blogs. I am so busy working on my own blog. When I do have time to browse the internet, I spend a lot of time watching YouTube videos. I really enjoy that.

Chris Crocker has been producing and starring in online videos for several years. He's currently pursing a career as a recording artist.

Chris Crocker

Internet Celebrity and Vlogger

Blog URL/Website: mschriscrocker.com

MySpace: myspace.com/chriscrocker

Chris Crocker has been actively producing and starring in online videos since 2005. However, it was his infamous "Leave Britney Alone" video that went viral and quickly made him a household name. Chris' videos have been seen by millions of people worldwide, making him one of the most popular and recognizable people on YouTube and on the web.

If you're a fan of his videos or if you've seen some of the worldwide publicity in the mainstream media that Chris continues to receive as a result of his "Leave Britney Alone" video and more recent endeavors, you've probably labeled him in your own mind as an outrageous crying lunatic who wanted his 15 minutes of fame, and who is willing to make himself look foolish to achieve it.

Describing Chris Crocker as a normal guy would be extremely inaccurate, but the description of "crying lunatic" or "freak" is equally erroneous. As you read this interview, hopefully you'll discover that Chris is a smart, down to earth, creative, ambitious, and extremely brave individual who has become famous by openly sharing some of his most personal thoughts and challenges with the world.

Although Chris helped put YouTube on the map by generating millions upon millions of hits to the site, according to Chris, the popular video hosting service has little appreciation or respect for his accomplishments, which is why Crocker has more recently turned his attention to launching his own website—mschriscrocker.com.

While you can still find his videos on YouTube, as well as on MySpace and several other sites, simply by doing an online search using his name, Chris is currently hoping his online fame will translate into real-world stardom as he embarks on a new career as a recording artist. His first single, entitled "Mind In The Gutter," was released on iTunes in October 2008. By selling official Chris Crocker merchandise online, making paid public appearances, and ultimately being hired as a consultant by several high-profile internet companies, Chris has achieved financial success, as well as online and real world fame. All is not perfect in his life, however. While he has millions of fans, he continues to receive threats from strangers, and has been forced to overcome tremendous life challenges.

Chris grew up in a small town in Tennessee, but now lives in Los Angeles.

Q: *How did you get started blogging?*

CC: In the beginning, I never set out to be a blogger, nor did I have any intention of making a series of videos with the goal of becoming famous on the internet. Initially, I made one video, which I posted on MySpace. It was to address the people in my hometown and to give them a piece of my mind after I was harassed at a local mall. I made this one video and it went viral. Within six months, more than eight million people watched it, but I did nothing to promote it or myself online.

As a result of inadvertently building an audience, I looked at the success of that first video, and decided I would take advantage of it by making additional videos and by speaking out about issues that I wanted to speak about.

These days, people always ask me where in Tennessee I am from, but I have never publicly revealed this for safety reasons. I get death threats on a regular basis, and my family members have been threatened as well.

Q: *How do you describe yourself and what you do?*

CC: It's hard, because I don't just want to be known as an internet celebrity, and at times I think its strange to be called a celebrity at all, because I haven't really done all that much. On the other hand, I think the title 'Internet Celebrity' is too limiting, because I plan to achieve fame in the real world as well. How I describe myself depends on the day, I guess.

Q: *What is your overall goal with producing and starring in your videos? What's your motivation for doing this?*

CC: In September 2008, I actually stopped posting videos on YouTube, because the service removed me from its 'Most Subscribed' list and stripped me of some of the honors I'd received as a result of being so popular. They never told me why this was happening. This led me to launch my own website [MsChrisCrocker.com] and focus on pursuing my passion for singing and becoming a recording artist. On the website, I'll still record videos and vlogs, but I think I have finished that whole chapter in my life where I produce video skits.

Q: *Where do you get your ideas and inspiration for the online videos that you produce and star in?*

CC: A lot of the videos are created spontaneously and I speak off the top of my head. Others are addressed to specific people in my life. All of the videos, however, deal with issues or situations that I have personally experienced or lived through, so I have strong emotions and opinions about what I am saying.

All of the videos have a message, although most people think they are just silly videos designed to get attention. Dolly Parton often says, "It takes a lot of money to look this cheap." For my videos, I've always had the belief that, "It takes a lot of thought to look this stupid." If you listen really closely, every one of my videos contains some type of message.

Q: *Are all of your videos recorded spontaneously, or do you script and rehearse your performances before recording and posting them?*

CC: It depends on the video. Some of them are really thought out and planned word for word, and each and every facial expression is rehearsed. Some of them are just me rambling.

Q: *How and why did the 'Leave Britney Alone' video come about?*

CC: One day, when Britney Spear's problems were starting to get really bad, I visited Perez Hilton's website and read his posts about her. I have looked up to Britney since I was in fifth grade. On a human level, I could not understand how anyone could be so mean to someone who they knew is going through such a bad time. I couldn't understand how I was the only person who seemed sympathetic to what she was going through. It wasn't the attacks on Britney as a performer that bothered me, it was the public attacks on her as a mother that I didn't understand. I recorded that video to let Britney know that she still had dedicated fans who were willing to stick up for her.

Q: *As a result of the 'Leave Britney Alone' video, how has your life changed?*

CC: It's changed a lot. I never recorded that video with the idea that it would go viral and that I would become famous. I look back and think I did a really brave thing, and I was one of the only people who stood up publicly for Britney when everyone else seemed to turn against her. I guess I should be proud for sticking up for her, but on the other hand, I wish that I could have showcased my personality on a broader scale, instead of being looked at as just a crying lunatic.

Now that I am in the public eye, the fame I have earned as a result of that video has created many new opportunities for me. In just one year, a lot has happened. Britney has gotten better and I went from crying over my idol and being seen as a crying lunatic to no longer having any idols and to working on my own music career.

Q: *When you record of your videos, do you have a formula in your head that you think will make it successful and go viral?*

CC: As time goes on, I have developed a formula in my head. I am tapped into my audience and know exactly what they want to see. With the 'Leave Britney Alone' video, however, I recorded it spontaneously. It came straight from my heart. Actually, after posting it, I planned to take it down right away. Before that video, all of my videos focused mainly on social commentary, not celebrities. The whole 'Leave Britney Alone' video and its success was basically an accident.

Q: *What advice about achieving online success can you share with someone who wants to produce and star in his or her own internet videos?*

CC: If you want to build an audience and have a viral video, there are many ways to do this. I am a force of nature who is naturally over the top. I was born this way, so I have always just been myself and stayed true to myself. I've always wanted to be successful in the entertainment industry, but I knew they'd never allow me in the front door. The internet has offered me a back door into the industry. It was my key to an otherwise locked door.

Q: *Back when your focus was on being a blogger and online celebrity, how much time each day or week did you put into your efforts?*

CC: I worked every day, day in and day out. I dropped out of high school as a freshman, because it became a scary and violent experience for me. From that point on, I put absolutely everything I had into my videos. I didn't have a set goal to be famous, but I put all of my hopes and dreams into my videos.

Q: *When you first got started blogging and producing videos, what type of equipment did you use?*

CC: I've always used the same Canon point-and-shoot camera that has a video record mode. I don't do any editing to my videos. I don't know how to edit.

Q: *What would you say is the biggest challenge a blogger faces these days?*

CC: When I first got started, it was when MySpace first launched its MySpace TV video feature and before YouTube really became popular. Today, I think people really need to use their face and their voice, as well as whatever it is they want to say, to make a name for themselves. It's important to make yourself stand out.

The only tip I really have is to avoid copying anything you've seen online before and to try your best to just be authentic. I see so many trying to copy other internet celebrities and personalities. People just need to be themselves.

People who hope to become famous online in order to cross over into the mainstream media should understand that this is an extremely difficult transition to make. When industry people hear the word 'internet,' you're really looked down upon and not taken seriously. This means that you'll need to really let people know how talented and smart you are as you try to break into the entertainment industry. Being from the internet has a stigma associated with it. I recommend staying strong and going with your gut.

Q: *What has been the highlight of your career so far?*

CC: I have gotten to meet so many famous people, but that really hasn't phased me. What I am most proud of is that I am now financially able to really pursue by dreams and fund my endeavors.

Initially, I earned money as a result of my online fame by selling T-shirts and getting paid for making public appearances. In addition to that, I now also earn money working as a consultant to several internet companies, that I am not allowed to reveal the names of.

Q: *Looking back, what's been the biggest mistake you've made as a blogger, and what can people learn from your mistake?*

CC: I think there is such a thing as putting too much of yourself out there in cyberspace. I did a lot of very personal soul searching on camera and looking back, I think there were times when the camera should have been turned off. People can spend too much time on the computer and making videos for the internet. I think people need to find a balance and do this in moderation. Some things I revealed online should have been kept private.

Q: *What tips can you share with someone about how to get started blogging?*

CC: If you're going to be blogging about a specific topic, you really need to keep up every day with what's going on. Figure out what you want to do, look at some successful examples of people who have done what you plan on doing, and then add some of your own flavor into the mix. It's all about being yourself. You have to be a true individual.

Q: *Do you have any tips for generating traffic for a new blog?*

CC: One the best ways to build an audience is to become popular and active on an online social network, like MySpace. At this point, I have almost 500,000 friends on MySpace, so when I post a new video online, I just need to post one bulletin to my friends on MySpace and the traffic to the video starts to build very quickly. For me, the online social networks, particularly MySpace, have always been the best tool for growing a fan base.

I became famous online initially because I posted a single video on MySpace which was serious, and it went viral. That led to people adding me as a friend on MySpace, so I started building up a fan base that way. Other people start by building their friends list on MySpace and other services, and then use those friends to promote their videos. Either method can work.

Be open to allowing accidents to happen and allowing an audience to build up for itself. I think if you try to follow a calculated path for becoming famous, it will backfire, because it's not as real.

Q: *How is your MsChrisCrocker.com website going to be different from what you've already done on MySpace and YouTube, for example?*

CC: I'm going through a lot of changes right now, so I'm not sure how exactly the website will evolve. Right now, it's like an internet home base for me. It's where my fans can go and know they will find me. YouTube hates me so much now, I didn't know from day to day if my account would be deleted. On my own website, I know I can say and do whatever I want. It's a place in cyberspace that's a little more Chris Crocker friendly.

For someone who is first starting out, however, building your own website is not necessary. I recommend using the tools and resources that are already there and that are available for free, and build around that. I got my start on MySpace and I continue to love MySpace. My advice is to build up your friends list on MySpace, or whatever online social networks you utilize, and use that to promote yourself and your blog.

Q: *What blogs do you access on a regular basis?*

CC: On Life Journal, I access a blog daily, called Oh No They Didn't [community. livejournal.com/ohnotheydidnt/]. It's always being updated and it's the most current place to go for entertainment and celebrity gossip.

Q: *So, if you're cutting back on producing and starring in online videos, what are you putting your time and effort into these days?*

CC: All of my effort is going into my music. My recording career is not a publicity stunt, it's something I am pursuing very seriously. My first single, called 'Mind In The Gutter,' was released on iTunes in October 2008. Being able to record this fulfilled my dream of recording a really good song. I am not yet signed by a major record label, but I have a bunch of really talented people from the music industry working with me. Right now, all of the production costs are being paid by me.

Currently, music is my main focus, but I also have a passion for acting. I have a friend who is starting a production company, so I am scratching my acting itch as well. I'm just a talent in all areas, so what happens next will depend on where I channel my energies. I'd also like to do a reality TV show. I am signed to the same reality TV production company that Paris Hilton and Tori Spelling used for their shows, but my project is on the back burner right now.

Q: *How would you describe your music?*

CC: Well, it's definitely influenced by Britney, and I am not ashamed of that. I would describe the music as "Britney Light," but my single "Mind In The Gutter"can best be described as a dark dance song.

Q: *What do you most want people to know or understand about you that they won't learn from watching your online videos?*

CC: Everything about me is out there on the web. They just need to take a closer look. I have a serious side and a silly side. I think people know everything they should know about me.

Q: *Do you take it personally when people say really harsh or mean things about you?*

CC: There are certainly times when I don't want to be Chris Crocker anymore. Sometimes, if I get upset, I will wonder what I've done to myself. But most of the time, I don't allow other peoples' opinions to matter to me. I just shut out that negativity. When I am depressed, the last thing I should do is read my comments. If I allowed people with negative things to say to really get to me, I would have been destroyed emotionally as a person back in kindergarten.

Q: *Because you stand up for who you are and what you believe in, do you consider yourself to be a role model?*

CC: No, not at all. I know some people look at me as a role model, but that's not at all how I see myself.

Ben Jelen

Recording Artist, Founder of the Ben Jelen Foundation, and Blogger

Blog URL: benjelen.com/foundation

Website: benjelen.com

MySpace: myspace.com/benjelen

At age 29, Ben Jelen is an accomplished singer, songwriter, and musician. For his first and second albums, he has worked with some of the best-known producers in the recording industry. He's released two albums and, in late 2008, began working on a third. He's had a few hit songs. He's toured around the world, and through hard work and with the help of the internet, he has built up a significant fan base.

In addition to his passion for music and performing, Ben Jelen is deeply concerned about global warming and in discovering what people can do to better protect the environment. This is a cause he's managed to rally his fans around, and one that he continues to support through a non-profit organization he founded, The Ben Jelen Foundation.

Throughout his career, Ben Jelen has utilized the internet as a promotional tool for his music, and he's used it to stay in direct contact with his fans through his MySpace page, website and his personal blogging efforts. He also writes a separate blog for The Ben Jelen Foundation. He currently lives in New York City.

Q: *How did you get started as a recording artist?*

BJ: In college, I pursued a biology degree. It wasn't until after I finished college that I first went into the recording studio. I recorded a few demos and wound up getting signed to Maverick Records. At the time, musicians, artists, and record labels were first discovering how to use the internet as a promotional tool. Back then, what I really loved about the internet, was that it allowed me to personally communicate with all of my fans and everyone who cared about me and my music.

Using the internet, I had my own website and used blogs to communicate. I think the internet played a huge role in helping me initially promote my music and build up my fan base.

Q: *How did your interest in protecting the environment come about?*

BJ: One of the reasons why I studied biology in school is because I have always been concerned with issues relating to the environment. Growing up, I moved around a lot, so I never had one place I considered home. Throughout my life, I'd periodically return to places I once lived and see firsthand how the environment was impacted by various changes. These changes seemed dramatic, because I wasn't there to see them happen over time. I only witnessed the before and after. I have been shocked by how we treat the world around us and how we build on it.

When I perform my music on tour, this was often a topic I talk about with my audience. This led me to start a foundation, which now allows me to educate people about the environment, raise money for worthwhile environmental causes, and share my own thoughts about environmental issues. In support of the foundation, I maintain a blog and use the internet to interact with others who share my concerns related to the environment.

Q: *What are some of the more goals of The Ben Jelen Foundation?*

BJ: The money we raise through the foundation goes to four distinct areas pertaining to the environment. These areas go along with my own philosophies about what's important. About 25 percent of the funds raised go toward education and awareness. There is a huge lack of awareness related to environment issues that are slow changing and hard to see from day-to-day, but that really are there and need to be addressed and dealt with. The next 25 percent of the funds raised goes toward political lobbying. We also use 25 percent of the money raised to invest in alternative energy sources, such as solar and wind energy. The last 25 percent of the money goes to individuals or groups that are dramatically impacted by environmental changes.

The main messages that I try to convey to my fans and to those who are interested in The Ben Jelen Foundation typically revolve around global warming issues.

Q: *In addition to having your own website, BenJelen.com, are you also active on MySpace and other online social networking sites?*

BJ: Yes, very much so. I think it's important if you want to communicate with people via the internet and you're interested in building up any type of following, that you be active on MySpace, and perhaps on other online social networking sites as well. These sites are popular, but they're also always evolving.

While MySpace was originally the main online social networking site, some of its popularity has decreased as new sites and services have launched and also become popular. So, as a blogger, it's important to stay up-to-date with which online social networking services are considered current and popular, and make yourself known on those.

Staying knowledgeable about the latest online trends is tricky. I try to follow where my fans and my friends go. It's not that an older service, like MySpace or even Facebook has become irrelevant, it's just that newer services pop up that capture peoples' attention as well, and these services gain market share. Since my goal is to promote myself, my music, and my foundation on the internet, I believe that it's important for me to be active on all of the popular sites and services.

Q: *How has the internet helped you and your foundation?*

BJ: Having a special website and blog set up for the foundation has allowed me to promote a cause that I believe is extremely important, and keep that somewhat separate from the online promotions I do for myself and my music. Whenever I work on a blog, whether it's related to my music or the foundation, I always take a very personal approach to it. I use blogging to share with people what's on my mind, whether it's being on the road and touring, or concerns I have about the environment.

Q: *How, where and when do you typically blog?*

BJ: I usually add to my blogs when I really feel like I have something important to add. I don't just blog for the sake of blogging. I don't blog on a daily basis. When someone visits my blog, they know they'll be able to access information and thoughts that I truly believe are important. I think followers of my blogs know that when something appears in one of my blogs, I am really passionate about whatever it is I am saying.

I do most of my blogging from home, because that's when I have the most time to sit in front of the computer and think about what I want to say. However, when I'm touring, I have blogged from all over the place.

Q: *When you're blogging, where do the ideas come from and how do you decide if you're going to use text, photos or video to make your points?*

BJ: I use text, video, and audio when I am blogging. When I use video, those blog entries are more planned out. For example, I'll record video blog entries while I'm on tour to give people a look at my life on the road or what happens backstage at a show. The environmental blog is completely text-based. I use pictures when they're relevant, but I always try to link my blog entries to other blogs or websites that publish related information that I think my audience would be interested in.

Often, what I blog about is inspired by books I'm reading or real life experiences I've had. Music I'm listening to, places I've been, and people I've met online have all inspired topics that I've blogged about.

Q: *Do you have any tips for someone who's interested in starting a blog?*

BJ: Yes. If you're someone who wants to start a blog, you are someone who has something to say. The way to get started is to figure out exactly what you want to say and who you want to say it to. That's what is going to make it interesting.

Your blog should appeal to a particular audience that you know and understand. Beyond that, stay current on whatever topic it is you choose to blog about so you can build yourself up as a reliable place to turn to for information about that topic.

Q: *For you, what is the hardest aspect of blogging?*

BJ: When I write and record music, it's a long process from the time I start writing to the time the music is heard on an album or when I perform it on stage. I am able to live with that creation for a while. When it comes to blogging, the content goes right from my head into the computer and onto the internet. It happens very quickly. It's a totally different style of creativity that I have had to get used to.

Q: *Do you have any tips for people on how to drive traffic to their blog?*

BJ: I think it's all about creating interesting and new content that you're passionate about. If you attract someone to you blog and they become interested in what you have to say, they'll come back, and they'll tell others about it. I also think that networking is important. Use online social networking sites to communicate with new people and to find people who share common interests.

In my opinion, I think the blog's subject matter should take priority over making the blogger the center of attention, but it all depends on what you're trying to accomplish. Sure, you can use the internet as a tool to get rich and famous, but if your focus is on using your blog to get some really important ideas or information out there, to help others, or to educate people, you have the power to have a really positive impact on the world.

Q: *What's next for you, in terms of your music career?*

BJ: I am about to get started writing my third album. I am now bringing all of my ideas together and I am in the process of figuring out what direction I plan to take with the album. I hope the new music will be released sometime in 2009 by my current record label. In my personal life, I am in a very different place then where I was when I worked on the second album, so this new music will probably be more fun, upbeat, and up-tempo.

I have experienced a lot as a recording artist and it's hard for me to envision how my career would have progressed if it hadn't been for the internet, blogging, and my involvement on the online social networks like MySpace.

Patrick W. Gavin

Political Journalist and Blogger

Blog URL: mediabistro.com/fishbowlDC

Patrick W. Gavin is a political journalist who coauthors *The Washington Examiner's* "Yeas & Nays" political gossip column. As a blogger, he is editor of Fishbowl DC, a blog that focuses on political journalism in Washington, DC published by MediaBistro.com. His articles have appeared in dozens of high-profile regional and national publications, including *The Financial Times, Christian Science Monitor,* and *The Washington Post.*

In the past, after moving to Washington, DC in 2003, Gavin served as a writer and media relations officer at the Brookings Institution, a non-partisan public policy think tank located in Washington. Prior to that, he taught 7th and 8th grade History and English at Princeton Day School in New Jersey.

Unlike many bloggers who start their blog as a hobby and hope to ultimately generate some type of income from it, Gavin started his writing career as a political journalist for the mainstream media, and was later hired by MediaBisto.com to edit and blog for Fishbowl DC, for which he receives a salary.

Q: *For the blogging that you do for Fishbowl DC, how would you describe the blog and the approach you take with it?*

PG: It's a blog with a very limited focus. It's about political journalism in Washington, DC. The blog reaches a very niche audience. It is not meant to have mass-market appeal. The blog is primarily for Washington, DC media insiders.

Q: *This blog targets a very particular niche audience; how do you promote the blog to that audience?*

PG: First and foremost, I strive to do a good job covering this topic. I know that if my blog does a superior job covering the topic, it increases the chance of my content being picked up by or quoted in larger media outlets. The Fishbowl DC blog is updated everyday, so our audience knows they can access the very latest information that's relevant. If someone wants current information, they know they need to access the Fishbowl DC blog at least once a day.

Another thing we do to promote the blog is to get ourselves out there in person to tell people in our audience about it. There are all kinds of political events in Washington, DC that we attend with the sole purpose of allowing people to put a face to the blog.

Something else we're in the habit of doing is that whenever we mention an individual within the blog, we forward a link from the blog to that person to tell them about it. This helps to get our name out there.

Q: *A lot of bloggers use their blog to voice an opinion, not necessarily report the news or hardcore facts. Is it important for bloggers to make it clear what they're doing and where their information comes from?*

PG: I think so. It all depends on what the mission of your blog is, however. I personally operate based on the assumption that nobody cares about my take on the stories we cover within Fishbowl DC. At the same time, it's sometimes appropriate to offer an opinion. The last thing a blogger wants is to simply become known as someone who cuts and pastes their content from other sources or just regurgitates news headlines.

There is a fine line between when you provide some analysis to content and when you don't. Don't write or provide commentary simply for the sake of hearing your own voice or to puff up your word count. Don't make people read more than they have to. Bloggers need to use their own judgment about when to allow facts to speak for themselves and when they should provide some of their own analysis. Try to create content that's of interest to your audience, but that doesn't waste their time.

To help your readers understand which are your words and what is content that's lifted from a press release or another source, you can format that content on the screen differently. For example, if I lift some content from a press release, I will use block quotes and indent that text, so that it visually looks different from the rest of the content on the page. Over time, my readers figure out that when content is displayed in block quotes and indented, it comes from another source.

As part of a story, one easy way to add your own opinion or point of view is to state within your content, "Fishbowl DC's take:…," for example. This makes it very clear that an opinion, as opposed to hard news, follows.

Q: *How do you choose the content for your blog?*

PG: You have to pursue stories and content that other blogs and news outlets are not covering. People who read Fishbowl DC also read other media blogs, so I try to avoid content that our competition is covering as well. I don't want our media blog looking exactly the same as every other media blog that's out there. I try to focus on topics or approaches that I will have exclusively, not necessarily the number one news story of the day.

Q: *How can someone find an exclusive approach to the content in their blog?*

PG: You have to become very aware of what your competition is doing and do your own research. Find a topic or a market that's not being covered. Few people read blogs because they care about the blogger's writing. Most people read their favorite blogs because of the information that's offered.

Having really good ideas for blog entries will help insure your content is unique. Try to come up with different types of ideas. Think outside of the box. For every good article you read in a newspaper, there's always an interesting follow up story that won't get pursued by most journalists. Always look for good follow up stories. That usually makes good content.

Q: *When and where do you do your blogging?*

PG: I spend at least 30 to 40 hours per week working on Fishbowl DC. The writing of the blog posts is always the easiest. What takes time is doing the research, networking, socializing, and brainstorming new content. I am in a unique position in that I get paid a salary for writing this blog. If I were not being paid, I don't know if I would invest this much time into it.

As for where I blog from, I can and do blog from anywhere, including from my cell phone. It's all a matter of where I am. If you have a strong following, however, it's important to have a strong and reliable mobile office from which you can do your blogging from anywhere. I use a wireless internet card from my laptop when I'm on the go, because I can't afford to rely on a hotel's internet connection or being able to find a Wi-Fi connection when I need one.

Q: Is there an ideal length for a blog?

PG: This is something I always wrestle with myself. I like using pictures within blog entries, but using a photo only works if it's relevant and adds to the overall blog entry. As for an ideal blog length, that varies. As a general rule, however, don't use more words than are needed to get your point across, and if you don't have something that's worthwhile saying, don't say it. Be mindful of your audience's time and don't waste it.

I believe that one reason why people enjoy reading blogs is because they can get content, news, or insight, for example, that they don't get from reading a traditional newspaper or watching a TV news program. Bloggers tend to put more of their own personality into their blogging approach, and that can make the content interesting and lively.

When someone visits your blog, you don't want them to feel overwhelmed by the amount of content being offered. A really long and wordy article can seem very intimidating. You might want to use a lot of white space and shorter formatted paragraphs to make the content seem more easily readable and digestible.

Q: Do you have any other advice for bloggers?

PG: Once you start publishing a blog, stick to it. Don't give up too quickly or get frustrated by the lack of response it receives early on. It takes time to build up a dedicated audience. Be patient. Also, make sure you possess the educated belief that you're offering something within your blog that will allow it to take off. Understand that blogging is a very competitive field, so you'll need to be persistent and self-promote.

Fashion designer/model Kiel James Patrick launched his own website to promote and sell his fashion line, but also uses blogging to interact with his fans and customers.

Kiel James Patrick

Fashion Designer, Model, and Blogger

Blog URL: KJPLife.blogspot.com

Website: KielJamesPatrick.com

At the age of 26, Cranston, Rhode Island-based Kiel James Patrick is an accomplished fashion model, having worked in the modeling and fashion industries since the age of 19. When in his early 20s, after rummaging through the attic of his parents' home and finding a chest chock full of his grandfather's old neck ties, he created a unique fashion accessory that involved cutting up the vintage fabrics and transforming them into ultra-trendy, hand-stitched bracelets that could be fashionably worn by males and females to compliment any wardrobe style. Patrick began wearing his creations every day while still in college. They quickly became a hit among his friends, all of whom wanted Kiel to create customized bracelets using similar vintage fabrics.

Over a two-year period, Kiel fine-tuned the design of his bracelets by adding a custom designed, oversized signature button to clasp the bracelets around the wearer's wrist, and he added a custom-made liner fabric to his creations. Soon, the Kiel James Patrick (KJP) brand was born.

Based on the demand among the people at Kiel's school for his bracelets, he soon decided to tap his entrepreneurial spirit, solicit the help of a few friends, and launch an online-based business to share his fashion accessory with the world.

Within weeks after launching and promoting his website, Kiel began receiving orders from high school and college students, as well as young adults from around the country, and he attracted the attention of fashion magazine editors, high-profile celebrities, and Hollywood stylists. This led to upscale boutiques expressing an interest in selling his unique products in their stores.

Prior to launching the KJP brand, Kiel was extremely active on both MySpace and Facebook, and had developed a following of fans as a result of his modeling career. So when it came time to launch the KielJamesPatrick.com website, one of the first things he did to begin promoting the new business was utilize his online friends network by sending out public bulletins, as well as direct e-mails.

As the online business continued to grow, he supplemented his direct and indirect interaction with his online friends through the social networking sites by running paid ads on Facebook that targeted his audience using keywords.

Yet another aspect to his marketing and promotional efforts for the KJP brand was to capitalize on and expand his personal fan base by launching a blog, called KJP Life, through which he could share details about his own life adventures, communicate more openly with his fans and the customers of his products, plus reach a broader audience to promote his company's fashion line.

According to Patrick, much credit for the success of the KJP brand and the eCommerce website has been a direct result of his active participation on the online social networks and his use of blogging to interact on a more personal level with fans and customers.

Q: *What made you start the Kiel James Patrick brand and bracelet product line, and then decide to sell the products online using an eCommerce website?*

KJP: I have always been interested in fashion. About six years ago, I was rummaging through a chest full of my grandfather's old neckties and admiring the different and unique vintage fabrics that were used to create men's fashions decades ago. The designs of the old fabrics captured my imagination. I began wearing the ties themselves, but one day decided to cut one of them up and sew it into a bracelet, which I began wearing to complement my preppy, New England style.

On the very first day I wore one of the bracelets, the guys and girls at school started asking me where I bought the bracelet, because they wanted to buy them for themselves. For the next several months, I started making bracelets for my friends and classmates. After about two years of making bracelets for friends and coworkers, I decided I could transform the idea into a business.

At the same time I was showing off the bracelets in-person, I also posted photos of myself wearing them within my MySpace and Facebook profiles. As a result of my modeling career, I had acquired thousands of friends online. When I launched KJP, I continued to focus heavily on building my online friends network. This has proved to be an excellent marketing strategy for my company.

Q: *Once you decided to launch a business based around selling your one-of-a-kind hand-crafted bracelets, what steps did you take to bring the idea to fruition?*

KJP: I knew I had created a very original fashion accessory product and for it to be successful, I needed to establish a unique and upscale brand through which to market the products. I wanted to create a brand that people would recognize outside of just the bracelets.

After having created my company name, logo, brand, and a unique product line, I quickly discovered this wasn't yet enough to obtain national retail distribution through upscale fashion boutiques. This is what lead me to establish an eCommerce website. I wanted to reach the broadest audience possible, comprised of fashion-conscious high school and college students, as well as young adults. I also wanted to take full advantage of the online fan base I had built up from working as a fashion model.

A few months after launching the website, I created a blog, called KJP Life, which would allow my fans and people interested in my products to learn more about me as a person, as well as about the KJP fashion line. Unlike the website, the blog is more of an informal online newsletter. It's more to entertain my fans and customers, as opposed to being a direct sales or advertising tool, like the website.

Q: *How did you go about launching the blog?*

KJP: The process was so much easier than designing and launching the KielJamesPatrick.com website. In less than three hours, I set up a free account with Blogger.com, chose a blog template, created a main title banner using Photoshop, and then posted my first blog entry, which was text-based. It incorporated one candid photo of me.

As I began to expand the blog, I later added some additional photos from my modeling portfolio, as well as a handful of candid photos that really showcased me as a person and my personality. I also shot a few short videos that were incorporated into the blog, again to allow people to get to know me on a more personal level.

Once the blog was established, we added a link to it from the KielJamesPatrick.com website, plus I promoted it heavily to my friends network on MySpace and Facebook. It didn't take more than a day or so to begin generating traffic to the blog.

Between my modeling career and my fashion line, I get a ton of e-mails from high school and college-age kids, so I wante d the blog to take a very light-hearted and informal approach. Yes, it helps to promote my company and the KJP fashions, but the sales and marketing approach used in conjunction with the blog is much more subtle.

Out of all of the business-related tasks that I manage, creating and maintaining the blog is one of the most enjoyable, because I get to really use my creativity when writing blog entries, plus I get to be myself and share my thoughts. People often see my photos and think they know me. My blog allows people to learn more about who I am as a person.

To promote the KielJamesPatrick.com website, we have done all sorts of advertising, marketing, promotional and public relations-oriented activities, just as any business would. The cost to implement some of these strategies, such as online advertising, or participating in trade shows, is rather high. Launching and managing the blog, however, cost us nothing but a little time. The positive impact, however, has been incredible and beyond expectations.

Q: *From a time investment standpoint, how long did it take from the time you decided to launch your eCommerce website to the time it went online? Also, how much time do you spend online these days?*

KJP: I invested two years of hard work into the business itself, and about three months of work into the website design. This is in addition to the time the website designer invested to program the site. Now, I spend at least 50 hours per week running the business, but a lot of this time involves handcrafting the bracelets themselves and handling the marketing for the website and the company.

This has become a full-time job which consumes my life, but in a good way. I invest a lot of time communicating with customers via e-mail, blogging, and on MySpace and Facebook. I spend at least two hours per day online answering e-mails and interacting with my online friends. To keep up with orders, my friends and I are often up until 2 a.m. sewing the bracelets.

Q: *What advice do you have for someone launching a blog?*

KJP: Start off on a small scale using a basic template and one of the free blog hosting services. You can set the blog up and get it online in a few hours. You can then see if you enjoy blogging and find it rewarding.

Tip

As a marketing strategy, on an ongoing basis, Kiel specially seeks out people on MySpace and Facebook with thousands or tens of thousands of online friends, and he asks these people to post bulletins and blog entries about the KJP brand using their accounts.

In exchange, Kiel provides these popular people with free product. "When a potential customer reads a blog post or bulletin from one of their own online friends, they are much more apt to check out the KielJamesPatrick.com website and place an order. This is a very quick and inexpensive, grassroots marketing approach that works better than paid advertising, if you can get the people with a ton of online friends to help you out," explained Kiel.

As the blog begins to grow in popularity, you can invest more time into adding features and functionality through widgets and by improving its overall design, for example.

When I created this blog, I wanted to share information about myself and voice my own opinions about topics and subjects that are relevant in my life and that I feel would be of interest to the young people who enjoy following my modeling career and the success of the KJP fashion line. If I were to offer advice to a fellow blogger first starting out, it would be to have fun with creating their content and to just be themselves.

If you don't have a huge budget to promote your new blog, definitely utilize the online social networking sites, like MySpace and Facebook. Use these sites to create a network of online friends and then become active in special interest online groups and forums hosted by these services.

For example, I know that many of my fans and my company's customer base is comprised of teenage girls who watch TV shows, like *Gossip Girl, 90210, One Tree Hill,* and *Greek.* So, I participate in online forums for fans of these and other shows, as well as special interest forums about fashion and modeling.

On Facebook, we've also created a special interest group based around the KJP brand which has attracted thousands of members. This is an open forum for customers and fans to interact amongst themselves, post photos of themselves wearing the KJP bracelets and talk about our latest designs and products. Setting up a special interest group on Facebook can be done for free, but it can't be used for blatant advertising.

In terms attracting traffic to the KJP Life blog, I guess I was lucky, because I already had an established fan base, so all I needed to do was post a few bulletins telling my fans and customers about the blog's launch. This generated a lot of initial traffic. The trick, however, has been to generate return traffic to the blog. The best way I have found to do this is to keep creating new content that the audience for the blog wants to access. Each time I post a new blog entry, I also post bullets on MySpace and Facebook telling people about the new content and that encourages them to check it out.

Final Thoughts

Blogging has become a tool for people to share their thoughts, ideas, knowledge, and opinions with the world in an extremely easy, inexpensive, and informal way. Some bloggers have become famous as a result of their efforts, and some have even discovered ways to generate rather significant revenues by creating, managing, and publishing a blog.

Anyone—yes anyone—can become a blogger, typically within a few hours and with no up-front costs. How popular your blog becomes, however, will depend on how effectively you promote it to the public. As you begin to explore the world of blogging, you'll discover that people from all walks of life have become successful bloggers. In fact, there are even teenagers that are among the most popular and entertaining bloggers in the world.

If you have an interest in blogging, the best thing you can do is to just get started! Follow the steps outlined in this book. Invest a few minutes to set up a blogging account with a service like Blogger.com, and then begin creating your first blog entries. You will soon discover how fun, entertaining, and rewarding blogging can be!

Glossary

Understanding the following terminology will help you better handle just about everything that's important when it comes to blogging.

AdSense: A revenue generating opportunity for bloggers that involves small, text-based, context-sensitive ads (or small display ads) be incorporated and displayed as part of a blog's content. The blogger receives a fee each time a web surfer clicks on the advertiser's ad. AdSense is a service, operated by Google, that works as the intermediary between bloggers (or web masters) and paying advertisers.

Advertising: This is a paid form of communication that allows you to market and promote your products/services (or a blog) to web surfers by conveying your exact marketing message. As the advertiser, you have total control over the message, as well as where and when it appears or is heard. Advertising can be done using many forms of media, including in newspapers, magazines, radio, television, billboards, and newsletters, as well as online.

Affiliate Program: A revenue generating opportunity for bloggers that involves showcasing online display ads, such as banners, within a blog. In exchange for providing the online ad space, the blogger receives a flat fee or commission each time someone clicks on an ad, makes a purchase, or sees the ad, depending on the compensation that's pre-arranged with the affiliate partner (the advertiser). There are several companies, like LinkShare and Commission Junction, that represent hundreds of advertisers each and that work as the intermediary between bloggers (or web masters) and the advertisers.

Audio Editing Software: Software used to edit digital audio files and transform them into podcasts.

Banner: A graphical display ad that can be displayed on a website or blog. Banners are typically created in a variety of standard sizes. The larger (horizontal) banners tend to be the easiest to read and thus generate the best response from web surfers.

Blog: A text-based diary or journal created by a blogger that is comprised of an ongoing series of entries, typically displayed online in order from newest to oldest. A blog can also incorporate photos, graphics, animations, video clips, audio clips, and other multimedia content. A blog usually focuses on a specific topic or theme.

Blog Hosting Service: An online-based service that hosts online blogs and that provides bloggers with the online-based tools needed to create, publish, and manage their blog. While services like Blogger.com are offered for free, there is a monthly fee for bloggers to use services, like TypePad, for example.

Blogger: The writer or creator of a blog.

Blogger.com: One of several popular online blog hosting services that offers a blogger all of the tools needed to create, publish, and manage a blog. Blogger.com is a free service operated by Google.

Blogging: The act of writing and publishing a blog.

Color Scheme: The combination of colors used to create a blog. Different colors can be selected for fonts, graphics, and backgrounds, for example, but the color scheme that the blogger utilizes should include colors that look good together and that are visually appealing.

Content: The combination of text, graphics, photographs, animations, audio, video, and other multimedia elements used to populate and create a blog, vlog, or website.

Conversion Rate: This is the percentage of people who actually click on and respond to an ad displayed on a blog or webpage, compared to the number of people who simply see the ad, but don't click on it. As a blogger looking to generate revenue from a blog, your goal is to create the highest conversion rate amongst your blog's visitors as possible.

Cost-Per-Click (CPC): How much it ultimately costs an online advertiser for each individual web surfer to click on an online-based ad (such as a banner). Some online ads are paid for based on the number of people who view them (impressions), while others are paid for based on the number of people who actually click on the ad.

Cyberstar: Someone who has achieve a high level of fame and notoriety as an online personality, blogger, webcaster or vlogger, for example.

Domain Name Registrar: These are the online-based services, such as GoDaddy.com and NetworkSolutions.com, where someone can register their blog or website's unique domain name, such as "[InsertDomainNameHere].com."

Downloadable: A digital product that can be purchased online and then immediately downloaded by the customer, such as a data file, website template, font, photograph, video file, audio file, or graphic image.

eCommerce Website: A website designed to sell products online that will ultimately be shipped or uploaded to the customer once payment is received. This type of website must quickly and accurately convey details about the product(s) being sold, plus have a shopping cart feature that allows customers (web surfers) to safely and securely place their orders using a major credit card or another online payment method.

Facebook (facebook.com): One of the most popular online social networking sites. In addition to allowing members to create their unique online profile, Facebook can also be used to host blogs and/or vlogs, and to communicate with online friends.

FireWire: This is a technology that allows two computers, or a computer and a peripheral (such as a video camera or digital camcorder), to be connected via a special cable so data can be transferred at extremely high speeds.

Font: A specific style of text that shares a common appearance or design.

Freelance Professional (Freelancer): Someone with specialized skills who is self-employed and who seeks out work from multiple clients. Someone who works on a freelance basis is not on any company's payroll. Bloggers can hire freelance blog designers, photographers, writers, search engine optimization experts, public relations professionals, and web marketers to help them create, manage, publish, and/or promote their blog. Freelancers are paid either on a per-project or per-hour basis.

Freeware: This is software available for a computer that is offered by the programmer(s) or publisher free of charge. Typically, freeware can be downloaded from a website.

Gigabyte (GB): This is how the amount of memory a computer possesses is measured. It can also refer to how much data can be transferred in one second. One Gigabyte (which is abbreviated "G" or "GB") contains 1,073,741,824 bytes of data or 1,024 megabytes (MB).

Google Checkout: A service of Google, this is a way for eCommerce website operators to quickly and securely accept and process online payments.

Hit: A single hit is equivalent to one visitor to a website or blog, or one person viewing a specific webpage.

Home Page: The main page of any website. It's where web surfers land when they enter a website's URL into their browser software. A blog can also have a home page, depending on how it's designed, or a blog can be accessed through a menu option found on a website's main page, for example.

HTML (HyperText Markup Language): A popular programming language used to create web pages, online documents, blogs and websites. HTML defines the structure and layout of a blog or webpage and allows for the use of hyperlinks. It is not necessary to understand how to program using HTML is order to be a successful blogger, especially if you use a blog hosting service. If you do know HTML programming, however, it gives you the ability to truly customize your blog and add features and functionality to it, without having to rely on templates, widgets or the tools offered by online blog hosting services.

iMac: An Apple Mac desktop computer suitable for most casual computer users.

Instant Message (IM): A method of sending text-based messages to other computer users via the Web in order to communicate in real-time using a service like AIM (America Online Instant Messenger).

iSight Camera: A tiny video camera, located at the top of Apple displays on iMacs, MacBooks, MacBook Pros, and MacBook Air units. The iSight can capture still digital images, or it can be used as a web cam to handle video conferencing, video blogging, webcasting, etc.

Links: Short for "hyperlink." This is a text-based link to another website, blog, or location on the web, for example, that a web surfer can access with a click of the mouse. One section of many popular blogs is a list of popular links to other topic-related websites that a blogger recommends.

Live Chat: The ability for two or more web surfers to communicate in real-time online using text messages. Many of the blog hosting services offer the ability to allow bloggers to add live chat functionality to their blogs in order to communicate with their audience. This functionality can also be added to a blog or website using a widget.

Logo: A single or multi-colored graphical image that establishes a visual icon to represent a company or blog, for example. A logo can also make use of a specific or custom designed font or typestyle to spell out your blog or company's name.

Main Title Graphic: This is a custom graphic that's placed at the very top of a blog's main page. It typically displays a blog's main title and logo.

Megabyte (MB): A measurement of computer memory equal to one million bytes.

Merchant Account: Offered by a merchant account provider, such as a bank or financial institution, this is what's required for a business operator to be able to accept credit card payments. The merchant will be charged various fees to be able to accept credit cards from their customers.

Meta Tag: This includes specific lines of HTML programming within your blog or website that are used to categorize its content in the various search engines and web directories. In addition to the blog's description, title, and a list of relevant keywords, within the HTML programming of your blog you'll need to incorporate a text-based, one-line description of your blog (which again utilizes keywords to describe your site's content). A meta tag must be placed within a specific area of your blog's overall HTML programming. In most cases, meta tags are automatically added to blogs that are created using one of the popular blogging services.

Microsoft Internet Explorer: The most popular web browsing software used by PC users who utilize the Windows operating system. A web browser is typically the software used by web surfers to access blogs and websites.

Mobile Blogging: The ability to create and publish blog content using a wireless PDA, cell phone, or a notebook computer that's connected to the wireless web. This gives people the ability to update their blog from virtually anywhere where there is cell service (or a Wi-Fi hotspot, depending on the technology being used).

Mouse Click: A single press of the mouse button when using a PC or Mac.

MySpace (MySpace.com): One of the most popular online social networking sites. In addition to allowing members to create their unique online profile, MySpace can also be used to host blogs and/or vlogs, and to communicate with online friends.

Niche Market: This is a narrowly defined group of people that make up a blog's target market. The people in your niche market (or target audience) can be defined by their age, sex, income, occupation, height, weight, religion, geographic area, interests, and/or any number of other criteria.

Online Personality: The persona a blogger or vlogger takes on when communicating with their audience.

Online Social Networking: Online services, such as MySpace or Facebook, that allow web surfers to communicate in a variety of ways in both real-time and through messaging, for example. The online social networks allow members to create profiles, plus showcase photos and host blogs or vlogs.

PayPal: An online service that allows web surfers to transfer money to each other quickly, though secure online transactions.

PayPal Express Checkout: A service of PayPal, this is a way for eCommerce website operators to quickly and securely accept and process online payments.

Photo Editing Software: Software used to edit, crop, and/or to enhance digital photos and graphic images.

Photoshop CS4: An industry standard photo editing and graphic creation software tool used by photographers and graphic designers, created by Adobe. PhotoShop Elements, a scaled-down and much less expensive version of PhotoShop, is generally adequate for most bloggers.

Podcast: An audio recording that is uploaded and broadcast over the web or made available for download so it can be listened to using an .MP3 player or iPod, for example. Unlike a blog or vlog, a podcast only utilizes audio.

Public Relations: A marketing strategy used to obtain free editorial coverage in the media in the form of product reviews, interviews, and/or product mentions in news stories.

RSS (Really Simple Syndication) Feed: A way for bloggers to syndicate and distribute their blog's content and make it available to a broader audience. RSS feeds also make it easier to access blog content, without someone actually having to visit a blog's URL.

Safari: A built-in application in the Mac OS X operating system used for surfing the web. Apple's premier web browser software offers similar functionality to Microsoft Internet Explorer and Mozilla's Foxfire. A web browser is typically the software used by web surfers to access blogs and websites.

Search Engine: An online service that web surfers use to find what they're looking for on the web. A search engine is a comprehensive and ever growing listing or directory of content found in websites and blogs.

Search Engine Marketing: Also referred to as keyword advertising. It involves paid, keyword (text-based) advertising using Yahoo Search Engine Marketing, Google AdWords, and/or Microsoft AdCenter. These short, text-only ads are keyword-based and appear when a potential customer enters a specific search phrase into a search engine, for example.

Search Engine Optimization (SEO): This involves getting your blog or website listed with the major search engines, like Yahoo! and Google, and then working to constantly maintain and improve your ranking/positioning with each search engine so your blog/website is easy to find and receives top placement.

Shareware: This is software that is offered to a potential user for free, on a trial period basis (usually 30-days), after which the software can be purchased and used indefinitely, or deleted from the computer. Shareware allows users to test out software on their own computer before paying for it. In most cases, a shareware edition of a program is identical to the full commercial version. In other cases, shareware editions of software have key features deactivated until the software is purchased.

Tag: One or more keywords or phrases created by a blogger to help categorize each of their blog entries and make them easier to search and find by web surfers and internet search engines.

Target Audience: This is the core group of people your blog will most appeal to and who will comprise your core audience.

Template: A pre-created design that can be customized into a blog, web page, website, or another piece of digital content. Templates can be purchased and downloaded online (and customized using web design or graphics software, such as Adobe Dreamweaver) or licensed for use with a blog or website, for example. The popular blog hosting services offer dozens or in some cases hundreds of free blog templates you can use to create your blog around so that it looks professional and contains all of the functionality you need, without having to do any programming.

Traffic: Refers to the number of web surfers who visit your blog or website on an hourly, daily, weekly, monthly, or annual basis. A visitor is someone who surfs over to your blog or website.

TypePad: One of several popular online blog hosting services that offer a blogger all of the tools needed to create, publish, and manage a blog. This is a fee-based service, but it offers more features and functionality than many of the free blog hosting services. A free version of TypePad called VOX, which offers fewer features, is also available. Unlike the free blogging services, TypePad offers live technical support for bloggers.

Typestyle: This refers to the appearance of any font or text. A typestyle can be regular, **bold**, <u>underlined</u>, *italic*, or customized in a variety of other ways, depending on the application. Text can also be displayed using combinations of these criteria, such as ***<u>bold, underlined, and italicized.</u>***

URL (Uniform Resource Locators): This is a blog or website's address. A typical URL has three main components. The first part typically begins with "www." or "http://" The second part of a URL is what you actually must select. The third part of a URL is its extension, which is typically ".com", however, a variety of other extensions are available, such as .edu, .org, .net., gov, .info, .TV, .biz, .name, and .us.

USB (Universal Serial Bus): A "plug-and-play" technology used for connecting various devices and peripherals to a computer, such as a mouse, keyboard, printer, webcam, or thumb drive. When such a device is connected to a computer, the computer automatically detects it and configures the appropriate drivers, without the user's intervention.

Video Editing Software: Software used to edit digital video footage (vlogs) on a personal computer and then save that footage in a format that's compatible with vlog and video hosting online services, such as YouTube and Yahoo! Video. This type of software also allows the editor (vlogger) to add graphic titles, special effects, transitions, and fades into their videos to give them more of a professional look.

Vlog: A video-based blog that is pre-recorded and published on the web.

Web Browser: The software used by web surfers to surf the web and access blogs. Microsoft Explorer, Safari, and FireFox are examples of popular web browsers. When creating a blog, it's essential that it be compatible with all of the popular browsers.

Webcam: An inexpensive video camera that connects directly to a computer that can be used to record video (vlogs) or for webcasting.

Webcast: A live video-based broadcast over the internet.

Widget: A program or utility that can easily be added to a blog in order to give it additional functionality or features. There are literally thousands of free widgets that can be incorporated into a blog, many of which provide for added interactivity.

Wireless PDA (Personal Digital Assistant): A handheld device, such as an iPhone, BlackBerry, Treo, or Sidekick that offers users access to the wireless internet. Most wireless PDAs also offer cell phone capabilities and a variety of other functionality.

WordPress: One of several popular online blog hosting services that offers a blogger all of the tools needed to create, publish and manage a blog. WordPress is a free service.

YouTube: Owned and operated by Google, YouTube is the most popular and largest video hosting service on the internet. It offers an easy and free way for anyone to publish video content on the web and make it available to the public.

Index

Additional Titles

The following books, written by Jason R. Rich and published by Entrepreneur Press are now or will soon be available wherever books are sold, and can be ordered online from EntrepreneurPress.com, Amazon.com, or BN.com. For more information about these and other books written by bestselling author Jason R. Rich, visit his website at JasonRich.com.

202 High-Paying Jobs You Can Land Without a College Degree

202 Things You Can Buy and Sell For Big Profits, 2nd Edition

Click Starts: Design and Launch an Online eCommerce Business in a Week

Click Starts: Launch Your Online Web Design, Photography or Graphic Arts Business in a Week

The Complete Book of Dirty Little Secrets: Money-Saving Strategies the Credit Bureaus Won't Tell You

Mac Migration: The Small Business Guide to Switching to the Mac

Smart Debt: Borrow Wisely, Live Rich

Entrepreneur Magazine's Personal Finance Pocket Guides

Buying or Leasing A Car: Without Being Taken for a Ride

Dirty Little Secrets: What the Credit Bureaus Won't Tell You

Get That Raise!

Mortgages & Refinancing: Get the Best Rates

Mutual Funds: A Quick Start Guide

Why Rent? Own Your Dream Home

Entrepreneur Magazine's Business Traveler Series

Entrepreneur Magazine's Business Traveler Guide to Chicago

Entrepreneur Magazine's Business Traveler Guide to Las Vegas

Entrepreneur Magazine's Business Traveler Guide to Los Angeles

Entrepreneur Magazine's Business Traveler Guide to New York City

Entrepreneur Magazine's Business Traveler Guide to Orlando

Entrepreneur Magazine's Business Traveler Guide to Washington, DC